PURCHASING SUBMISSION

Purchasing Submission

Conditions, Power, and Freedom

PHILIP HAMBURGER

HARVARD UNIVERSITY PRESS

Cambridge, Massachusetts

London, England

2021

FIRST PRINTING

Publication of this book has been supported through the
generous provisions of the S. M. Bessie Fund.

Library of Congress Cataloging-in-Publication Data

Names: Hamburger, Philip, 1957– author.
Title: Purchasing submission : conditions, power, and freedom / Philip Hamburger.
Description: Cambridge, Massachusetts : Harvard University Press, 2021. |
Includes index.
Identifiers: LCCN 2021010319 | ISBN 9780674258235 (cloth)
Subjects: LCSH: Duress (Law)—United States. | Constitutional law—United States. |
Consent (Law) United States.
Classification. LCC KF450.D85 H36 2021 | DDC 342.73 / 041—dc23
LC record available at https://lccn.loc.gov/2021010319

For Jim Lindgren

Contents

Preface

This book has its origins in a memorable after-dinner conversation. Two decades ago, at the home of a friend and fellow scholar, I asked him why he had not yet published one of his most interesting and important articles. To my astonishment, he replied that it was not publishable under the rules of his university's institutional review board.

He explained that he had forgotten to obtain prior permission for his research from the IRB and that if he published without its permission, he would probably have difficulty getting permission to publish his future scholarship; he might even lose his job. Therefore, he explained, he was circulating his work only in manuscript, like Russian samizdat.

I was puzzled and horrified. What was an institutional review board? Why did my friend need its permission? Why was this not unconstitutional? The answers involved federal funding. My friend's research was not federally funded, but in funding his university, the federal government had pressured it to impose prior licensing even on unfunded research and publication.

In the ensuing years, I devoted much time to studying federal censorship of academic inquiry and publication. But that turned out to be only the tip of the iceberg. It was merely part of a much larger problem of control through conditions. An entire realm of subterranean governance thus gradually came into view. Although it is an increasingly prominent mode of power, the purchase of submission is only glancingly addressed in standard texts on the Constitution, administrative power, and political theory—as if it were a marginal rather than a central form of power. And even when discussed, it is not well understood. So I have struggled to wrap my mind around it. The result is this book.

PURCHASING SUBMISSION

Introduction

The purchase of submission is a poorly understood mode of power. It is widely recognized that government exercises influence through its distribution of money and other privileges. But it is only dimly perceived that this is a new pathway of power—a mode of control that now rivals binding statutes and even administrative edicts. In place of promulgating rules, either congressionally or administratively, government nowadays often offers inducements at the price of compliance with its conditions. This transactional mode of control needs to be recognized and analyzed as seriously as the older modes of power that it increasingly is displacing.

Conditions are the fulcrum of this method of control. When the government offers its largess or other privileges, it places conditions on its generosity so that recipients get the money or other benefits only if they conform. Compliance with the conditions sometimes must occur entirely before the distribution of benefits, and sometimes it must continue or occur afterward; but one way or another, conditions are mechanisms for control.

Of course, most conditions are entirely lawful and desirable. The government, for instance, can purchase airplanes on the condition it will not owe money if the plane does not fly at a specified height and speed. And it can distribute confidential government information on the condition that it be used only for limited purposes on specified secure computers. Such conditions not only clarify the government's expectations but also provide a convenient remedy, for where a government condition is not met, the government need not sue to recover damages, but can just stop the flow of money or information and often can demand the return of any money it has already paid. Far from being dangerous, these mundane conditions can be advantageous.

Other conditions, however, are more interesting. Consider these examples:

- The 1939 Hatch Act took aim at federal employees who actively spoke in political campaigns, even if on their own time, by providing that they could be fired.

- Some state statutes offer parole to sex offenders on the condition that they submit to regular injections that temporarily reduce their testosterone—what is known as "chemical castration." Some states, such as California, add that offenders can avoid the injections upon parole if they voluntarily submit to permanent surgical castration.

- In 1961, after Jimi Hendrix was twice caught riding in stolen cars, the local prosecutor told him he could stay out of prison if he would join the army. He chose to enlist and was assigned to the 101st Airborne. Fortunately, for both him and the army, he was soon discharged. The rest is rock and roll history.

- Most criminal cases end in plea bargains that, on average, offer a defendant a two-thirds reduction in prison time for giving up his jury and other trial rights. Thus, a charge that at trial would result in a fifteen-year sentence is apt to be reduced in a plea bargain to five years, which means a defendant typically faces a threat of triple prison time if he refuses a plea bargain and its conditions.[1]

- The Department of Justice makes grants to states and localities to pay for criminal justice personnel, training, equipment, and supplies, and in July 2017, the department announced that such grants would no longer go to cities that refuse to cooperate with US Immigration and Customs Enforcement (ICE). As a result, more than two hundred sanctuary cities faced federal financial pressure to share information with ICE and give it access to their correctional facilities.

- When the US military discriminated on grounds of sexual orientation, notably under its "Don't Ask Don't Tell" policy, many academic institutions barred the military from recruiting through their career development offices. In response, beginning in 1995, Congress in the Solomon Amendment—and the Defense Department in its interpretation of it—limited the ability of such institutions to get federal funding, thereby pressuring them to permit military recruiting.[2]

- The federal statute known as Title IX bars federal funding for educational institutions that discriminate on the basis of sex. The Department of Education interpreted this condition to require such institutions to bar not only sexual harassment as traditionally understood but also much student speech on sexual matters. Adding to the constitutional concerns, the department interpreted the condition to require institutions to enforce these requirements through little inquisitorial tribunals, which tended to be systematically prejudiced against the accused.

- New York State's version of Aid to Families with Dependent Children offered assistance to families on the condition that they permit caseworkers into their homes to evaluate their needs, thus systematically pressing the poor to accept intrusions into their domestic spaces.

The policies underlying these conditions will provoke diverse reactions, depending on one's view of their merits. But even more interesting than the policies is the process by which they are imposed.

The point is not to suggest that all of these conditions run afoul of the Constitution but rather to introduce a sobering question about how Americans are to be governed. By law, as authorized by the Constitution? By administrative edict? Or perhaps increasingly by something even more distant from the Constitution, the government's purchase of compliance? This transactional mode of control—it scarcely deserves to be considered even administrative—is the subject of this book.

The focus here will be on a particularly disturbing aspect of this mode of governance: the degree to which it becomes the purchase of submission to an unconstitutional regime. By offering subventions and privileges, government persuades Americans to subject themselves to an unconstitutional pathway of power and even unconstitutional restrictions. It is a strange mode of governance, in which Americans sell their constitutional freedoms—including their self-governance, due process, and speech—for a mess of pottage.

William Wordsworth feared that the world was too much "getting and spending." Little did he imagine that spending and getting would become a formidable avenue for government power beyond the Constitution and in violation of its freedoms.

Layers of Constitutional Dangers

The constitutional threat is typically thought to be one of unconstitutional conditions—the conditions that impose unconstitutional restrictions. And even this problem tends to be understood very narrowly as one of conditions in violation of constitutional rights. This book will spend many pages on conditions imposing unconstitutional restrictions, for they are all too common and dangerous.

There are, however, other difficulties, for even when conditions do not impose unconstitutional restrictions, they can be an unconstitutional pathway for control. Most notably, conditions can function as a mode of regulation that sidesteps the Constitution's regulatory process. Whereas the Constitution envisions that Congress will ordinarily regulate by enacting binding statutes, the government nowadays often regulates by placing conditions on its largess—as when federal Aid for Families with Dependent Children came, in New York, with the condition that caseworkers be allowed into the recipients' homes. This condition did not, according to the courts, violate the Fourth Amendment prohibition against unreasonable searches, but the condition required a large swath of poor single mothers to open up their homes to government. It is improbable that Congress or the New York State Assembly would have directly imposed so intrusive a regulation on poor single mothers, but by means of a condition, government could push itself into their homes with ease. Thus, quite apart from the constitutionality of the requirements imposed by conditions, the process of regulating through conditions comes with profound constitutional risks, including that of displacing the Constitution's regulatory pathway through binding statutes.

The full extent of the constitutional dangers will unfold gradually over the course of this book, but the key point, as illustrated already by regulatory conditions, is that conditions can be dangerous for different reasons—sometimes because of the substance of their restrictions and sometimes more fundamentally because they evade the

Constitution's processes and structures. Overall, therefore, conditions need to be recognized as an irregular mechanism, which threatens the Constitution's structures of power as well as its rights.

The Federal Budget

To understand how federal conditions could become a broad unconstitutional avenue for regulation and even for denying rights, one need only consider the size of the federal budget. Federal grants to states and localities have increased from over $18 billion in 1970 to a current total of over $550 billion—that's $550,000,000,000.[3] Overall federal spending has increased from $195 billion in 1970 to nearly $4,500 billion today—that's $4,500,000,000,000.[4] For example, the Department of Health and Human Services (HHS) spends an average of more than $100 billion per month, which means about $3.3 billion per day or nearly $138 million per hour.[5] With this much money to distribute, the federal government can lean heavily on recipients.

Federal conditions are particularly far-reaching and thus are the focus of this book, but states and localities also impose conditions, which are no less interesting than their federal cousins, and sometimes even more worrisome. So this inquiry cannot be exclusively federal.

Viewed from below, the financial considerations are pressing. The states now get about 30 percent of their budgets from the federal government, and many individuals are even more dependent. The finances of most Americans include much government aid, including Social Security benefits, government pensions, welfare, public education, educational loans and guarantees, Federal Deposit Insurance Corporation guarantees, subsidized housing and medicine, and so forth.

The accompanying conditions affect Americans in almost all aspects of their lives, including education, health, publishing, science, religion, and sex. The purchase of submission is thus pervasive in its reach, digging deep into society and personal experience.

Censorship

The best way to get a quick measure of the threat is to consider the twentieth-century revival of the licensing of speech. At stake, it will be seen, is not merely the regulatory process, nor even merely constitutional rights, but even human life.

The First Amendment completely bars the prior review or "licensing" of speech or speakers. It is worrisome enough when speech is punished after the fact in legal proceedings, but in these retail proceedings the government at least must prove before a judge and jury that a particular defendant said particular words that are particularly harmful. In contrast, when government requires speakers to submit to "licensing"—that is, when it requires them to get permission before speaking—it can simply deny them permission without proving anything about their words. Licensing thus lends itself to wholesale suppression, and the First Amendment unsurprisingly bars this method of control, forcing government to regulate speech only through retail judicial proceedings against particular persons for particular words.[6]

Nonetheless, by means of conditions on its largess, the federal government has revived the licensing of speakers and words. The First Amendment and other constitutional guarantees of rights generally bar governmental constraints on Americans, and this focus on constraint has seemed to create an opening for the government to interfere with rights through its largess and other grants of privileges. By placing conditions on its generosity, the government has found that it can often escape constitutional rights that would severely confine it if it acted directly.

For example, the Federal Communications Commission (FCC) licenses broadcasters on the condition that they allow candidates equal time. The Internal Revenue Service exempts nonprofits from income tax on the condition that they submit to Internal Revenue Service determinations that they have largely given up persuading voters in elections and lawmakers as to legislation. And HHS uses its funding of academic research to impose prior licensing on much research speech and publication.

These licensing systems, though well intentioned, predictably lend themselves to the suppression of political opinion. Presidents Franklin Delano Roosevelt and John F. Kennedy already used the FCC to deny radio licenses to their opponents.[7] And political suppression is only the most salient problem, for the licensing of speech introduced through conditions inevitably does damage across the full spectrum of human endeavors, ranging from the arts to science. This is most painfully apparent from HHS's prior restraint of speech in and about research. This censorship stymies medical knowledge and consequently has a high cost for human health. There is even (as will be seen in Chapter 2) a substantial body count. It thus becomes clear that the purchase of submission has profound consequences for speech and life itself.

From Status to Contract

The purchase of submission has developed as part of a broader shift from status to contract. Whereas individuals in traditional societies could not easily escape their status, those in modern societies are relatively free to choose their fate, not least by entering contracts and other consensual arrangements.[8] The result has been a broad expansion of freedom.

The shift from status to contract, however, has not been an unmixed blessing. At the personal and social level, the costs include alienation and a loss of cohesion. And more centrally here, the shift toward something like contract as a mode of governance threatens a peculiarly valuable sort of status—the egalitarian status shared by persons in this country.

All citizens have an equal claim to vote, and all persons owing allegiance have an equal claim to the protection of the law, redress in the courts, and constitutional rights. For example, the First Amendment guarantees its freedoms without confining them to any particular sort of persons.[9] Rather than narrowly the equal protection of the laws guaranteed by the Fourteenth Amendment, this underlying equality cuts across the nation's entire constitutional order, and as will be seen (in Chapter 6), it is of profound significance in garnering broad societal support for otherwise merely legal freedoms.[10]

This egalitarian status, though, is now at risk. The shift from status to contract has gone so far that the government now pays Americans to submit to a loss of constitutional freedoms—often leaving Americans without the full rights and other freedoms enjoyed by fellow Americans. To be sure, different conditions deprive different Americans of different rights, and the inequality thus varies from condition to condition. But being subject to conditions, Americans do not equally enjoy their freedom to be governed by law, they cannot be equally confident of getting their day in court, they do not equally enjoy the security of federalism, and they are not equal in constitutional rights such as speech, juries, and due process. The purchase of submission thus deprives many Americans not only of particular constitutional freedoms but also of their status as persons equally secured by the Constitution's freedoms.*

---

*Although this book locates conditions within the shift from status to contract, it does not adopt the terms *commodification* and *inalienability*. These labels are commonly used in connection with conditions, and this footnote therefore explains why they are not employed here.

The term *commodification* could be used to describe some effects of conditions. But the word is often used in a manner suggestive of profound discontent with modernity, and it is not at all clear that either commodification or modernity deserve so much disdain. For example, contract was widespread even in premodern society, and over time it has been an essential escape from premodern constraints based in status—as when, for example, Englishmen purchased their way out of the obligations of vassalage and even out of serfdom. Commodification thus has often been a path toward freedom.

An Alternative Mode of Governance

Unfortunately, the problem explored in this book is often understood as a narrow or even technical matter of conditions. Being complicated mechanisms, which displace direct constraints with consensual arrangements, conditions can make it difficult to discern whether the government has violated constitutional rights. Conditions are therefore widely understood as a constitutional conundrum—a technical problem rather than a distinctive avenue for power.

But they are a pathway for power. Ruth Grant, in her book *Strings Attached*, recognizes aspects of this point: "incentives are a form of power as well as a form of trade," and thinking about them "as a form of power . . . brings to light important concerns about democratic politics." She worries, among other things, about the tendency to "shape people's choices without the sort of public discussion and consent that ideally characterize democratic processes of decision-making."[11] In more concrete legal terms, as will be explored here, the difficulty is that in seeking to regulate through the distribution of privileges, government sidesteps the avenues of power established by the Constitu-

---

The word *inalienability* may seem relevant because conditions sometimes require the sacrifice of rights that cannot reasonably be given up. Certainly, some rights may be inalienable. For example, on the view that faith is owed only to God, an individual cannot sacrifice his freedom of belief to anyone, whether government or even another individual. But the argument here concerns only what cannot be given up to government; it raises no objection to sacrificing one's freedom to private persons, except to the extent this is engineered by government. The argument from inalienability thus goes far beyond the questions examined in this book. Put another way, the inalienability argument is too powerful for purposes of this inquiry, and at the same time that argument is too narrow, for so powerful an argument can plausibly apply to only a small number of freedoms and thus cannot reach the breadth of regulatory and other problems examined here. Last but not least, this book can adequately pursue its inquiry about the Constitution by focusing on constitutional limits without delving into the deeper philosophical waters inhabited by ideas of inalienability.

tion and thereby threatens both constitutional self-governance and constitutional rights.

Accordingly, the first step, in Part I, is to begin to consider the problem not merely as a technical difficulty but as an evolving pathway of power, which can circumvent constitutional structures and rights.

It is in this sense that the book treats the problem as the purchase of submission. At stake is not merely personal compliance but submission to a reconfigured constitutional order in which the government takes an end run around the Constitution's pathways for power, around its enumeration of particular powers, around its separation of powers and federalism, and even around its guarantees of rights. This is, in other words, an alternative and dangerous mode of governance.

Constitutional Analysis

Having begun in Part I to recognize the problem, this book then turns to constitutional analysis. Although the book's main goal is to expose the grim reality of a new pathway of power, this danger cannot be fully understood without systematically pursuing the constitutional questions.

Conditions have long been considered too knotty to be unraveled by conventional legal concepts. But when the breadth and significance of the problem is understood, it becomes possible to take a fresh look at the legal responses and to see that they can be surprisingly familiar and concrete. The very expansiveness of the danger brings into focus some reassuringly narrow correctives.

Part II lays out the structural objections to the purchase of submission. Many conditions serve as irregular pathways of government control—paths that evade the Constitution's legislative and judicial avenues of power, its separation of powers, its federalism, and its procedural rights—and on this ground alone, many conditions are unconstitutional. That is, even when conditions do not impose restrictions that conflict with particular constitutional rights, they still are often unconstitutional because they depart from the Constitution's avenues of power.

Of course, some readers may hesitate to embrace this book's structural analysis, especially because the Supreme Court has gone far in abandoning the Constitution's structures. But those structures are not merely structural; they are also protections for freedom. Structural dangers, moreover, usually need structural responses. Accordingly, when the problem is understood structurally—as an unconstitutional pathway that threatens freedoms and needs an adequate solution—the Constitution's old structures may not seem so out of date.*

Part III turns to more conventional questions about unconstitutional conditions—the conditions that include unconstitutional restrictions, usually in violation of particular constitutional rights. Though often understood to be fraught with difficulty, such conditions actually have relatively clear solutions in the Constitution's guarantees of rights. By examining such guarantees, one can often discern whether a condition imposes an unconstitutional restriction.

There remains the difficult question of whether conditions come with the sort of federal action that would render them unconstitutional, but this question turns out in Part IV to be less intractable than is usually supposed. Many conditions are accompanied by the force of law or other constitutionally significant pressure, and for some constitutional questions, such force or pressure is not requisite. Moreover, even without force or other pressure, conditions that come with

---

* Whereas this book uses the word *rights* to refer to the Constitution's enumerated rights, it uses the word *freedoms* more broadly to refer to all of the Constitution's freedoms, including not only its enumerated rights but also its more structural freedoms, such as its protections for self-governance at the federal and the state level, its judicial power, and its separation of powers.

undue influence or that violate public policy are void and unenforceable under the law on consensual arrangements.

This might seem the end of the matter, but some conditions do not neatly fit within a consensual model. Part V therefore examines the use of conditions beyond consent—as instruments of governmental extortion and even as mechanisms by which the government gets agents to do what it constitutionally cannot.

Range of Constitutional Problems

Because of the host of possible constitutional defects, one cannot evaluate conditions under a single test. Instead, any condition must be examined from multiple angles:

- *Spending and Other Privileges.* Is the condition within Congress's power to spend or otherwise distribute privileges?

- *General Welfare.* If the condition involves spending—at least if it involves any tax funds—does it promote the general welfare?

- *Regulatory.* Is the condition regulatory—in the sense that it serves as a mode of regulation and thus displaces the Constitution's legislative avenue of power? For example, even if such a condition is specified entirely by Congress, it would appear to shift regulation from publicly enacted laws—even from publicly adopted administrative rules—to private decisions, thus divesting and even privatizing regulatory decisions that the Constitution envisions as public enactments. Such a condition also divests the courts of their judicial power, vesting it instead in agencies or even private institutions. And when these agencies or private bodies adjudicate, they systematically deny the Constitution's procedural rights.

- *Federalism.* Does the condition commandeer the states? And even when a federal condition does not go so far as to commandeer the states but rather merely conflicts with state law, does the Supremacy Clause really permit it to defeat state law?

- *Unconstitutional?* Is the requirement imposed by the condition unconstitutional? To be precise, does the applicable constitutional limit leave room for consent to the condition? If not, the condition is apt to be unconstitutional.

- *Federal Action?* Is there sufficient federal action for such a condition to be held unconstitutional?

- *Undue Influence and Public Policy.* Even when there is insufficient federal action to hold a condition unconstitutional, is the condition nonetheless void and unenforceable under conventional doctrines relating to consensual transactions—either because it was obtained through undue influence or because it is against public policy?

- *Regulatory Extortion.* Has the condition been imposed through threats of regulatory harassment, such as a threat to delay or adjust a licensing decision?

- *Regulatory Agents.* Does the federal government, instead of acting by itself, use the condition to corral states or private institutions into serving as agents to carry out federal regulatory policies or impose unconstitutional restrictions?

These are the sorts of questions that need to be considered in evaluating conditions.

Three Foundations

In making such arguments, this book relies on three foundations: the Constitution, precedent, and utility.

Most fundamentally, the book rests on the Constitution—indeed, the Constitution as understood historically. Even if one is not attached to the original Constitution, one still may want to understand it—if only to understand what has been lost, what has been gained, and where we may be heading.

Judicial precedents form a second foundation for this book's arguments. It is notorious that judicial decisions on conditions are poorly developed and often simply wrong. All the same, they can deserve attention. In some instances (such as on the germaneness and proportionality requirements and the anti-commandeering doctrine), they come close to recognizing requirements of the Constitution—even if they do not fully understand what is at stake and do not state the issues as accurately as might be desired. In other instances (such as on the spending power), they are so deeply imbedded that one must at least acknowledge them, even if without approbation. And even more commonly, one must mention precedent to observe how far it has gone astray. Thus, even when precedents deviate from the historical Constitution, they can be illuminating—sometimes for inchoate but still useful intuitions about the Constitution, sometimes for a second-best constitutional order, and sometimes simply to illustrate intellectual error.

Third, this book often recurs to utilitarian concerns about consequences in health, safety, liberty, and so forth—if only because such considerations are a useful reminder that departures from the Constitution are not merely of theoretical concern. They often come with practical dangers.

Each of these intellectual foundations will move different readers to different degrees, depending on their taste. The underlying point is akin to that of the old advertisement: "You don't have to be Jewish to love Levy's real Jewish rye." You don't have to be an originalist to worry about conditions.

The Way We Are Governed Now

Going beyond a legal argument about the constitutionality of conditions, this book opens up a question of political theory: How are we governed now?

The reality is sobering. Americans are now governed along pathways very different from those laid out in the Constitution—administrative commands being one of these new pathways and another being the purchase of submission.

My 2014 book *Is Administrative Law Unlawful?* observed that the government increasingly controls Americans not merely along the Constitution's avenues of control—which run through acts of Congress and the courts—but also along an additional pathway, administrative power.[12] Indeed, administrative edicts and adjudications nowadays vastly outnumber congressional statutes and court decisions. Put another way, though the United States remains a republic, there has developed within it a very different sort of government. The result is a state within the state—an administrative state within the Constitution's United States.

This book follows up by pointing out another irregular pathway of power—not by administrative command but by purchase. By paying for acquiescence, the central government co-opts individuals, states, and private institutions and ultimately secures submission to an unconstitutional mode of governance and unconstitutional restrictions.

The effect of these irregular pathways—both administrative and pecuniary—in evading the Constitution's avenues has largely escaped the attention of American political theory. That discipline often focuses on the Constitution and even more commonly recasts the Constitution's republic as a democracy, but it rarely observes that very different sorts of governance have developed within the Republic. One of the irregular modes, administrative power, has attracted much attention; but even administrative power is not sufficiently recognized as an alternative pathway of governance, which bypasses the Constitution's avenues. And the other leading irregular method, the purchase of submission, has scarcely been understood as a pathway of power.

This lack of recognition is especially troubling because the purchase of submission is even more dangerous than the administrative state as an evasion of the Constitution's avenues of power. Administrative edicts at least tend to be publicly adopted and promulgated as rules binding on the public. In contrast, conditions are ultimately adopted only in private transactions. And because they come with government largess and so are not themselves binding, they have thus far been peculiarly effective in defeating constitutional rights. Therefore, even if one were willing to live with administrative power, one should hesitate to accept this more dangerous irregular pathway for control. Nonetheless, it is scarcely even recognized as an alternative mode of power.

To be sure, there are valuable intimations. Ruth Grant (as already noted) hints at some of the risks for self-government.[13] Martha Derthick illuminates the losses at the state and local level.[14] Further exploring the implications for federalism is the work of Judge James Buckley, Thomas McCoy, and Barry Friedman.[15] And myriad other legal scholars have examined the loss of constitutional rights.[16]

Perhaps the most important recognition of conditions as a mode of power is Charles Reich's 1964 article "The New Property." Admittedly, he frames government largess in terms of property and therefore misses the depth of the problem of power. But at least in the course of pursuing his property vision, he sees that privileges enable power.[17]

Yet even with all of this prior scholarship, the question of power remains in need of systematic analysis. And the threat as a whole from conditions—including the full range of constitutional dangers—is largely unrecognized. This book, therefore, explains how the purchase of submission serves as an alternative pathway of power, which enables the federal government to sidestep congressional lawmaking, adjudication by the courts, the enumerated federal powers, federalism, and a host of constitutional rights.

All of this amounts to a new power. The growth of federal spending in the 1960s prompted much excitement about the new property and concomitant new rights, such as due process for government benefits. The reality, however, has been very different. The process gains were negligible and even destructive of real due process (as explained in Chapter 11). And the expanded federal funding came with massive regulatory, commandeering, and unconstitutional conditions.[18] Americans acquired not so much a new property as a new mode of being controlled.

Long ago, Alexis de Tocqueville presciently hinted at the dangers of government benevolence—anticipating that it would undermine private authority and life and subvert political self-government.[19] Yet even the most prophetic generalities of the past are no substitute for understanding current realities. This book, if nothing else, calls for Americans to consider how in fact we are governed now.

PART I

The Problem

Although the problem is severe, it is not well or widely understood. Even lawyers who specialize in the subject fail to recognize the scope of the danger, and most of the public remains blissfully unaware. This book in Part I therefore begins to explore the danger, after which it will turn to systematic constitutional analysis.

1

Poorly Understood

A host of potential misconceptions could derail a clear understanding of the purchase of submission. This chapter therefore addresses some such impediments—if only to get past them.

Counterintuitive

The most basic obstacle to understanding the purchase of submission is simply the counterintuitive nature of governance through spending. In this strange substitute for governance through law, money moves in one direction and power in another. If one focuses too much on the largess, one can miss the resulting control. The unfamiliarity of this give-and-take leaves many Americans, even specialists, struggling to understand what is really happening, let alone to respond to it with conventional and thus plausible legal tools.

Accordingly, it is important to avoid thinking about the problem merely in terms of the technical-sounding word *conditions*. Though that word cannot be avoided, one should remember the danger that the government is sometimes purchasing submission to an unconstitutional mode of governance. With this in mind, the logic of the problem will never be elusive.

Not Just Unconstitutional Conditions

As conventionally understood, the problem is centrally one of unconstitutional conditions—in particular, conditions imposing restrictions that violate particular constitutional rights. The Constitution's
rights mostly bar the government from constraining Americans, and
the government consequently feels relatively free to ignore such rights
when acting through conditions on its benefits.

But the risk from unconstitutional conditions is only one of the
dangers, and not the most common. Accordingly, it is necessary to
step back, so as to get a broader view of the landscape.

For example, quite apart from unconstitutional conditions, there
is the risk that government increasingly regulates through conditions
on its largess rather than through law. Thus, even when conditions
do not conflict with constitutional rights, conditions can threaten the
freedom of Americans.

The problem must therefore be understood expansively. It includes
unconstitutional conditions, but is much broader—with wide-ranging
implications for self-government and freedom.

Nudging

Although broader than unconstitutional conditions, the purchase of
submission is a more specific problem than the government's use of
financial incentives and similar devices to shift behavior—what is
sometimes called nudging.[1] While the government often uses benefits to move Americans in one direction or another, this nudging is
not necessarily unconstitutional.

Of course, even incentives that do not collide with the Constitution can be worrisome for a host of reasons. For example, though incentives can motivate virtue (in the sense of good behavior), they
can also crowd out virtue (in the sense of a personal commitment to
such conduct).

This book, however, does not concern the general problem of crowding out virtue; instead, it focuses on the use of incentives to crowd out the Constitution's pathways of power, its guarantees of rights, and its other limits. That is, although all sorts of government incentives can undermine personal self-government, the problem of purchasing submission concerns the use of incentives in ways that more directly threaten constitutional governance and freedom.

Submission

The word *submission* may seem harsh. Nevertheless, it makes sense here, precisely because this book focuses on the conditions that ask Americans to submit to a new pathway of power.

If this book concerned the vast number of mundane conditions that do not require submission to unconstitutional governance, it could have spoken merely about the purchase of *compliance.* Similarly, if this book focused on government support for Roman-style bread and circuses, it would have complained about how the government purchases *contentment* and offers *distraction.* And if the book protested against Bismarckian-style spending to overcome divisions, it would have emphasized the purchase of *loyalty* or *consensus.* Such uses of spending could, and may yet, undermine America's political system. But they do not necessarily conflict with the Constitution, and this book does not question them.

What this book does challenge is the use of government largess to induce Americans to submit to a new path of governance, which displaces the Constitution's avenues of power and its rights. Rather than merely the purchase of compliance, this is something much more serious—submission to an unconstitutional mode of power—and to capture this reality, the book speaks about the purchase of *submission.*

Historical Baseline

As should be evident by now, the baseline for this inquiry is the Constitution—that is, the Constitution unaltered by the living constitution. That enactment of the people does not solve all problems faced by Americans, and it creates some problems of its own. But at the very least, it is a good measure of losses in freedom. A historical understanding of the Constitution is useful for evaluating the fate of freedom in this country.

Put another way, one does not have to be an originalist to mistrust the growing tendency of government to devolve powers and purchase rights. Nor must one be an originalist to value regulation by law over regulation by purchase—or to appreciate due process and the freedom of speech.

Thus, even readers who are not inclined to interpret the Constitution historically should find value in this book's approach. The trajectory of freedom is at least as important as its location at any one time, whether the past or the present, and therefore whatever one's approach to constitutional law, there is reason to consider its development, including where it has been and where it is going.

Academic Theories

Academic theories can be a mixed blessing. Though many illuminate unconstitutional conditions, they tend to address only this one element of what is a much broader problem. And even within this restricted realm, the most prominent theories tend to evaluate the constitutional dangers in socioeconomic terms.

One theory, proposed by Seth Kreimer, proposes that when the government denies benefits that are considered normal—on historical, egalitarian, or predictive grounds—the denial should be considered a penalty or constraint, which would then be subject to the Constitution's limits.[2] Though this approach has much appeal, it does not wrestle with conditions on their own terms. It is true (as will be seen in Chapter 11) that the distinction between constraints and benefits has been eroded, but the reality is that the Constitution pervasively makes this distinction and that government exploits it—using conditions on benefits to avoid constitutional limits on constraints. Rather than engage with this deeply ingrained problem, Kreimer's theory sweepingly recategorizes common benefits as constraints. And yet not sweepingly enough, for in finding constraint in the government's denial of common or "normal" benefits, his theory does nothing to illuminate the myriad conditions on less common or normal benefits.

Another prominent academic theory—from Richard Epstein—evaluates unconstitutional conditions in light of consensual ideals and consequently focuses on force, fraud, monopolies, and threats to third parties.[3] This book will pursue versions of some of these concerns. But Epstein's theory elaborates these questions in terms of economic freedom and market failure and therefore does not adequately work through conditions in legal terms. Indeed, it moves the inquiry to a level of generality far above constitutional law.

The other leading theory, Kathleen Sullivan's, observes that conditions alter the distribution of power—between government and the people and among the people—even to the point of creating a caste hierarchy. Sullivan notes, for example, that the poor have nothing to trade but their rights.[4] Again, an economic vision—this time about distributive effects—is very suggestive but does not concretely sort out the legal difficulties.

What is needed in place of these theories is an understanding that is simultaneously broader and more concrete—broader in confronting the full problem of the purchase of submission, not just unconstitutional conditions, and more concrete in analyzing it in practicable legal terms.

Fortunately, some of the existing scholarship offers precisely the sort of practical analysis that is needed, and this book relies on such work where it can—mostly to understand unconstitutional conditions and federalism. But otherwise—for example, as to spending, regulatory conditions, evasion of the courts and their due process, force, regulatory extortion, and the use of regulatory agents to control their personnel—this book must strike out on its own, with only occasional echoes of prior work. Most broadly, this book offers a new vision of the problem by recognizing the purchase of submission as an irregular pathway of power.

Precedent and Doctrine

Although it may be expected that a law book will follow existing precedent and doctrine, this is difficult when it comes to the purchase of submission. Even as to unconstitutional conditions—a relatively familiar component of the problem—the case law is all over the map. And in many other areas involving conditions, the Supreme Court has not even recognized that constitutional questions are at stake.

This book accordingly must often discuss issues that the Supreme Court has never or scarcely considered. Though the book draws on existing precedents and doctrines where it can, it does not pretend to reconcile them, let alone to reconcile all of them with its arguments. Readers who want a narrow analysis of existing precedent and doctrine are advised to look elsewhere.

Just how independent of the Supreme Court's doctrines this book must be becomes evident from the court's doctrine on disproportionate and nongermane conditions. The court is surely correct when it intuitively focuses on these characteristics, but exactly why they matter needs further attention. It will be seen that they can be revealing about a range of questions—including whether a condition fits within federal authority to spend, whether it is regulatory, and whether it comes with force.

Although the undeveloped and scattered character of existing judicial doctrine means that this book must sort through the constitutional problems without clinging to precedent, it also means that such doctrine remains open to maturation. Accordingly, even when this book makes unfamiliar arguments, this is not to say it is entirely at odds with what has come before. In going beyond precedent, it often is simply exploring the problems in greater depth and breadth than the courts have thus far attempted.

This book therefore asks judges not so much to abandon their doctrine as to develop it—sometimes by adjusting it to recognize the full analytic strength of what they have already incompletely discerned, and sometimes by recognizing the familiar doctrinal tools that are lying at hand but have not yet been used.

Evolving and Recent Development

Another impediment to understanding the purchase of submission is that it has evolved in an ad hoc manner, without much public fanfare, and has developed into a common mode of governance only during the past half century.[5] As a result, it is still strangely unfamiliar to many judges and other Americans.

The purchase of submission was an improbable mode of power at a time when the federal government could scarcely afford to support itself, let alone the states and a vast swath of the populace. In such circumstances, the government's occasional purchase of submission lacked much salience, and such purchases did not seem a serious alternative to more traditional pathways of power.

Judicial decisions therefore long focused on a relatively narrow range of unconstitutional conditions—indeed, on seemingly technical questions, of little interest to the public—as if there were no broader danger that the government was using its generosity as a mode of power. In the late nineteenth and early twentieth centuries, for example, the Supreme Court went back and forth in decisions about out-of-state corporations—in particular, as to whether a state could bar such a corporation from doing business in state, unless it first agreed that, if sued in state court, it would not remove the case into federal court.

Even the cases concerning individuals were relatively technical. A 1927 Supreme Court decision, *Hess v. Pawloski,* held that Massachusetts could admit out-of-state drivers to drive on the state's highways on the condition that they submitted to the state's jurisdiction, thus enabling injured persons to sue them.[6] The most interesting decision concerning individuals was a state case. In *McAuliffe v. Mayor & Board of Aldermen* (1892), a Massachusetts police officer was fired for soliciting money and for being a member of a political committee—in violation of municipal regulations. Sitting on the state's Supreme Judicial Court, Oliver Wendell Holmes forcefully declared that the policeman "may have a constitutional right to talk politics, but he has no constitutional right to be a policeman."[7]

These early judicial opinions stand out for their failure of imagination—for their inability to see the larger stakes. Only rarely before the 1920s did courts squarely recognize that government was exploring what might become a new mode of governance.

Since then, American governments, especially the federal government, have vastly expanded their use of subsidies to purchase submission. Certainly, lawful conditions on government privileges have been commonplace since the beginning of the nation—for example, in plea bargains and land grants. But increasingly in the twentieth century, federal conditions subverted the Constitution's pathways of power, its rights, and its other limits.

The underlying reality has been the growth of federal spending. Federal spending has grown from about 4 percent of gross domestic product in 1900 to about 20 percent. And in the last decade alone, it has increased from $3 trillion to almost $4 trillion.[8]

Not least significant (as pointed out by Judge Buckley) has been the increase in federal grants in aid to the states. In 1970, federal grants to states and localities totaled over $18 billion. By 1980, this became nearly $70 billion; by 1990, over $100 billion; and by 2000, more than $230 billion. Then came the greatest leap, when in 2010 such funding reached $500 billion. And today, it is well over $550 billion.[9] The funding has thus multiplied more than five times since 1990, and it now provides the states with about 30 percent of their budgets.[10]

Such grants shape almost the full range of state policies—including matters as varied as health care, child care, foster care, prekindergarten classes, education, policing, the environment, welfare, highways, airports, mass transit, low-income and senior housing, community and regional development, job training, clean water, voting processes, water and sewer systems, community and youth centers, libraries, employment assistance, labor market information and job training, law enforcement, community-oriented policing programs, juvenile justice programs, prevention and prosecution of violence against women, combating drug trafficking, and so forth. No wonder federal conditions increasingly overshadow much American government and life!

Perhaps Americans are doomed not to recognize problems until they are overwhelming. But at least at this stage, there is little excuse for failing to understand that the purchase of submission is a prominent mode of government power, which is growing more pervasive every year.

Regulatory Effects

It cannot be overemphasized that this book does not argue against regulation. Even when protesting regulatory conditions, it does not question that many of the regulations imposed through conditions are valuable. Rather than raise doubts about regulation, the book questions the use of conditions for this purpose.

All the same, the book's arguments have regulatory costs—as is inevitable whenever one elevates constitutional mechanisms over regulatory ends. It can be more difficult to regulate when one must act through Congress and have open political debate, when one must enforce the law with the due process of the courts, and when one cannot sidestep the Constitution's enumerated powers, its federalism, and its rights.

Regulation, however, is not the only valuable feature of government. Also desirable are the Constitution's representative and judicial processes, its division of power between the federal government and the states, and its procedural and other freedoms. And if these desiderata are to be cast aside, it surely should be done more openly and deliberately than through the purchase of submission.

Whatever the need for regulation—and there certainly are areas in which more is desirable—there also needs to be a reconsideration of the process by which regulation is adopted and imposed. Many of the regulations imposed by conditions would be entirely constitutional if imposed directly by Congress. Yet the use of conditions to adopt such regulations can be more dangerous than the problems thereby addressed. Although administrative regulation raises its own constitutional difficulties, even that would often be better than the pecuniary mode of regulation that ends up privatizing regulatory decisions.

Private Transactions

A further difficulty for understanding the problem is that the purchase of submission comes into existence through private transactions. Although often authorized by public statutes or at least administrative rules, the purchase of submission ultimately occurs in private arrangements—prototypically between government and those whose submission it purchases.

This shift of public power to private transactions comes with many dangers, including a loss in visibility. Much of what is really happening in the purchase of submission cannot be discerned merely in the statute book or the federal register. On the contrary, the details, even crucial substantive elements, must often be found in agency guidance, scattered assurances, letters, emails, and mere conversations.[11] An agency site inspector, for example, can orally share his understanding of what the agency expects and can thereby secure conformity not merely to the agency's formal conditions but even to its more expansive desires. He can do this, moreover, by raised eyebrow—with little more than ambiguous expressions of concern, which prompt funded organizations to restrain themselves beyond what is expressly demanded. In many instances, accordingly, basic questions about the submission (such as who has submitted and to what) can be answered only by securing documentation of the private arrangements—something that is not always documented, let alone publicly available. The phenomenon is consequently difficult to measure.

Conditions are thus like submerged icebergs—only partly visible on the surface of the law. The full measure of the submission is difficult to discern. But if one looks into the depths, one can see enough to be worried.

Contractual or at Least Consensual?

Yet another impediment is that commentators talk about conditions in stereotyped ways, drawn from contract, that obscure the realities. The result is to lump conditions together in ways that miss their distinctive features.

Most basically, judges and scholars often describe conditions as contractual. For decades, the Supreme Court has (in its own words) "repeatedly characterized" conditions as being "much in the nature of a *contract*."[12] But the Supreme Court once said otherwise, and many government agencies still take that older view. Carefully avoiding any suggestion of contract, many agencies state their

conditions not in contracts, nor even in promises, but instead in mere
"assurances"—recitations of existing facts, which an applicant must
sign before being considered for a grant.[13] This self-conscious avoid-
ance of a contractual framework suggests that the contractual vision of
conditions is disputed and that many agencies are thinking about conditions differently from the judges and other commentators.*

Another common assumption is that, whether or not conditions are
contractual, they are two-party consensual transactions. This, however, misses the growing use of conditions to control third parties,
whose consent is sometimes explicit, sometimes merely implied, and
sometimes vanishingly elusive.

The government often works in roundabout ways—corralling one
group of Americans in order to create incentives for others to comply
with government policy. For example, it gives taxpayers charitable deductions for donating to churches and other charities, but only if the
charities comply with government-stipulated restrictions on their political speech. These speech restrictions, which are tied to deductions,
are no different from those imposed on charities in exchange for their
exemption from income tax, but it is the pressure from donors who
want deductions that typically leads charities to submit to the speech
restrictions. This strategy of indirection—of using a condition on one
group (donors) to create incentives for another group (charities)—

---

* Recognizing the limits of the contract analogy, some commentators compare government grants to conditional gifts, and certainly for many grants, the conditional gift
analogy is helpful. But it is, at best, an incomplete analogy, as it is often clearly inappli-
cable. For example, procurement contracts are not conditional gifts. Nor are plea bargains, regulatory licenses, or any of the other conditional government privileges that
cannot be understood as spending. Even as to government grants, the gift analogy is not
entirely accurate, for grants (as will be seen in Chapter 3) have become an avenue of
regulatory power, and they often (as will be explored in Chapters 11 and 12) come with
varying degrees of federal action.

redoubles public pressures with private pressures and thereby makes it easier for the government to deprive Americans of their constitutional freedoms.[14]

Even more intrusively, the government controls individuals through conditions on states and private institutions. That is, the federal government funds states and private bodies on the condition that they regulate persons within their domain. The potential for power over third parties increasingly motivates federal conditions on states and private entities. It is a triangular mode of control that stands in sharp contrast to the typical two-party model of conditions.

Another misguided assumption about consent is that its presence means the absence of force—as if consent and force were mutually exclusive. But one cannot forget to inquire whether the consent was induced through force and whether there can be subsequent force. Consent is thus merely the beginning of the inquiry, and it does not displace a separate inquiry into the possibility of force, let alone lesser degrees of pressure. Indeed, it will be seen that some alleged conditions are better understood as a matter of extortion.

Pre- and Post-Grant Compliance

Government grants can require compliance at different times. Under some government programs, performance of a condition must occur before a grant will be made or distributed, and no further performance is required. Under other programs, compliance must continue or occur afterward, or the benefits will stop or even have to be returned.

Important as this distinction may be for government agencies, it does not matter much for constitutional purposes. And as the Supreme Court has observed, if the government could manipulate the difference, it would be able to evade its constitutional limits by simply shifting from one sort of condition to the other.[15] This book therefore does not differentiate the two kinds of conditions, except for the narrow purpose of understanding (in Chapter 12) when a condition is backed by force or other pressure.*

Conditions versus Considerations

It is widely assumed that the considerations that enter into government decisions do not amount to conditions. In *National Endowment for the Arts v. Finley* (1998), a performance artist, Karen Finley, challenged a 1990 statute that required the National Endowment for the Arts, when awarding grants to artists, to "tak[e] into consideration general standards of decency and respect for the diverse beliefs and values of the American public."[16] If the statute had actually barred the distribution of grants to artists whose work did not meet "general standards of decency" (whatever that may mean these days), there would be no doubt that this would be a condition on funding. But is a mere consideration of such standards a condition?

The Supreme Court upheld the statute on the ground that it imposed its disputed standards not as "categorical requirement[s]" but rather merely as "considerations."[17] And at least initially, this conclu-

---

* The Supreme Court has summarized the distinction between the two kinds of conditions by speaking about conditions precedent and conditions subsequent—for example, in *Koontz v. St. Johns River Water Management District* (2013). This shorthand, however, could prove misleading. In traditional contract law, whereas conditions precedent were those that had to be met before a promise would become obligatory and thus enforceable, conditions subsequent were those that, if satisfied, could defeat the obligation of a promise and render it unenforceable. It is therefore unsurprising that the words *precedent* and *subsequent* come to mind in discussions of conditions. Nonetheless, these traditionally were labels for conditions that trigger or defeat the obligation of promises, not the conditions required for grants.

The appropriation of these promissory labels could thus introduce confusion about the sort of conditions at stake here, which at times are tied to promises but typically are not. There is already more than enough confusion in this area of law, and accordingly, for the sake of clarity, this book avoids the Supreme Court's catchy but misplaced terms.

sion makes sense. If a condition unequivocally bars receipt of a grant or justifies its revocation, then one can distinguish a mere consideration as something that may or may not affect the grant. From this perspective, considerations are not constitutionally significant for purposes of understanding conditions until they harden into conditions.

But there is another point of view. If a condition is unconstitutional, why should the government be able to justify it merely by calling it a "consideration" and making its application slightly unpredictable? In other words, what distinguishes considerations from conditions is merely a matter of probability. When a barrier to receiving funding or some other privilege is relatively unequivocal, it is called a *condition*, and when its application is somewhat open-ended or discretionary, it is called a *consideration*. It thus makes sense to treat considerations as conditions of uncertain probability.

This is not to say that the consideration weighed by the National Endowment for the Arts in *Finley* was an unconstitutional condition. On the contrary, as will be seen in Chapter 10, it probably was entirely lawful—but not for the reason given by the Supreme Court when it mistakenly drew a sharp distinction between conditions and considerations.

Exactly when considerations are unlawful conditions—whether because they are regulatory, commandeering, unconstitutional, or otherwise—will be pursued further in Chapter 10. For now, it is enough to observe that considerations have the potential to be unlawful as conditions.[18]

Not Just Spending but Privileges

Even when commentators focus on the narrow question of unconstitutional conditions, there is much confusion on something as basic as what constitutes a condition—one source of difficulty being a narrow focus on spending. Many commentators speak in terms of "conditions on spending," and this is not entirely unreasonable, as spending is central. The government typically ties its conditions to its expenditures, whether in the form of cash or other valuable benefits. It will be seen, however, that many conditions cannot easily be considered a matter of spending.

When a prosecutor offers a plea bargain reducing criminal charges, he may ask the defendant to waive his right to a jury trial and perhaps his right against self-incrimination. Similarly, when a local zoning board allows a landowner to build on her land, the board may ask her to accept limits on her use of the property. Such conditions are difficult to understand as limits on spending; far from being conditions on government payments, they are not even conditions on government benefits.

The spending paradigm is therefore misleading, and one must take a more capacious view of the problem. Rather than rest merely on spending, conditions rest on the full range of government privileges.

Privileges versus Constraints

Of course, it may be doubted whether the distinction between privileges and constraints is tenable in a world of widespread dependency on vast government benefits. Certainly, the distinction between constraints and privileges has lost some of its luster, and the Supreme Court and some eager academics have even declared it moribund. Its death, however, has been greatly exaggerated.

The legal reality is that the Constitution clearly places a host of restrictions on government constraints (such as takings, searches, judicial process, and criminal punishments)—restrictions that it does not impose on the government's distribution of privileges. And it bars laws abridging the freedom of speech and the right to bear arms, without requiring the distribution of government grants supporting speech and guns. It thus should be evident that although government privileges can be of great importance, the Constitution typically limits constraints rather than privileges.

This is why conditions are so significant. They have thrived precisely because they play upon the traditional difference between constraints and privileges. Being conditions on privileges, they apparently avoid the Constitution's avenues for lawmaking and adjudication, and even evade its enumerated powers and rights, thus becoming an all-round escape hatch for eluding constitutional limits. Accordingly, even if the distinction between constraints and privileges has lost much traction in some areas of law, it cannot be considered obsolete as to conditions.

Both a Duty and a Condition

It may be thought that all laws impose conditions. For example, when a law imposes a duty, subject to a penalty, it could be understood as stating the condition on which one can avoid paying the penalty. And when a law directly regulates interstate commerce, it could be viewed as reciting the conditions of engaging in such commerce. From this point of view, conditions can be found everywhere.[19]

The constitutionally important feature of conditions, however, is their capacity to limit without the direct imposition of a legal duty. This is what has enabled conditions to evade so many rights and other constitutional limits. Accordingly, if one were to understand conditions so broadly as to include all direct restraints, one would miss what has been distinctively interesting about conditions.

All the same, there is some overlap. In most instances, a condition is not a legal duty, and a legal duty is not a condition of a privilege. Put in terms of remedies, a condition is indirectly enforceable through a denial or loss of funding, and a duty is directly enforceable through some sort of legal constraint. The two categories may thus seem mutually exclusive. A sizable minority of conditions, however, are also legal duties. In other words, the government can impose a requirement both directly as a constraint and indirectly as a condition.

Imagine a mid-twentieth-century state statute requiring public school teachers to take a loyalty oath, or a twenty-first-century state statute requiring them annually to make a vow of their commitment to diversity. Leaving aside the merits of requiring affirmations of belief, note that such a statute could take the path of either a condition or a legal duty. On the one hand, it could make the affirmation a condition of continued employment—so that a noncompliant teacher would lose her government job. On the other hand, it could directly require teachers to make affirmations of their views—that is, it could make the affirmation a legal duty, such that each teacher would have a legal obligation to recite it. And to secure compliance, the statute could impose a criminal fine of $500 for any violation of the duty. Under this version of the statute, the oath is not a condition of serving as a public school teacher, for a teacher could simply refuse to swear and then pay the fine without worrying about her job.

But now imagine that the statute makes the oath both a legal duty for public school teachers *and* a qualification for serving as a public school teacher. Under such a statute, the duty would also be a condition of government employment.

A direct legal requirement can thus also be a condition. And because a requirement can be both a constraint and a condition, what distinguishes a condition from a constraint is not the absence of legal obligation or penalty. Instead, the distinguishing feature of a condition is that it demarcates when one can get or lose a benefit or other government privilege. If a failure to satisfy a requirement results in the loss of a privilege, the requirement is a condition—whatever else it also might be.

In short, many conditions are also direct constraints; these modes of power can overlap. But the requirements that are or seem to be merely conditions are especially worrisome, as the government uses them to evade its constitutional limits.

The Economically Vulnerable

Conditions bear down harshly on the poor—even more than is widely recognized. At the same time, to understand the problem as a whole, it is important to recognize that all sorts of Americans are economically vulnerable to conditions.

Focusing on the poor, Kathleen Sullivan argues that conditions "can create an undesirable caste hierarchy in the enjoyment of constitutional rights."[20] Unpacking Sullivan's argument, Daniel Farber explains:

> If benefits are made available only to the poor, who are then encouraged to waive their constitutional rights, the result is to leave constitutional rights distributed according to a hierarchy. One message of Sullivan's analysis is that funding conditions on welfare for the poor are particularly suspect, since they may result in creating constitutional second-class citizens, who not only have fewer material goods than others but also fewer basic rights.[21]

Unequal economic status facilitates a loss of rights and thus ultimately unequal legal status.

Legislators so far have not adopted the most intrusive proposals for conditions on the poor. But the risks are clear. It has been proposed, for example, that aid for indigent mothers should be conditioned on their not having further children or on their using the contraceptive Norplant.[22] At one point, the federal government seriously proposed that its support for local public housing be conditioned on the consent of tenants to police searches of their apartments.[23] Sullivan is therefore surely correct in worrying that the poor will face conditions that distinctively deprive them of their rights.

Of course, conditions on the poor are apt to be severe even when the conditions do not target constitutional rights. It has already been seen that, under the federal program for Aid to Families with Dependent Children, New York State provided assistance on the condition that families permitted caseworkers into their homes to evaluate their eligibility. By the same token, under the Anti-Drug Abuse Act of 1998, the Department of Housing and Urban Development conditions funding for local public housing on the inclusion of one-strike drug provisions in all leases—so that a lease can be terminated whenever a tenant or a member of the household engages in any drug-related criminal activity (including possession with intent to sell or use).[24] The public housing authority in Oakland, California, has expanded on this by allowing termination for the mere possession of illegal drugs or drug paraphernalia.[25] This may not be unconstitutional, but it is very harsh on the relatives of those who go astray. Entire families can lose their homes. They even may hesitate to call 911 in the event of an overdose. Aid aimed specially at the poor tends to come with especially hard conditions.

Even under the conditions that apply to all sorts of Americans, the poor are most at risk, as they are least able to meet the conditions. For example, the repayment conditions on student loans, though onerous enough for the middle class, are all the more difficult for the indigent.

It is not just the poor, however, who are economically vulnerable. Amid the justified concern about a caste hierarchy of rights, it is often forgotten that economic vulnerability cuts across American society. Much of the middle class, many states, and most academic institutions operate on the margin of what they can afford. States and private institutions, ranging from banks to universities, usually feel they cannot turn down subsidies and their attendant conditions, and the sense of exigency is especially strong when the private institutions (banks, again, are a good example) must comply with the conditions to secure licenses to do business.

Inasmuch as the wealthiest states and private institutions cannot easily resist the siren song of federal money, let alone the necessity of federal licenses, the point about economic vulnerability reaches far beyond the poor. The indigent are particularly apt to feel pressures and suffer under harsh conditions. But one cannot understand the threat from conditions without recognizing that the financial pressures are pervasive; they threaten the freedom of all Americans. The danger is thus not merely a hierarchy of rights but more generally a fragmentation of rights in which nearly everyone is vulnerable to a separate and unequal peace, and vast numbers are deprived of one constitutional freedom or another.

Agency but Not Administrative Power

Are conditions part of administrative power? Although the purchase of submission is usually done by government agencies, it is not administrative power. Rather than control Americans through binding public rules—statutory or administrative—conditions secure submission through allegedly optional private arrangements.

Traditionally, Americans could be bound only by acts of Congress and the courts. But increasingly, Americans have also been controlled by other mechanisms. The primary alternative mechanism is administrative power, by which a host of government agencies issue administrative rules and adjudications, not to mention other administrative edicts. But administrative power is only one evasion of the Constitution's pathways for binding Americans. Another evasion takes place through agencies' conditions on government largess.

This mode of regulation differs from administrative power because it does not purport to bind. Congress sometimes specifies federal conditions or, more typically, leaves agencies to do this in their rules, interpretations, and guidance. Mere conditions, however, do not pretend to bind in the manner of law. Instead, they are qualifications that come with the acceptance of funding or other privileges. Though conditions increase the power of agencies, they are different from administrative power.

Accordingly, in evading the Constitution's routes for binding law-making and adjudication, the government and in particular its agencies can choose between two illicit pathways. They can impose binding administrative edicts, which purport to have the binding force of law, or they can place conditions on privileges—a mechanism that purports to be without the force of law.

Administrative power and conditions should thus be considered feral cousins. Both give agencies power by allowing them to escape the Constitution's avenues, but whereas administrative power candidly purports to bind Americans, the conditions more subtly pretend not to bind. And this makes their evasion of political and constitutional limits especially dangerous.

So much for the standard sources of confusion. Having been recognized and (hopefully) resolved, they need not stand in the way of understanding the purchase of submission.*

---

* A further possible source of confusion is the public forum doctrine. This doctrine bars government from viewpoint discrimination in the distribution of some types of benefits, and it is therefore often assumed to be a matter of unconstitutional conditions. But rather than ordinarily apply to the distribution of general government funds or privileges, the doctrine most predictably and centrally applies to only a narrow class of such things.

The public forum doctrine stands on strongest ground when the government discriminates in barring access to common property, such as common land, for this is property shared by the public. In such circumstances, when the government denies someone access on account of their views, it is denying them their freedom of speech in using property that they hold in common with others. And the public forum doctrine is almost as strong as to government property that has been dedicated to public purposes. The difference is that the government can withdraw this public dedication—something it cannot do with common property. But until it withdraws its dedication of the property to the public, it cannot discriminate on the basis of viewpoint in cutting off the public's use of the property.

The public forum doctrine is also strong as to special assessments. Whereas government can spend general tax funds as it pleases, the benefits of a special assessment must be distributed among those who were required to contribute to it. In other words, those who contribute have a right to receive their share of benefits, and this means that government cannot discriminate in distributing the benefits.

This sort of reasoning about special assessments underlies *Rosenberger v. University of Virginia* (1995). When distributing funds collected out of student fees, the University of Virginia discriminated against a student publication on account of its religious orientation. The Supreme Court held that the distribution of the funds created a limited public forum and that the discriminatory denial of funding in this context violated the First Amendment. Of course, the court would not have reached such a conclusion about the university's distribution of general funds, but its decision makes sense because the fees functioned as a form of special assessment. The university therefore could not discriminate on the basis of viewpoint when allocating the resulting pool of money.

In short, although the public forum doctrine and the doctrine on conditions sometimes apply to the same facts, the public forum doctrine is much narrower, for its requirement of nondiscrimination arises from the public or shared interest in the distributed property. Of course, the public forum doctrine could be expanded to reach generic government benefits or privileges, but at its core, this doctrine is distinct from that on conditions.

2

Examples

To get a feel for conditions—to get a sense of their texture and how they are used—this chapter offers some examples. It begins with lawful and valuable conditions. It then turns to more troubling instances, which illustrate some of this book's arguments: regulatory conditions, commandeering conditions, unconstitutional conditions, and those imposed through agents. Of course, most conditions do not depart from the Constitution. Many, however, are more worrisome.

Generally Lawful and Valuable

All sorts of conditions are lawful and very useful—not just those in government contracts for airplanes, software, and supplies but also some of those that serve as instruments of governance. For example, it can be valuable and lawful for student loans to be conditioned on student attendance and repayment and for welfare to be conditioned on the recipient's needs.

Among the most interesting of conditions that effectuate government policy are plea bargains. An astonishing 97 percent of federal prosecutions result in plea bargains—in part because, as has been seen, defendants typically face a threat of triple prison time if they refuse a plea bargain and its conditions. Such conditions are highly coercive. They also (as will be explained in Chapter 3) may be regulatory. And in some instances, their terms are unconstitutional (a point to which Chapter 10 will return).

But notwithstanding such risks, there is nothing necessarily unlawful about plea bargains. And they often are valuable. They can induce cooperation from defendants, offer them lower sentences, and relieve the judicial system of unnecessary burdens.

Thus, even conditions that may make one pause can be welcomed as lawful tools of governance—up to a point. Beyond that, as now will be illustrated, there are dangers. Even when conditions are in some sense valuable, they can be constitutionally worrisome.

Regulatory: AFDC

Some conditions are regulatory, meaning that they serve as a mode of regulation. Although the regulatory policies carried out by such conditions are often reasonable, this conditional pathway for regulation is troubling because it displaces the Constitution's statutory avenue for regulation.

Recall that New York State's program of Aid to Families with Dependent Children (AFDC) assisted families only if they allowed caseworkers into their homes to determine their needs. Although the Fourth Amendment prohibits unreasonable searches, the Supreme Court in *Wyman v. James* (1971) upheld the New York AFDC condition on the ground that the searches did not occur in the criminal context and were a "reasonable administrative tool."[1] Indeed, it surely was useful for the government of New York to enter the homes of the poor to determine their eligibility.

There are other ways of measuring need, however, and the condition requiring recipients of aid to admit government agents into their apartments was a systematic intrusion into the homes of the poor.

Nationally, over 5 million families benefited from AFDC in the mid-1990s, when there were about 7.5 million families in poverty.[2] This means that in states such as New York, which conditioned aid on home visits, a large percentage of impecunious families and especially poor single mothers depended on AFDC and so were subject to the condition.[3] One therefore must consider not merely whether the condition violated a constitutional right but also, more fundamentally, whether it was regulatory and was thus displacing the Constitution's avenue for regulation—namely, binding statutes. Conditions that impose constraints on a large segment of the population, or on much of a distinctive part of it, function as a mode of regulation, and so one must wonder about the AFDC conditions that intruded into the homes of so many poor single mothers and other indigent families. Did these conditions function as a means of regulating them? And would this home invasion have been imposed if it had had to be adopted through the Constitution's statutory avenue for regulation?

Commandeering: Drinking Age and ICE Enforcement

Even when conditions are not regulatory, they can be problematic because they direct or "commandeer" the states—an initial example being the use conditions to impose a federal minimum drinking age. In accord with an act of Congress, the federal Department of Transportation withholds a percentage of federal funding for highway construction when a state fails to adopt a minimum drinking age of twenty-one. Although the Supreme Court upheld this condition in *South Dakota v. Dole* (1987), the condition is nonetheless sobering.

Most basically, the condition is regulatory. Congress itself openly describes this condition as an attempt to impose a "national minimum drinking age."[4] But in addition the condition directs the states in their policies. That is, by pressuring states into adopting federal drinking policy, the condition interferes in the states' own governmental decisions. As will be seen (in Chapter 8), this is known as "commandeering"; for now, it is enough to observe that it threatens federalism.

Congress could have just directly adopted a federal minimum drinking age. Under the Constitution's Supremacy Clause, the federal law would then have defeated any contrary state law. But if Congress had taken this approach, it would have faced a public debate on the merits of a nationally imposed drinking age. And its statute would have been tested against the Constitution's enumerated congressional powers. Instead, Congress used its funding to regulate, even to direct states in their regulation.

Another example can be found in the conditions requiring cooperation with Immigration and Customs Enforcement (ICE). The federal government (as already noted) restricts Justice Department funding for municipalities that fail to cooperate with ICE's immigration enforcement, and though this condition is regulatory, it is also an example of a condition that directs or "commandeers" the states—in this instance, their municipalities. In particular, the conditions deprive cities of their funding unless they provide ICE with access to their correctional facilities for purposes of immigration enforcement, unless they provide notice to ICE of the release date for detainees, and unless they certify that they are in compliance with a federal statute prohibiting state and local governments from restricting information sharing with the Department of Homeland Security.[5]

One might think that states and their municipalities ought to cooperate with the federal government's immigration enforcement. But when the federal government uses conditions to demand access to municipal prisons and information, it is requisitioning buildings and information belonging to portions of the states and is directing the states in policies that are distinctively theirs in the Constitution's federal system. It thus should be evident how conditions can commandeer the states and undermine the Constitution's federal structure.

Unconstitutional: FCC and IRS Licensing of Speech

Some conditions, whether or not they are regulatory or commandeering, are interesting for another reason—that they impose restrictions that violate the Constitution. The 1939 Hatch Act has already
been mentioned, and unfortunately, that is only one of many conditions that appear to abridge the freedom of speech and the press.

An additional set of examples involve federal licensing of the airwaves. The Federal Communications Commission (FCC) licenses
the use of the airwaves and in this way regulates both radio and tele-
vision broadcasters. By statute, it must issue a license if this will serve
"public convenience, interest, or necessity," and its licenses come with
conditions limiting content that (in descending order of offensiveness)
is "obscene," "indecent," or "profane."[6] The government thereby
uses conditions tied to the licensing (a.k.a. prior review) of speakers to
regulate sexual speech on the airwaves.

The FCC also for a long time used such licensing to limit political
speech under the "fairness doctrine." Beginning in 1949, the commission interpreted the "public interest, convenience and necessity"
standard to mean that broadcasters had to cover "public issues" adequately and had to provide a "reasonable opportunity for the presentation of contrasting viewpoints on such issues." This interpretation
aimed at fairness, in the sense of requiring the presentation of both
sides, and certainly, in purporting to limit speech ecumenically, it
avoided any narrowly discriminatory suppression of speech. Yet, even
if it did not discriminate between left and right, the fairness doctrine
limited broadcasters in their freedom to express distinctive points of
view, and it was used under at least two presidents to suppress political
opposition. Although the Supreme Court upheld the fairness doctrine
in *Red Lion Broadcasting Co., Inc. v. FCC* (1969), the commission in
1985 stopped enforcing it as a condition of broadcast licenses, explaining that it "inhibit[ed] the presentation of controversial and
important issues." Recognizing that it probably did not comply with

the First Amendment, the commission finally in 2011 repealed the underlying regulation.[7]

Still on the books is the "equal time rule"—another condition of holding a broadcasting license. This rule, stipulated in the Federal Communications Act, requires licensed broadcasters, when they give time to one political candidate, to give equal time to other legally qualified candidates—with only limited exceptions.[8] At first glance, this may seem a nondiscriminatory rule, for it applies to all broadcasters and requires them to be inclusive. But it constrains those who support only one candidate—thus dampening down outlying and even merely distinctive opinion. Like the fairness doctrine, the equal time rule discriminates on the basis of viewpoint.

The commission's speech restrictions are widely justified as conditions on a government subsidy—the theory being that the airwaves are government property. The airspace above the United States, however, is in the "public domain."[9] And similarly the airwaves are common property, which the FCC allocates to prevent congestion. The FCC's licensing conditions therefore cannot be understood as conditions on the use of government property. Instead, the government is generally barring the use of the airwaves, and then offering the privilege of a license to selected applicants, as long as they comply with the FCC's conditions. As will be seen later (in Chapters 12 and 14), this sort of licensing is very different from the sort used by licensors to give access to their property. Instead, it is regulatory licensing—the use of licensing to demarcate the boundaries of regulation. And the licensing conditions are also regulatory in the sense that they serve as a means of regulation—in this instance, regulation in violation of the First Amendment.

Of course, the FCC's fairness doctrine is history, and its equal time rule for broadcast media does not apply to the expanding realm of web media. Nonetheless, the FCC conditions remain prominent examples of how the government can rely on conditions to regulate in ways that would otherwise violate the Constitution. That document

enumerates no congressional power over speech and, in the First
Amendment, even bars Congress from abridging the freedom of
speech. All the same, by working through conditions, the FCC has
imposed licensing of speakers and ultimately of their speech.

Another even more prominent set of speech conditions comes from
the Internal Revenue Code. Section 501(c)(3) of the code exempts religious, educational, and charitable organizations from federal income tax, but only if they refrain from central modes of political
speech. To be precise, they must completely avoid campaign speech
and must not make substantial efforts to influence legislation. Section 170 reinforces section 501(c)(3) by making contributions to the
exempt organizations deductible for the donors—as long as the organizations comply with the speech conditions. Churches, charities,
and nonprofit schools thus must choose between tax exemption—with
the advantages of deductibility—and the full freedom of political
speech.[10]

To be sure, the deduction is a tax subsidy, and both the exemption
and the deduction are privileges.[11] But even so, churches, charities,
and nonprofit schools face powerful government incentives to limit
much of their political speech.

Their Hobson's choice—between paying a higher tax rate or limiting their speech—is especially disturbing when one considers that
the government is singling out idealistic organizations. Although it
is often said that the speech conditions in sections 501(c)(3) and 170
affect "nonprofits," this fails to capture the reality that in focusing on
religious, educational, and other charitable organizations, the conditions take aim at the central types of idealistic associations as opposed
to business or political associations. In contrast, for example, the Internal Revenue Code exempts political organizations without such
conditions on their political speech.[12]

Tellingly, moreover, sections 501(c)(3) and 170 do not limit political
speech *outside* political contests. Instead, they limit speech *in* poli-

tics. In other words, they create a loose cordon sanitaire between the political process and idealistic organizations.

Why would Congress seek such limits? At very least, politicians do not like to be held to account by idealistic organizations. The speech conditions were introduced by Senator David Reed in 1934 and Senator Lyndon Johnson in 1954 in response to opposition—thus confirming that the goal was to suppress political criticism. But that is not all, for underlying the conditions was a raft of prejudice. The first person who prominently proposed both of the speech restrictions was Hiram Evans—the imperial wizard of the Ku Klux Klan. He cultivated influence in Washington, and four years after he made his suggestion in 1930, Congress began to give it effect through the tax code.[13] This is not to say that his ideas were determinative, but they were typical of the era. Nativists and many others feared the speech of churches and churchy organizations and wanted them to quiet down.

One might find it reassuring that nonprofits can find alternative avenues for speech through section 501(c)(4) organizations and section 527 Political Action Committees (PACs). These alternative pathways, however, are subject to their own speech limitations and so, as a practical matter, cannot fully compensate for the loss.[14] And even if they were not so burdened, they still could not solve the constitutional problem, which is that idealistic organizations have been denied their freedom to speak—that is, their freedom to speak in their own voices.[15]

Consider the fate of churches. For religious reasons, many churches must pray, witness, confess, profess belief, petition, and plead in their own voice. Only when speaking in its own voice, or in the united voices of its members, can such a church speak with religious authority and authenticity, let alone with passion and moral force. It is therefore a profound affront to the freedom of speech, not to mention the freedom of religion, to suggest that churches can find adequate substitutes for their own voices in government-approved contraptions, such as 501(c)(4) organizations or 527 PACs.

None of this is to deny that deductions could become an avenue for government-subsidized political contributions. This is a very reasonable concern. It could be fully addressed, however, by permitting deductions only for gifts that are not misused—for example, gifts processed through restricted accounts (such that the funds cannot be used for campaigning or much lobbying). The availability of this relatively unrestrictive solution makes abundantly clear that the current solution, which sweepingly suppresses the speech of exempt organizations, is grossly disproportionate—the opposite of narrowly tailored.

The reality is that although the speech restrictions come as conditions on privileges, they regulate idealistic organizations, denying them speech rights that would otherwise be assiduously protected. Imagine what the Supreme Court would do with a statute that directly imposed such sweeping limits on political speech. Even more than the FCC conditions, the conditions in the tax code illustrate the danger for freedom of speech.

Through Agents: Title IX and IRBs

Adding to the menagerie of conditions are those that the federal government imposes through other institutions, including states and even private institutions. Some such conditions are regulatory, some are commandeering, and some are unconstitutional in abridging speech and other rights. But they are particularly interesting because they enable the federal government to control individuals by working through intermediate institutions, which thus operate as agents for regulating individuals or even depriving them of their rights.

Academic institutions are among the most notable of such intermediaries—as is familiar from Title IX of the Education Amendments Act of 1972 (as amended in 1988). This federal statute bars discrimination on the basis of sex in any academic institution receiving federal financial assistance. Such policy, at first glance, is appealing. As will become apparent in Chapter 3, however, the imposition of policy through conditions is regulatory. And as will be seen in Chapter 7, Title IX has been used to abridge the freedom of speech and the due process of law in violation of the Bill of Rights. The condition, as interpreted for nearly a decade by the Department of Education, required educational institutions to prohibit much sexual and related political conversation and to enforce these restrictions through petty inquisitorial tribunals, which all too often were substantively and procedurally biased against the accused. The department, in other words, used academic agents not only to regulate and suppress speech but also to evade the due process of the courts.

Even now that the department has backed away from its most speech-stultifying interpretation of Title IX, the legacy of its interpretation remains in place. Many academic institutions continue with the speech suppression and still maintain their petty academic tribunals with all of their prejudices and at least some of their procedural failings. Thus, although the especially overbearing version of the condition has been pulled back, the remaining version continues to legitimize privatized regulation and adjudication. The damage seems to be permanent.

An even more serious example of conditions requiring agents to regulate, and to violate the First Amendment, is the licensing of academic speech and publication by institutional review boards (IRBs). By means of these conditions, the federal government turns funded academic institutions into agents to regulate third parties, even researchers who do not receive government funding—subjecting them to licensing of academic speech and publication. These complex conditions reveal how, by means of elaborate conditions, the government can control Americans with an indirection and opacity that defies public and even judicial understanding, thereby enabling the government to do what it otherwise could not. It is therefore important to conclude this chapter's examples with a detailed account of IRBs.[16]

The Department of Health and Human Services (HHS)—together with a host of other federal agencies—funds "human subjects research" on the condition that the research is licensed. But unlike the FCC, HHS itself does not do the licensing. Instead, it funds individual research through academic institutions, and as a condition of its funding, it asks the institutions for "assurances" that they have established IRBs, which will license the research done by the institution's students, faculty, and other personnel.

Like so many others, these conditions were adopted for ostensibly good reasons: in this instance, to protect the human subjects of research. Although many doctors in HHS's predecessor agency, the Department of Health, Education, and Welfare (HEW), hoped already in the 1960s to regulate human subjects research, the opportunity arose only when in 1972 the government's Tuskegee Study was exposed by the *New York Times*. The Tuskegee Study was a longitudinal study of tertiary syphilis in Black men. HEW's Public Health Service ran the project on the theory that it was providing the men with health care, but it did not give them penicillin after it became publicly available. Like the other American research projects that seem especially appalling—such as the army radiation studies on soldiers and the Willowbrook study of hepatitis in disabled children—Tuskegee was government research. In contrast, private academic research (which has always been subject to negligence law and the cost of insurance) did not have such a bad record.*

After the Tuskegee Study was exposed, however, the government's medical establishment was less interested in facing up to its own dangerous role than in using the occasion to regulate all human subjects research. It seized the opportunity to impose sweeping new

---

* A well-known 1966 study by Thomas Beecher allegedly showed the ethical failings of human subjects research in general, but it reached this conclusion only by including non-American research and by obscuring how much of its data concerned government or government-funded research.

conditions that subjected all government-funded human subjects research to prior licensing by IRBs. Indeed, it used its funding to pressure academic institutions to accept IRB licensing for all human subjects research, even if not federally funded.[17]

In extending IRB licensing to privately funded research, the government used its conditions to inculcate the impression that IRB licensing was the standard of care for human subjects research. That is, the government used its conditions on government-funded research to make IRB licensing of human subjects research seem a requirement of state negligence laws.[18]

As a result, almost all such research in the United States is nowadays subject to IRB licensing. State universities, private academic institutions, and even many grade schools (public and private) now require IRB licensing of human subjects research, regardless of its source of funding—thereby inculcating the idea, even among children, that one needs permission before publishing such work and even before making inquiries.

And the institutions are draconian in enforcing the licensing because the government cross collateralizes its conditions. That is, even if only one privately funded researcher violates only one HHS condition in one research project, this constitutes a breach of the conditions on funding for all research projects at his institution, thus allowing the federal government to withdraw all funding for the slightest infraction by one person.[19]

The focus on speech and the use of speech is relentless. Although the HHS conditions require licensing for human subjects research, they define such research in terms that refer to information, inquiry, reading, publication, and even thought. For starters, they define a "human subject" as a living individual about whom a *researcher* directly obtains "*information*" or "*biospecimens*" and then "*uses, studies, or analyzes*" the information or biospecimens. Alternatively, they define a "human subject" as a living individual about whom the *researcher* otherwise "*obtains, uses, studies, analyzes, or generates"* any *"information"* or "biospecimens" that make the individual identifiable.[20]

Then the conditions define "research" as a "systematic *investigation"* designed to produce *"generalizable knowledge"*—meaning any research that aims to develop a general statement or theory, this being what scientifically oriented academics consider publishable.[21] The result is to cover a vast amount of academic research and publication.*

Under the regulations, a student or faculty member who wants to do human subjects research generally needs to get prior IRB permission. For example, if a religious studies student interviews preachers to study the prevalence and character of religious attitudes about race—let alone, if he records their names or expects responses that might have reputational consequences—he needs prior permission.[22] The regulations, in other words, treat speech (both in the course of research and afterward in publication about it) as a potential medical harm. They therefore limit what researchers can read, say, and

---

* The conditions governing human subjects research have recently been altered with what is widely assumed to be an exemption for enumerated fields in the humanities or social sciences: "the following activities are deemed not to be research: . . . Scholarly and journalistic activities (e.g., oral history, journalism, biography, literary criticism, legal research, and historical scholarship), including the collection and use of information, that focus directly on the specific individuals about whom the information is collected."

This exception, however, is only for activities that "focus directly on the specific individuals about whom the information is collected." Such activities, which concentrate on an individual, are not ordinarily assumed to aim for "generalizable knowledge." Given that the government's definition of "research" already excludes activities that are not in pursuit of "generalizable knowledge," this purported exception does not really exempt much from the licensing system. At best, it merely confirms that the government's definition of "research" in terms of "generalizable knowledge" does not extend to narrowly individualistic inquiries. And, of course, very little research in history, journalism, literary criticism, law, and even biography has so confined a focus.

publish—all on the basis of the IRB's evaluation of whether the benefits outweigh the risks.

The HHS conditions even demand that in evaluating risks and benefits, IRBs "should not consider possible long-range effects of applying knowledge gained in the research."[23] Thus, when deciding what to censor, IRBs must not consider the primary biomedical and policy benefits of acquiring and sharing the biomedical information.

Those who do not sufficiently cooperate with the censorship are usually subject to more severe censorship in the future. If an IRB is troubled by a researcher's noncompliance, it can simply delay her future work until she submits to additional restrictions on what she can learn or publish. More aggressively, it can outright bar her from doing the research project or publishing it. It can even declare her unfit to do research, thereby entirely precluding her from doing her work. As if that were not enough, colleges and universities make clear that faculty can be fired for noncompliance with an IRB.

Much academic speech is thus now subject to prior licensing. Whether in biomedicine, epidemiology, education, sociology, literature, history, religion, or law, scholars and students often need prior permission to read, ask questions, record answers, analyze results, and share resulting information in books, periodicals, or even academic talks. All of this is licensing of words—a method of controlling speech and the press that the First Amendment emphatically prohibited.

The results are perverse, for although the licensing is justified as a means of protecting human subjects, its focus is on speech. Dangerous physical interactions require no permission as long as they are not done in pursuit of "generalizable knowledge"—the sort of knowledge that scientifically minded academics consider publishable. But entirely harmless interactions (including observation, reading, or conversation) require permission if one is aiming for generalizable knowledge. The target of the licensing is the production of what, in the scientific world, is considered publishable knowledge rather than harm.

And even though the licensing probably prevents some harms, it does so through prior review, which in order to prevent harms inevitably ends up imposing undeserved delays, clerical burdens, and prohibitions on much inquiry, speech, and publication that is entirely harmless. For example, most of the covered research speech and publication does not cause any legally cognizable harm, but because IRBs aim to *prevent* research speech and publication from causing harm, they limit vast amounts of such speech and publication just in case it turns out to be harmful.

IRBs thus illustrate why licensing is always an overly restrictive means of addressing speech harms. Being a mode of prior review, it is always vastly overinclusive, not narrowly tailored.

Adding to the First Amendment problems, HHS tells IRBs to protect the mental well-being of human subjects. Indeed, in accord with long-standing HHS guidance, IRBs tend to assume "Stress and feelings of guilt or embarrassment may arise simply from thinking or talking about one's own behavior or attitudes on sensitive topics such as drug use, sexual preferences, selfishness, and violence."[24] It is difficult to think of more stifling grounds for licensing speech.

The IRB licensing has squelched much empirical research in fields as diverse as education, sociology, religion, and politics. And because IRBs tend to enforce their sensitivities about speech along the lines of locally prevailing prejudices, inquiry and publication that is socially or politically unpopular is especially likely to be censored.

The human costs are high. Most seriously, when one limits (or even merely delays) biomedical inquiry and its publication, there inevitably is a cost for those who would have benefited from the research.

To be sure, studies of new drugs and devices can be dangerous, and the Food and Drug Administration (FDA) uses IRBs to license such studies under FDA regulations, thereby probably saving some lives every year. But that is a different regulatory scheme. At stake here are the HHS conditions that more generally require IRB licensing for human subjects research.

Undoubtedly, IRBs acting under HHS's human subjects research conditions have saved some lives. But there is no serious empirical evidence of any substantial number of lives saved. In contrast, there is overwhelming evidence that IRBs impede biomedical research and its publication at the cost of innumerable lives.

The body count is suggested by Peter Pronovost's study of catheter-related bloodstream infections. Although HHS shut down this study out of concerns that there had not been sufficient IRB approval—stopping further collection of data—it was published in 2006 with the effect of saving at least 17,000 lives per annum in the United States alone.[25] To date, that means over 250,000 lives (again, just counting the United States). And that was just one study. If one very conservatively supposes that the IRB system impedes only a few profoundly lifesaving studies each year, the lost lives since the imposition of IRBs in 1972 runs into the millions.

IRBs protect the lives of human subjects at a rate that is arithmetical, for a medical research project can directly harm only its participants. When IRBs suppress medical knowledge, however, the losses in life can increase geometrically—that is, at an accelerating rate—for reasons that are obvious enough. The number of lives saved by the publication of biomedical research is apt to be a multiple of the number of those studied. Moreover, the censorship cuts off not only the censored research but also the research that would have built on it.

The costs are especially high for minorities because HHS's conditions set a distinctively high standard for research on them—ostensibly to protect them from the burdens of research. As put by the HHS conditions, the selection of subjects should be "equitable" so as to protect "subjects who are vulnerable to coercion or undue influence, such as children, prisoners, individuals with impaired decision-making capacity, or economically or educationally disadvantaged persons."[26] All of this sounds reasonable, except that it comes with a cost for such persons, and not only them. It is widely understood that the protected

persons prototypically include Blacks. In the aftermath of the Tuskegee
Study, all of this may seem only prudent and just (though the
Tuskegee Study was governmental rather than private). But in im-
peding research on minorities and their distinctive medical problems,
the conditions have predictable results.

For example, Black men have a higher death rate during cardiac
surgery than White men. This has led to speculation about racial indifference or prejudice in the medical profession, which certainly
may be a contributing factor, but at the same time, IRB licensing must
also be considered.[27] Pregnant women often need to take drugs, for
their own health or that of their unborn babies, but not enough is
known about efficacious and safe dosages, and again IRBs stand in
the way.[28] Licensing speech in and about research costs lives, and
when such licensing discriminates against research on minorities, it
has discriminatory costs.

Like the FCC conditions, the HHS conditions are a means of regulation, they commandeer state universities, and they even enable
the government to impose licensing of speech and the press. Yet
HHS's conditions go even further. Rather than merely require recipients of federal benefits to give up their speech, these conditions openly
ask recipient institutions to censor their personnel—illustrating how
conditions can operate through agents to affect the rights of third
parties.

Other examples of conditions will be discussed later. What has been
seen thus far, however, should suffice to introduce readers to the
problem, including questions of regulation, commandeering, violations of rights, and control through agents. It should be evident that
conditions have become a powerful mode of governance, which offers an unexpected pathway for regulation and for cutting through
constitutional limits.

3

Regulatory Conditions

M any of the problems with conditions arise when the government uses them as a mode of regulation. This book makes no complaint against conditions that merely define what government is lawfully buying or supporting with a grant. The government, for example, should be able to buy medicine on the condition that it works and distribute it on the condition that it be used by the recipient for a specified disease.

But rather than merely defining the government's purchases or generosity, many conditions serve as a mode of regulation. Of course, the regulatory policies imposed through conditions can be valuable. But though there is a wide range of regulation that can be valuable, the use of conditions to impose regulation is another matter, as such conditions evade the Constitution's avenues for regulation and adjudication. Over the course of this book, regulatory conditions will be seen to be dangerous and unconstitutional.

The Scope of Regulatory Conditions

The question at this stage is to understand the scope of regulatory conditions. Although many scholars (including Lynn Baker, Barry

Friedman, Renée Lerner, and Thomas McCoy) have explored such conditions, it remains to be understood what exactly makes them regulatory.[1] All too often, such conditions are understood as a residual category—those that are left over after one has identified the conditions that define spending or purchases. This approach, however, omits many conditions that serve a regulatory function.

For example, Justice Sandra Day O'Connor, in her dissent in *South Dakota v. Dole*, assumed that the relevant constitutional provision was the spending power, and she therefore understood regulatory conditions to be those that are unsupported by that power—to be precise, those that go "beyond specifying how the money should be spent."[2] But there are other pertinent constitutional provisions, such as those vesting legislative powers in Congress and judicial power in the courts, and to understand the implications of these provisions, it is important to adopt a broader and more natural understanding of regulatory conditions.

The danger is that when conditions function as a mode of regulation, they displace the Constitution's congressional avenue for regulating and its judicial route for adjudication—a point that will be elaborated in Chapter 5. At this stage, as a foundation for that argument, it is important simply to identify the conditions that serve as mechanisms for regulating, regardless of whether or not they are authorized by the alleged spending power.

To be sure, when a condition goes beyond the underlying spending, this can reveal that the condition is regulatory. But an inquiry about conditions that regulate and thereby supplant congressional regulation cannot be confined to the scope of the spending power.

Put in terms of purchasing, if one were concerned solely about the government going beyond its spending authority, the goal would be to identify purchasing conditions—on the theory that purchases are securely within the government's power. If, however, one is worried about the displacement of the Constitution's regulatory mechanisms, then there is no safety in purchasing conditions, as even these may be regulatory.

The key is therefore to understand which conditions function as a mode of regulation—regardless of whether they also could be viewed as part of a government purchase. Put another way, regulatory conditions are those that substitute for statutes in regulating Americans.*

Recognizing Regulatory Conditions

How exactly can one know which conditions are regulatory? In most instances, there are relatively visible criteria.

One way of discerning such conditions is simply to examine what the government says about them. Frequently, the government bluntly explains that it is using its conditions as a mode of regulation, as when the Office for Human Research Protections—the Health and Human Services (HHS) office that enforces the conditions establishing institutional review boards (IRBs)—declares that it "maintains regulatory oversight" over "biomedical and behavioral research."[3] The government has a similar justification for withholding highway construction funds from states that do not adopt a minimum drinking age of twenty-one; as seen in Chapter 2, Congress openly describes this as an attempt to impose a "national minimum drinking age."[4]

Even when government is not so candidly regulatory, its conditions often reveal themselves to be regulatory—for example, when they are disproportionately large, nongermane, or otherwise "off." Of course, some conditions are disproportionately small, and it cannot be con-

---

* Allied with the overemphasis on purchases is a related argument—that what government does in its private capacity (notably, purchasing) is not confined by the constitutional limits on what it does in its public or governmental capacity (such as regulation). The effect is to justify regulatory conditions that could be considered elements of purchases. But the Constitution's provisions for legislative and judicial powers and its guarantees of rights do not come with an exception for whatever the government can characterize as done in its contractual or otherwise private capacity. On the contrary, the Constitution limits government generally, without any such exception. And this is fortunate, as government all too often uses apparently private transactions to purchase submission to what is constitutionally forbidden.

cluded from this that the conditions are regulatory, but when conditions are excessive or otherwise overbearing, this is a strong signal that
they are regulatory. Here are some examples of the circumstances that
reveal conditions to be regulatory:

- *Conditions on Sorts of Things Not Funded (a.k.a. "Crossover
  Conditions").* Conditions are regulatory when government
  leverages the funding for one sort of thing to impose conditions
  about other sorts of things.[5] It has been seen, for example, that
  the Department of Transportation will withhold a percentage of
  federal funding for state highway construction if a state fails to
  adopt a minimum drinking age of twenty-one. This condition is
  regulatory not merely because Congress confessed as much but
  more basically because the drinking age is not an element of
  highway construction.[6] Recognizing the regulatory implications,
  Justice O'Connor dissented in *South Dakota v. Dole:* "When
  Congress appropriates money to build a highway, it is entitled to
  insist that the highway be a safe one. But it is not entitled to
  insist as a condition of the use of highway funds that the state
  impose or change regulations in other areas of the state's social
  and economic life because of an attenuated or tangential
  relationship to highway use or safety. Indeed, if the rule were
  otherwise, the Congress could effectively regulate almost any
  area of a state's social, political, or economic life on the theory
  that use of the interstate transportation system is somehow
  enhanced."[7] When funding for one thing (highway construction) comes with a condition on something else (the minimum
  drinking age), this reveals the condition to be regulatory.

- *Conditions on Similar but Unfunded Things.* A disconnect
  between the funding and the condition is also evident when the
  condition restricts similar but unfunded things. HHS uses its
  support for human subjects research to get academic institutions
  to impose IRB licensing not only on federally funded research

but also on privately funded research. In contemporary Supreme Court parlance, the conditions are "nongermane." More concretely, this is an overapplication of the HHS conditions to similar but not federally funded research, and it means that the government is regulating.

- *Conditions beyond the Funded Program or Activity.* Conditions are also regulating when they extend not merely to the funded program or activity but beyond it—for example, when they apply (as noted by Renée Lerner) to the funded organization as a whole.[8] In *United States Agency for International Development v. Alliance for Open Society International, Inc.* (2013), the government financed work against AIDS / HIV on the condition that the funded organizations have "a policy explicitly opposing prostitution." In holding this condition void, the Supreme Court observed that one must distinguish "between conditions that define the limits of the government spending program—those that specify the activities Congress wants to subsidize—and conditions that seek to leverage funding to regulate speech outside the contours of the program itself."[9] Although the court said this to hold the condition in violation of the First Amendment, its analysis also reveals the regulatory character of the condition.

  Another example can be found in the evolution of the Solomon Amendment. As adopted in 1995, it denied Department of Defense funding to schools or subunits of academic institutions that "in effect, prevent" military recruitment on campus. But the condition was soon adjusted. Of particular interest here, the Department of Defense adopted regulations broadening the condition to apply to "all sub-elements of such an institution." Even if the condition originally was not regulatory, its extension beyond the funded program or activity—in this instance, to entire institutions—reveals the condition to be regulatory.[10]

This reasoning—about conditions that extend beyond funded
programs and activities—may be painful to recognize, as it
requires a reevaluation of some civil rights statutes. At least
four federal civil rights statutes barring discrimination
operate not as direct constraints or duties, but as spending
conditions. Reflecting this design, the conditions in the
statutes were originally drafted to apply only to federally
funded programs or activities, not to any funded institution
as a whole. But the federal government increasingly interpreted the conditions to reach entire institutions, and after
this interpretation lost in the courts, Congress in 1988
amended all four conditions by defining "program or activity"
to include "all of the operations" of the funded institutions.
Since at least 1988, therefore, the anti-discrimination
conditions in these four civil rights statutes have applied
to programs and activities not funded by the government,
and at least to this extent, they are regulatory—a conclusion
confirmed by Congress's candidly regulatory ambitions for
its 1988 amendment.*

- *Overreaching Relative to Funding or What Is Being Funded.*
  When government imposes conditions that are overbroad or

---

* The relevant civil rights statutes are Title VI barring racial discrimination, Title IX
barring sex discrimination in education, section 504 of the Rehabilitation Act barring
discrimination against the handicapped, and section 303 of the Age Discrimination
Act. There has been concern about the constitutionality of these federal anti-
discrimination conditions on the theory that the conditions are not really germane to
the government spending. That theory, however, is unpersuasive. When the federal
government funds education and other such endeavors, it is surely relevant for the
government to avoid subsidizing discriminatory programs or activities. The constitutional difficulty is therefore not a generic lack of germaneness or relevance but rather
that the conditions became regulatory when they moved beyond funded programs and
activities.

overreaching in relation to the amount of the funding or what is being funded, the conditions cannot be viewed as merely a purchase and, in fact, are regulatory. For example, although the federal government contributed only 8 percent of the cost of elementary and secondary education, its 2001 No Child Left Behind Act required funded states to adopt performance metrics that reshaped much curriculum and teaching.[11] Similarly, in *FCC v. League of Women Voters* (1984), the government made modest grants to noncommercial educational radio stations on the condition that they not "engage in editorializing." Though this condition was held unconstitutional by the Supreme Court on account of its abridgment of the freedom of speech, the condition was also overreaching in relation to the subsidy and on this account was regulatory.[12] Another example concerns sections 501(c)(3) and 170 of the Internal Revenue Code—sections that, together, impose sweeping speech conditions on tax-exempt organizations. As seen in Chapter 3, the danger that donations to tax-exempt organizations will be used as a conduit for tax-deductible political spending could have been addressed simply by barring deductions for donations used for such ends. Accordingly, quite apart from any First Amendment violation, the restrictive speech conditions are grossly overreaching and regulatory.

- *Undifferentiated.* The overreaching and regulatory character of conditions can also be evident when they do not differentiate those who benefit substantially and those who do not. For example, when the government, in section 501(c)(3) of the Internal Revenue Code, exempts churches and other idealistic organizations from federal income tax on the condition that they suppress much of their political speech, the conditions go too far, as they apply to many idealistic organizations that have negligible income and thus little benefit from the exemption.

Such conditions not only are at odds with the First Amendment but also are regulatory.[13]

- *Numerous Recipients.* When a government condition reaches most or many individuals, institutions, or programs in a field, the condition will usually be regulatory. For example, when the same condition appears in vast numbers of plea bargains, one must worry that it is regulatory. Federal educational funding, moreover, comes with conditions governing everything from teaching methods to discrimination, and because such conditions affect almost all students and institutions, it is difficult to avoid the conclusion that they are regulatory. Similarly, section 501(c)(3)'s speech conditions confine so many churches and other idealistic organizations that they apparently are regulatory. Indeed, section 501(c)(3)'s conditions and many of the educational conditions are often justified on candidly regulatory grounds.

  Notwithstanding this point that conditions affecting numerous individuals or institutions are regulatory, it probably should be considered only a rebuttable presumption. For example, conditions that merely stipulate the return of government money or compliance with government accounting standards are ordinarily not regulatory. Similarly, generic conditions that affect many Americans, such as that federal money be spent on food or on education, need not be considered regulatory. More specific versions of such conditions, however, can easily become regulatory. For example, to the extent that student aid conditions press vast numbers of students and institutions into a narrow range of government-approved educational models, such as community college or four-year undergraduate programs, there is a high risk that the conditions functionally regulate education. Of course, a law or condition can be regulatory even if it affects only a few individuals or even just one. Accordingly, the absence of a large number of affected persons and so forth cannot be taken to mean that a condition is not regulatory. But when most or very substantial numbers of individuals, institutions, or programs in a field are affected, it often is difficult to avoid the conclusion that the condition is regulatory.

- *Cross-Collateralized Conditions.* The government sometimes cross collateralizes its conditions. That is, it requires a recipient to agree that a breach of a condition on one grant will amount to a breach of the conditions on various other grants it receives from the government. This is a powerful indicator that the condition is disproportionate and regulatory.

    Cross-collateralized conditions must be distinguished from the better-known phenomenon of crossover conditions. Those conditions (it has been seen) cut across subjects of federal concern—as when a grant on highway funding comes with a condition requiring a state drinking or environmental policy. Such a condition, not being germane, signals that the federal condition is regulatory.

    In contrast, cross-collateralized conditions cut across grants and so can concern similar subjects. Recall that HHS links the conditions on all of its grants for human subjects research at each university, and thus a single violation of a single condition by a single human subjects researcher amounts to a breach of the conditions on all of HHS's funding for human subjects research at his institution. Quite apart from questions about the germaneness of conditions that cut across subjects, conditions that are cross collateralized even within a subject are highly dispropor-tionate. Coming close to recognizing this, Chief Justice John Roberts opined in *National Federation of Independent Business v. Sebelius*—the 2012 Affordable Care Act case—that conditions not "govern[ing] the use of the funds," including those that "take the form of threats to terminate other significant independent grants," "cannot be justified" on the basis of a federal spending power.[14] To which it need only be added that such conditions are regulatory.

- *Running into the Future.* When the government seeks conditions that run into the future, there is a risk that the conditions are regulatory. Of course, some conditions that run into the future are not regulatory. For example, HHS's Health Resources and Services Administration pays tuition, fees, and other costs for medical school students—on the condition that they afterward work for a while in rural communities not well served by doctors.

  But at least when a condition restricts the future exercise of a constitutional right—that is, when the future exercise of the right could affect funding or defunding—the regulatory character of the condition is clear. It is one thing for the government to ask a defendant in a plea bargain to waive his jury rights or his privilege against self-incrimination in his current trial, but quite another to ask for any such waiver as to future trials. Not merely a deal about a current pro-ceeding, this looks like an attempt to regulate.

  The Supreme Court already in *Home Insurance Company v. Morse* (1874) held that a person "may omit to exercise his right . . . in each recurring case. In these aspects any citizen may no doubt waive the rights to which he may be entitled. He cannot, however, bind himself in advance by an agreement, which may be specifically enforced, thus to forfeit his rights at all times and on all occasions, whenever the case may be presented."[15] Although in focusing on specific enforcement, the court aimed too narrowly, it aptly noted that rights-restricting

conditions running into the future raise constitutional
problems—one of which is that such conditions are regulatory.

In short, regulatory conditions often have telltale characteristics.

It is difficult, all the same, to give a complete taxonomy of such
beasts. Government is adept at reformulating regulations as conditions on privileges, and it will be equally adroit in disguising its regulatory conditions—for example, by recasting them as mere purchases
or grants. It is therefore important to recall that the question of whether
a particular condition is regulatory cannot turn on whether it is a purchase or grant, but rather must come to rest on whether it serves as a
mode of regulation. Far from being reducible to any simple formula,
this inquiry requires a careful evaluation of the regulatory realities.

It is disturbing that so many conditions are regulatory, as this points
to the possibility that many conditions do more than merely define
government benefits or other privileges. Although it has long seemed
that conditions are worrisome only when they restrict constitutional
rights, the regulatory character of many conditions suggests that, even
without imposing unconstitutional restrictions, they may be dangerous for more basic reasons.

Of course, not all regulatory conditions are unconstitutional. At
least when (as will be seen in Chapter 5) they reinforce direct legal
duties, they are less apt to run afoul of the Constitution. On the whole,
however, it will become apparent that regulatory conditions raise serious constitutional difficulties.

The broader point of Part I is that conditions, far from being merely
a technical conundrum, are a profoundly worrisome problem of
power. This book therefore now turns to constitutional analysis for a
more complete understanding of what is at stake.

PART II

Unconstitutional Pathway

Although the Constitution lays out broad avenues for lawmaking and judging, conditions increasingly evade these public boulevards of power by creating a private shortcut. Thus, even before one gets to unconstitutional conditions—those which impose unconstitutional restrictions on rights—one must consider how conditions create an alternative pathway for governance.

It will be seen that, regardless of whether a condition violates a constitutional right, the purchase of submission can be unconstitutional. In particular, conditions can collide with the Constitution by violating the government's power to spend or otherwise distribute privileges, by divesting Congress and the courts of the powers placed in them by the Constitution, by circumventing procedural rights, and by slicing through the separation of powers and federalism.

4

Spending

The conventional assumption among judges and lawyers is that conditions are exercises of Congress's spending power. From this perspective, conditions rest securely in the broad authority of the federal fisc. Nonetheless, it is worth pausing to consider in what sense this is true.

Non-Spending Conditions

At the outset, note that however expansive any federal spending power, it does not authorize conditions that rest on nonspending privileges. To be sure, many federal conditions are tied to federal money—or at least to benefits purchased by the federal government—but at least some rest on privileges that do not involve spending.

Where, for example, is the spending when a prosecutor offers a plea bargain subject to a condition? And where is the spending when the Food and Drug Administration gives a drug company permission to do research on a new drug or device? And where is the spending when the Federal Communications Commission gives a broadcaster a license to use the airwaves? The airwaves (recall from Chapter 2) are not really government property but common property, and their allocation therefore cannot be understood as spending.

The point is not that these nonspending conditions are unconstitutional but simply that they cannot rest on any spending power. They thus must find authorization in other government powers. Whatever the breadth of federal spending, it does not include some important federal conditions.

No Spending Power

Still, it may be assumed that at least the vast majority of conditions are exercises of federal spending. Perhaps. But the question is complicated by the reality that the Constitution, at least as written, does not actually contain a spending power.

Instead, the Constitution enumerates a series of other congressional powers (for example, to tax, coin money, borrow money, regulate interstate commerce, and do what is necessary and proper to carry out other powers). From this point of view, Congress has the power to spend only to the extent it can do so through these enumerated powers. And this is not an accident, for the Constitution thereby limits the objects of government spending.

"But wait a minute," you may protest, "surely the Constitution authorizes spending!" In fact, what is taken to be the "spending power" is only a limit on the taxing power. According to the relevant paragraph of the Constitution:

> The Congress shall have Power To lay and collect Taxes, Duties, Imposts and Excises, to pay the Debts and provide for the common Defence and general Welfare of the United States; but all Duties, Imposts and Excises shall be uniform throughout the United States;

As evident from the words and the placement of the semicolons, this is merely a taxing power—the power being qualified by the requirement that the taxes be for general public purposes, namely paying the *nation's* debts and providing for the *common* defense and *general* welfare of the United States. The supposed spending power is thus merely a barrier to imposing taxes for purposes that do not serve the interests of the nation as a whole.

That this requirement merely confines the taxing power, rather than establishing a spending power, is especially clear because of the drafting history of the punctuation after the word *Excises*. The Constitutional Convention initially placed a comma there, but Gouverneur Morris attempted to alter the punctuation. Although he wanted a general spending power, he knew he could not accomplish this openly. So, while serving on the convention's Committee of Style, he surreptitiously introduced a tiny change. Following the word *Excises*, he added a dot above the comma, thereby turning the restriction on the taxing power into a separate spending power. Rarely has a single dot been so significant![1]

But the convention noticed the change and restored the punctuation. It is thus abundantly clear that the phrase about "providing for . . . general welfare" was merely a limitation on the taxing power, not a spending power.

Already in the 1791 debate over the Bank of the United States, Alexander Hamilton departed from the text and intent to suggest that Congress had a general spending power in the Constitution's words about "provid[ing] for the common Defence and general Welfare."[2] James Madison responded, however, that "the power as to these general purposes, was limited to acts laying taxes for them."[3]

Of course, it cannot be taken for granted that the judges will promptly reconsider their creation of a general spending power. Certainly, commentators still try to sustain such a power. But it is telling that they do this by using interpretation to alter the text, saying that the fateful comma should be read akin to a semicolon—as if to restore the text that the convention rejected.[4]

In short, the Constitution does not contain a spending power that cuts through the government's otherwise limited powers. Instead, the document leaves the federal government to spend through its various enumerated powers, subject to their limits.

This point is useful, at the very least, as a reminder that one need not worry much about whether a condition rests on government spending. The word *spending* has little constitutional significance, as it does not appear in the Constitution. Even the Constitution's words *providing for* have little relevance for understanding conditions, as these words are merely part of a limitation on the taxing power. Accordingly, rather than worry about whether a condition is tied to spending, one need only inquire whether it is part of a lawful government privilege. Put simply, it is unnecessary to strain to understand any condition as a mode of expenditure.

Spending outside the Enumerated Powers

Notwithstanding the clarity of the Constitution's text and history, the Supreme Court has interpreted the taxing power to include a broad power to provide or spend. That is, it has turned a limit on the taxing power into a spending power. The court has thereby liberated the federal government to impose spending conditions that regulate Americans beyond the scope of the Constitution's enumerated powers.

One might have thought that the government would be content with the Supreme Court's highly expansive interpretations of the interstate commerce power and the necessary and proper power. As currently interpreted by the court, such powers scarcely limit federal legislation. But the government relies on the supposed spending power to go further—to regulate in a manner unconfined even by the federal government's judicially expanded powers. It thereby exercises, with private consent, a breadth of regulation it cannot pursue with public consent.

Recall that the Constitution enumerates only limited powers for the federal government (regulating interstate commerce, coining

money, and so forth), and it further confines federal powers by enu-
merating rights (such as freedom of speech and jury rights). Beyond
these boundaries, it leaves power to the states and the people. Pressing
this point home, the Tenth Amendment declares, "The powers not
delegated to the United States by the Constitution, nor prohibited by
it to the States, are reserved to the States respectively, or to the people."
In other words, the powers that the Constitution did not give to the
federal government (and that the Constitution did not take from the
states) remain in the states or the people.

Nonetheless, the Supreme Court has held that when Congress
places conditions on its funding, it is not limited by either the Tenth
Amendment or the underlying enumeration of federal powers. As the
court summarized in *South Dakota v. Dole,* "a perceived Tenth
Amendment limitation on congressional regulation of state affairs"
does "not concomitantly limit the range of conditions legitimately
placed on federal grants."[5] Translation: conditions are not restricted
to the federal government's limited powers.

No wonder the federal government regularly uses conditions to
regulate far beyond its powers—most egregiously to license academic
speech through IRBs and ecclesiastical speakers through the IRS. The
federal government thereby exercises a power over inquiry, science,
religion, speech, and politics that the Constitution does not entrust to
it—indeed, that the Constitution denies to it—and that judges would
never tolerate in direct congressional regulation.

As summarized by the Supreme Court in *National Federation of
Independent Business v. Sebelius*, the federal government now enjoys
"considerable influence even in areas where it cannot directly regulate." To be sure, the federal government "may enact a tax on an activity that it cannot authorize, forbid, or otherwise control." But now,
more formidably, it allegedly is unlimited in its spending and thus can
use conditions on its spending to regulate beyond its powers—even
to "induce the states to adopt policies that the Federal Government
itself could not impose."[6]

Again, it cannot be assumed that the judges will immediately re-consider their creation of a general spending power, but the observa-tions here may at least have moderating effects. In particular, the use of a general spending power to evade constitutional limits is apt to be tempered when one recognizes that the Constitution actually contains no such power. The judges, rather than the Constitution, established the government's authority to spend outside its enumer-ated powers. Accordingly, where federal spending conditions go be-yond federal powers, the judges cannot blame the Constitution. The judges created this danger and will eventually have to consider whether they really want the responsibility of ratifying their error.

Must Be Part of Spending

Even if an alleged spending power continues to enjoy a place in judi-cial doctrine, it cannot justify conditions, except where they are part of the spending. This point has been widely recognized, not least in *South Dakota v. Dole* (1987). But rather than be taken seriously, it has merely led to doctrine requiring that any condition be "germane" to the spending.

This could have been a good first step toward ensuring that condi-tions are part of the underlying spending. But as the Supreme Court acknowledged in *Dole*, it has yet to "define the outer bounds of the 'germaneness' or 'relatedness' limitation."

An initial problem is that the court has hesitated to require that conditions be *directly* related to the underlying spending. Without a requirement of a direct relationship, conditions can easily move be-yond defining spending. *Dole* itself illustrates the danger. The fed-eral statute in the case gave states funds for highway construction, but withheld a percentage (5 percent in that case) from states that did not impose a minimum drinking age of twenty-one. The court should have recognized that this condition did not relate *directly* to the supported highway construction and therefore should have held it to be outside the alleged spending power. Instead, the court upheld the condition as germane, and neither in *Dole* nor in later cases has the court required conditions to be directly related to the underlying spending.

The Supreme Court has further eviscerated the germaneness inquiry by suggesting that a condition need not be germane narrowly to the government's spending but can instead be germane to its broader interests and purposes. In *Massachusetts v. United States* (1978), the court accepted a connection to such interests, saying that conditions must be related to "the federal interest in particular national projects or programs."[7] And earlier, in *Ivanhoe Irrigation District v. McCracken* (1958), the court even mentioned broader objectives or purposes, explaining that the federal government may "establish and impose reasonable conditions relevant to federal interest in the project and to the over-all objectives thereof."[8] By saying that conditions can be germane merely to the government's interests or its overall objectives or purposes in its spending, the court has left the door wide open for conditions that go beyond what the government is actually purchasing or supporting and that thus exceed the supposed spending power.

Again, *South Dakota v. Dole* is a good illustration. Remember, that case did not require a *direct* relationship of any sort. But with the governmental purpose measure, the court had no difficulty in concluding that the condition in *Dole* was "directly related to one of the main purposes for which highway funds are expended—safe interstate travel."[9] Using this "purpose" standard, which goes beyond the spending to consider its broader ends, the government can fund one thing (such as highway construction) and impose conditions on another (such as drinking).

Such a condition (as noted in Chapter 3) is really a mode of regulation. And here, it can be added that although attached to spending, such a condition is not part of it. Whatever one thinks of drinking under the age of twenty-one, a condition that does not directly relate to what is actually being funded cannot be considered part of the spending.

Similarly, one may have to distinguish between immediate and more remote limits. The most immediate conditions are those that define the product that the *federal government* gets for its money. More removed are conditions on a *recipient* of federal money—that is, on the recipient's use of it or, even more remotely, on other conduct or characteristics of the recipient. Yet further removed are the downstream conditions that, even if they formally apply only to recipients, actually govern *persons who deal with the recipient*, and so forth. As conditions become more removed, they are less obviously part of federal spending, and the downstream conditions are particularly apt to raise such questions.

Ultimately, what matters is not one doctrinal test or another, but the underlying problem. Chief Justice Roberts came close to recognizing this in *Sebelius* when he observed (as already noted) that where a condition does not "govern the use of the funds," it "cannot be justified on that basis."[10]

He understood, moreover, that the problem can arise when "conditions take the form of threats to terminate other significant independent grants"—that is, when the breach of a condition on one grant will jeopardize another grant. This is a common danger, for the government often cross collateralizes its grants, extending the condition on one grant to cut off another. It is therefore good to have some candid judicial recognition that if spending is to justify a condition, the relevant spending is the underlying grant, not spending in the abstract, and that when a condition on one grant affects another, it is reaching beyond the relevant spending.

When conditions go further than the underlying spending, they are not really part of the spending. They consequently cannot be justified as such.

Must Provide for the General Welfare

Whatever the foundation of spending conditions—whether a supposed spending power or Congress's enumerated powers—one must attend to the Constitution's words about imposing taxes to "pay the Debts and provide for the common Defence and general Welfare of the United States." It would seem to limit spending conditions to general purposes.

If the providing-for-the-general-welfare phrase is recognized as merely a limit on the taxing power, it would appear to limit the disposal of tax funds—in contrast to federal property such as territorial lands, which the Constitution allows Congress to "dispose of" without any general welfare requirement. From this perspective, the conditions on spending from tax funds must serve general purposes. On the other hand, if the providing-for-the-general-welfare phrase is understood to establish a general spending power, then all federal spending conditions are limited to providing for general ends. Either way, almost all federal spending must be for the general welfare. And this means, as recognized by the Supreme Court in *Dole*, that the associated conditions must serve the "general Welfare."

But the court in *Dole* added that, "in considering whether a particular expenditure is intended to serve general public purposes, courts should defer substantially to the judgment of Congress." The court even questioned "whether 'general welfare' is a judicially enforceable restriction at all."[11]

Certainly, Congress has authority to legislate within its enumerated powers. The Constitution, however, recites "the general Welfare of the United States" as a limitation on congressional taxing—confining Congress to taxing for the welfare of the whole nation, as opposed to narrow state or local benefits. And however much this power (taxing) is adapted to other purposes (spending), there is no reason to think that the Constitution leaves this portion of the Constitution for Congress to judge for itself. Justice O'Connor, dissenting in *Dole*, protested: "If the spending power is to be limited only by Congress' notion of the general welfare, the reality, given the vast financial resources of the federal government, is that the Spending Clause gives power to the Congress to tear down the barriers, to invade the states' jurisdiction, and to become a parliament of the whole people, subject to no restrictions save such as are self-imposed." This, she added, "was not the framers' plan and it is not the meaning of the Spending Clause."[12]

Of course, even after judges employ all of the interpretative tools at their disposal, it still will often be unclear whether spending fails to serve the general welfare—in which case the judges should not hold the spending unlawful. But at least in some instances, they can and should question whether spending provides for the general welfare.

For example, does Congress provide for "the common Defence and general Welfare of the United States" when it transfers funds to or for states and other localities? Surely, the federal government can support its own facilities and programs wherever they are located—as when the Federal Emergency Management Agency distributes aid in battered towns and counties. When, however, the federal government gives its support not merely within states and localities, but to them, it is not providing for the *general* welfare. In theory, federal grants in aid to states and localities could be understood to benefit the whole nation, but the Constitution's vision of providing for the general welfare of the United States was understood in opposition to aid for the states and their localities.* And this remains a valuable limitation.

---

* That the general welfare clause was understood to bar federal payments to or for the states is confirmed by the 1790 congressional debate over the federal assumption of state debts. The states had incurred burdensome debts to pay for the Revolutionary War and needed federal assistance, but an act of Congress paying their debts would not "pay the Debts and provide for the common Defence and general Welfare of the United States." So Hamilton proposed that the federal government should assume the state debts and then pay them—once they were federal debts and thus within the scope of the Constitution's

Federal funding of these lesser jurisdictions distorts their taxing and spending, commandeers their regulatory and other policies, and eviscerates their political accountability and fiscal responsibility.[13] It also enables federal majorities to divert the nation's wealth to their political allies in the states. It therefore is important to recall that the general welfare requirement bars federal funding to or for states or localities.

It also must be considered whether spending provides for the general welfare when it comes with conditions that violate or otherwise undermine the Constitution. When conditions sidestep the Constitution's avenues for legislative and judicial power, they do not promote the general welfare. When conditions allow the government to escape its enumerated powers, they do not provide for the general welfare. When conditions enable the government to avoid political accountability by buying off opposition for some Americans and weakening the others, they do not serve the general welfare. When conditions impose restrictions that violate constitutional rights, they do not contribute to the general welfare. And so forth.

All government conditions rest on government privileges, and all such conditions and underlying privileges must have constitutional authorization. Accordingly, the federal government's authority to spend or otherwise grant privileges comes with inherent limitations.

---

limitation. Opponents protested the sleight of hand, arguing that state debts could not be converted into federal debts, but the debate over the assumption of state debts at least reinforces the conclusion that the general welfare clause does not permit federal aid to or for the states.

Tellingly, Hamilton was an early advocate of an open-ended spending power. Yet even he believed, as he summarized the next year in his *Report on Manufactures*, that "the object to which an appropriation of money is to be made" must "be *general* and not *local*."

Most basically, there is no general spending power. It thus does not matter whether a condition is tied to spending or another sort of privilege. Regardless, under the Constitution, conditions must specify privileges that are founded in Congress's enumerated powers.

Even when one relies on a judicially created general spending power, there evidently are limits. If conditions are to be justified under such a power, they must specify the use of the funds.

Last but not least, spending conditions must provide for the general welfare of the United States. The Constitution allows taxation only for the general welfare, thus precluding the use of tax funds for other purposes. And if one assumes a general spending power, then all spending must advance the public welfare.

5

Divesting and Privatizing Government Powers

The Constitution authorizes the federal government to bind or regulate Americans through acts of Congress and decisions of the courts. Nonetheless, with regulatory conditions—the conditions (identified in Chapter 3) that regulate Americans—the government increasingly has developed another pathway for legislating and adjudicating.

One consequence is to divest Congress and the courts of the powers vested in them by the Constitution. Although administrative power also has this effect, regulatory conditions are even worse, for they take effect not through public administrative edicts, let alone public congressional consent, but through private consent.

Ultimately, therefore, the danger is the privatization of powers that the Constitution places in government. The risks of privatization are increasingly recognized.[1] What is not so clearly understood is that regulatory conditions go much further than most other privatization, as they displace much legislative and judicial power out of the Constitution's avenues and into private channels.

Of course, one might imagine that privatized governance through conditions enables the government to accomplish what it otherwise could not—in particular, that government can impose regulatory policies that otherwise would be unavailable to it. But except where such policies violate constitutional limits, the government could surely enact the same policies by statute. Accordingly, once one puts aside unconstitutional conditions, the advantage of working through conditions is really one of process, and this is worrisome for reasons of policy as well as process. When government takes a private sideline around the Constitution's avenue for regulation, it all too often pursues policies that, perhaps for good reason, would not survive the Constitution's more regular and public process.

Evading the Constitution's Avenues for Binding Power

Much of the freedom enjoyed by Americans is secured by the Constitution's avenues for binding power. But by means of regulatory conditions, the government evades those public roadways, and when it engages in this off-road driving, one must wonder what happened to the Constitution's guardrails.

Under the Constitution, the government's power to bind (in the sense of imposing legal obligation) runs exclusively along two avenues: acts of Congress and of the courts. The government, under the Constitution, can regulate and otherwise make legally binding rules only through acts of Congress (or treaties ratified by the Senate). And it can make legally binding adjudications solely in the courts. These dual modes of creating legal obligation are not the exclusive mechanisms at the nation's jurisdictional edges—such as in territories and some cross-border matters.[2] But generally, in national domestic matters, the Constitution allows the federal government to impose legal obligation only through congressional statutes and judicial decisions.

This bifurcation of the government's power to bind is essential for the liberty of Americans, because legislative power and judicial power are practically opposites. The government can make law only through the will of a legislature that is politically accountable to the people in elections, and it can adjudicate the law only through the independent judgment of judges who are immune from political accountability.

The point is not merely that the government can bind Americans only through two institutions—Congress and the courts—but that it can create this sort of legal obligation only through their laws and judgments—through acts of Congress and decisions of the courts. Laws and judgments are the Constitution's pathways for binding Americans. Nonetheless, the federal government systematically evades these paths—most notoriously, by regulating Americans through administrative commands, but also, less familiarly, through conditions on benefits and other privileges.[3]

Even when Congress fully specifies such conditions, the government is regulating ultimately through acts of private rather than congressional consent—this being the legislative aspect of the evasion. And close behind is the judicial version of the evasion, in which the government relies on agency determinations about conditions, thereby avoiding binding judgments in court.

Conditions are thus near the bottom of a cascade of evasions. Dissatisfied with the Constitution's requirement that it govern through acts of Congress and the courts, the government shifts to regulating and adjudicating through formal administrative commands. Going further, it moves to ever less formal versions of administrative power. And discontent even with this, it increasingly seeks to regulate and adjudicate through conditions.

Of course, government has good reason to impose limits on what it will purchase or support. But when federal subsidies become an opportunity to reroute federal power outside the Constitution's pathways for binding Americans, they become yet another evasion of the Constitution's avenues for lawmaking and adjudication. And as now will be seen, this is constitutionally significant because it points to how regulatory conditions divest Congress and the courts of the powers that the Constitution vests in them, and how such conditions thereby deprive Americans of basic freedoms of self-governance and due process.

Divestiture of Legislative Powers

The Constitution vests legislative powers in Congress, and this has two constitutional implications. Congress cannot divest itself of such powers and, further, Congress cannot vest them elsewhere. This dual barrier to any relocation of legislative powers—summarized here as "divestiture" or "divesting"—has consequences for any attempt to shift regulation to agencies, let alone to private transactions.

That regulation is to be done through congressional lawmaking is sometimes explicit, as when the Constitution gives Congress the power to "regulate" interstate commerce. And even when the Constitution does not expressly mention regulation, it clearly recognizes regulation as part of Congress's legislative powers, by which that body has the nation's power to impose binding laws.

Of course, judges frequently consider whether Congress has "delegated" legislative power.[4] Beyond speaking of delegation, judges additionally muddy the waters by saying that the obstacle to delegation is an ephemeral "nondelegation doctrine"—a mere judicial doctrine—which purports to bar congressional delegation of legislative power to agencies, but actually permits it, as long as Congress provides the agency with an "intelligible principle." Congress therefore can relocate its power under the nondelegation doctrine if it maintains the pretense of nondelegation by providing an intelligible principle.

But the Constitution does not generically delegate its powers, for it states that legislative powers shall be "vested" in Congress. Thus, what ultimately is at stake is not mere delegation but more specifically vesting.

Rather than doctrine, let alone a farcical one on nondelegation, it is the Constitution's vesting of legislative powers that impedes Congress's relocation of its powers. The question, accordingly, is whether Congress can divest itself of the powers that the Constitution vests in it and, moreover, whether it can vest those powers where the Constitution did not vest them. Once the problem is put this way, it becomes evident that the Constitution bars any such divesting from Congress or vesting elsewhere.[5]

All the same, by means of conditions, the government nowadays divests and privatizes the regulatory authority that the Constitution locates in Congress. When Americans are regulated by conditions, they typically are governed not so much by acts of Congress as by agency-formulated conditions. Regulatory conditions thus divest legislative power at least partly to agencies. Worse, even when Congress itself spells out regulatory conditions, it is relegating decisions about regulation to the private transactions in which Americans decide whether to submit. Regulatory conditions take effect only with private consent, and so legislative power is shifted out of Congress not merely to agency decisions, but ultimately to private bargains.

Regulatory conditions, in other words, divest Congress of its legislative powers in two stages. Initially, in the formulation of regulatory conditions, legislative power often gets divested from Congress to agencies. But regardless, because regulatory conditions need consent, legislative power in the end is reduced to private transactions. Though regulation was once a matter of public congressional enactment, it nowadays is divested to agency decisions and even private deals.*

---

* Just how much regulation was traditionally a matter of public congressional enactment rather than private deals is evident from the historic reluctance of Congress to use conditions as a means of national domestic regulation. To be sure, regulatory conditions were long part of regulatory licensing schemes for the District of Columbia and the territories, where Congress acted in the place of state and local governments. They also were used in federal licensing of cross-border matters, such as Indian traders and steamboats. However, prior to the twentieth century, conditions do not seem to have had a significant role as a mode of national domestic regulation.

Regulatory conditions are thus alarming for many reasons. One danger is that when agencies regulate through conditions, they exercise both executive and legislative power, which the Constitution separates. Even more basically, regulatory conditions undercut the elective basis of regulatory power. Congress is the body in which the public is represented by their elected representatives. The Constitution vests legislative powers exclusively in Congress centrally to ensure that regulations and other binding rules of law—the rules that constrain freedom—come from the joint decision of persons directly accountable to the people. Such rules and regulations, in other words, enjoy the binding effect of public elective consent. In contrast, when agencies formulate regulatory conditions, the decisions about how Americans will be regulated move away from the elected lawmakers—shifting regulation from the representatives of a diverse people and into the hands of a relatively homogenized class of unelected bureaucrats. And even without agency participation in formulating regulatory conditions, when Americans consent to such conditions, the decisions about who will be regulated move to private interactions—thus privatizing what traditionally belonged in the public acts of Congress.

Not merely a matter of constitutional structure—or of congressional power—this divesting and privatization of regulation threatens the freedom of Americans to govern themselves through elective consent. In shifting legislative power to agencies and even private decisions, conditions displace public representative self-government not merely with agency edicts, but with private barter.

An Exception: Reinforcing Conditions

Of course, the argument thus far—that regulatory conditions divest and privatize legislative power—loses much of its force when regulatory conditions merely reinforce binding laws. Consider, for example, the government's tendency to condition its grants on compliance with various laws that already bind the persons receiving the grants—such as anti-discrimination laws, environmental laws, and laws barring disclosure of the government's proprietary and confidential information. Or consider a program offering parole and housing for prisoners on the condition that they not break the law. The restrictions in these conditions are binding independently of the conditions. And because these restrictions are already required by statute, it is not clear that the conditions really divest or privatize legislative power.

Perhaps, in some circumstances, these reinforcing regulatory conditions could threaten to displace legislative power—for example, when such conditions are disproportionately harsh. But a displacement of legislative power cannot be assumed when regulatory conditions merely echo direct statutory constraints.

All the same, the regulatory conditions that merely reinforce existing legal duties still run into difficulty—not for displacing legislative power, but for relocating judicial power. When regulatory conditions are adjudicated by the courts, they obviously do not divest the courts of the judicial power. But judicial decisions about regulatory conditions are relatively rare. Even when such conditions reinforce directly imposed legal duties, any breaches are usually decided by agencies—sometimes initially in denying funding and later in cutting off funding. It is therefore now necessary to consider how the full range of regulatory conditions—both those that reinforce statutory duties and those that do not—divest the courts of their judicial power.

Divestiture of Judicial Power

Just as bad as the divesting of legislative power is the divesting of judicial power. Statutes that leave agencies to adjudicate violations of their own conditions—most worrisomely, their own regulatory and unconstitutional conditions—displace the judicial power of the courts. That is, they divest the courts of judicial power and vest it where the Constitution did not.

Statutes establishing conditions almost always leave agencies to adjudicate whether their conditions have been violated—first, when an agency makes or does not make a grant and, second, when it reconsiders the grant. For example, when the National Institutes of Health—part of the Department of Health and Human Services—considers whether to support research at a university, it makes an initial determination about the university's compliance with the department's conditions. And it may later determine that the university has violated the conditions. In both instances, the department is adjudicating its own conditions.

When a recipient of a federal grant breaches a condition, the relevant federal agency can pursue relatively formal administrative proceedings. That is, the agency can ask its administrative adjudicators to determine whether the recipient of a grant is in "noncompliance" with a condition and then give a remedy. Remedies can include the temporary suspension of payments, a partial or complete termination of the award, the return of prior payments, the suspension or debarment of the recipient from future federal grants, an order requiring the recipient to cease and desist its violations, and even a penalty.[6]

But these administrative proceedings usually come with risks for the agency, notably judicial review.[7] Many agencies therefore avoid formal administrative proceedings in order to pursue less formal mechanisms—first for gathering information, then for determining the existence of violations, and finally for securing compliance. Some agencies even deliberately inculcate fear about their formal remedies, and then feel especially free to make very intrusive informal demands. Overall, agencies usually have the capacity, more or less at will, to make informal adjudicatory demands—to demand information, decide about violations, and ultimately insist on remedial action—including certifications, representations, and additional conditions.[8]

It may be objected that when agencies informally decide that their conditions have been violated, they are doing no more than private parties do when negotiating how to resolve breaches of contract. Yet agencies are government actors, which formally adjudicate violations of their conditions in administrative proceedings under color of law. Thus, when they informally decide that their conditions have been violated, they are adjudicating in the shadow of their more formal adjudicatory powers. And as so often when agencies act informally in the shadow their more formal powers, the informality of the proceedings allows them to be all the more coercive.

Especially when an agency's conditions are regulatory, it is clear that its decisions about compliance amount to the exercise of judicial power. The application of laws regulating the people is part of the core of judicial power. Accordingly, when agencies adjudicate regulatory conditions, they are displacing the courts—divesting them of their judicial power and assuming that power for themselves.[9] As put long ago by Charles Reich, "government largess" has given rise to "special tribunals, outside the ordinary structure of government."[10]

The Constitution vests the judicial power of the United States in the courts—thereby precluding any divestiture of this power outside the courts. The Constitution reinforces this conclusion by staffing the courts with judges. Whereas judges in the Roman law tradition could subdelegate their judicial role, judges in the common law tradition cannot delegate their judicial office, whether to clerks, executive agencies, or anyone else.[11] Even clerks, though they can assist the judges, ideally cannot exercise the office of judging, as this belongs exclusively to the judges.

These constitutional barriers to any divesting of judicial power from the courts, and any vesting of it elsewhere, are profoundly important because Americans cannot expect much justice when adjudication shifts from courts to agencies. The costs for procedural rights must await the next chapter, but already here it is obvious that when agencies formally or informally adjudicate their own conditions they are not disinterested, and that at least when the conditions are regulatory, the agencies are displacing the role of real judges. And because regulatory conditions typically are specified by agencies, the agencies end up with a dangerous combination of legislative, prosecutorial, and judicial power—a combination in which their judging is often a further expression of their legislative and prosecutorial policies. This is the very opposite of the Constitution's separation of powers and a perfect illustration of why the separation of powers matters.

The dangers are even greater when judicial power gets devolved by regulatory conditions to state or private institutions. When imposing regulatory conditions on states and private institutions, the federal government often asks them to impose such conditions on persons within their control and then to adjudicate the conditions—a familiar example being Title IX tribunals in state and private universities. Judicial power is thereby not merely divested, but defederalized and even privatized, and (as will be seen in Chapters 7 and 15) the resulting regulatory adjudications are often untamed by even the most basic due process or other procedural rights.

Like the displacement of legislative powers, this displacement of judicial power is a question not merely of structure, but of freedom. Just as the Constitution guarantees Americans the freedom of living under laws made by their elected legislature, so it guarantees them a freedom to be held to account only in the courts, with all of the process due in the courts. By divesting the underlying powers, however, conditions, especially regulatory conditions, throw these most basic freedoms to the winds.

Consent Decrees and Other Settlements

The displacement of Congress's legislative power often comes in the form of settlements. Many commentators have noted the abuse of consent decrees and other settlements; less well recognized is that such agreements can be unconstitutional.

Rather than use benefits to impose regulatory conditions, some agencies or state attorneys general sue in federal court and then settle in exchange for regulatory conditions, which the courts embody in "consent decrees." For example, after forty-six state attorneys general sued the tobacco industry, they settled on the condition that the tobacco firms submit to a consent decree imposing advertising restrictions. Such restrictions would have faced political and constitutional objections had the regulation come through Congress, but now they are imposed by a court's consent decree.

In an administrative version of such tactics, some agencies stay out of court, relying instead on harsh administrative proceedings to secure consent to regulatory conditions. The Federal Trade Commission, for example, uses this approach to get submission to regulatory conditions it could not have imposed by law (as will be seen in Chapter 14). Mimicking the "consent decrees" of the courts, the commission embodies its regulatory conditions in administrative "consent orders."

Yet another variation can be found in nonprosecution agreements. Instead of prosecuting and then getting a settlement approved by some sort of tribunal, federal prosecutors and agencies, such as the Securities and Exchange Commission (SEC), often secure settlements merely by threatening prosecution. They thereby use their power in court to impose regulatory conditions without going to court—indeed, often without disclosure to a court or the public.[12] Similarly, the government often seeks deferred prosecution agreements. Though these settlements are at least filed with the courts, they face very limited review.

Regardless of whether regulatory conditions come through consent decrees, consent orders, or non- or deferred-prosecution agreements, such conditions divest Congress of its legislative powers and vest such powers in prosecutors or agencies. The wayward conditions mostly confine how Americans can conduct their businesses, charities, and other organizations, and they mostly impose restrictions beyond what is required by law—all without working through the legislative process.

Adding to the danger from such settlements, many also require defendants to refrain from seeking any judicial reconsideration in court, or even disputing the settlements in public—notwithstanding that this may be the only way to hold government accountable for its unlawful use of conditions. The SEC, for example, requires settling defendants to submit to gag orders. One advantage for an agency in using consent decrees (judicial or administrative) is that the agency can treat each violation of a decree as a contempt. The effect is to avoid regular judicial processes, even abbreviated administrative processes, and instead impose the summary process available when imposing sanctions for contempt.

Magnifying the constitutional problems, the settlements that appear in consent decrees often lead judges to go beyond judicial power. Far from being merely settlements, consent decrees are judgments of courts. The Constitution vests judicial power in the courts, and the judges have what James Iredell called "the duty of the power," which, he explained, was the duty "to decide in accord with the laws."[13]

On this foundation, there has long been concern about consent decrees containing conditions that depart from law. As put already by an English court, judges should not "give a judgment which they know would be against the law, although the plaintiff and defendant do agree to have such a judgment given."[14] That is, judges have a duty to follow the law, and they therefore cannot, even with the parties' consent, issue decrees that they know depart from law. So when a court enters a consent decree containing a condition that the judge knows (or should know) to be less or more than is required by law, the condition should be considered beyond judicial duty, and thus beyond the judicial power and unlawful and void.*

---

*Among these illicit conditions in consent decrees are those requiring payments not required by law—whether made to a prosecuting party or to a third party who did not participate in the underlying lawsuit. Attorneys general often seek these distributions in order to mobilize political support and finance political allies. Such settlements,

But the most basic problem with settlements that impose regulatory conditions is that they divest Congress of legislative power. This alone—apart from violations of rights and of judicial power—is enough to render them unconstitutional.

Necessary and Proper

Can the divestiture of legislative and judicial powers be justified by the Necessary and Proper Clause? This clause authorizes Congress to make such laws as are "necessary and proper" for carrying out other governmental powers, and it is often interpreted to mean that Congress can do whatever it considers expedient. But this interpretation is contrary to the Constitution's text and would enable Congress to undo the Constitution's allocation of powers.

The Constitution authorizes the president to recommend to Congress such measures as he judges "necessary and expedient." This phrase is revealing, for in contrast, the Constitution empowers Congress to enact what is "necessary and proper." The Constitution thus clearly limits Congress, in its pursuit of what is necessary, to what is proper. At a minimum, this means Congress cannot rely on a claim of necessity to justify divesting Congress or the courts of the powers that the Constitution vests in them, or to justify vesting such powers elsewhere. However expedient it may seem to Congress, such things are not constitutionally proper.

The Necessary and Proper Clause, moreover, speaks of "vested" powers and thereby specifically avoids authorizing any divestiture of such powers. It is often assumed that this clause gives Congress the power to enact what is necessary and proper to carry out other government powers in the abstract—a breadth that might justify

---

however, impose sanctions that Congress did not authorize and subsidize persons for whom Congress did not appropriate funds.

Congress in rearranging such powers. But the clause confines Congress to making "all Laws which shall be necessary and proper for carrying into Execution the foregoing Powers, and all other Powers vested by this Constitution in the Government of the United States, or in any Department or Officer thereof." The clause, in other words, restricts Congress to carrying into execution only the powers *vested* by the Constitution in different persons and parts of government. The clause thus reinforces vested powers and carefully does not authorize Congress to divest any part of government of its powers or to vest such powers elsewhere.

The Necessary and Proper Clause, evidently, is not an opportunity to undermine the Constitution's avenues of power and other structures. It offers no justification for conditions that displace regulation from congressional statutes to private transactions or that enable adjudication outside the decisions of the courts.

Excused by Administrative Power?

Notwithstanding that regulatory conditions on privileges displace the constitutional powers of Congress and the courts, one could take perverse comfort in the existence of administrative power. This mode of governance allows agencies to evade the Constitution's avenues for legislative and judicial power, and if administrative power is nonetheless acceptable, then perhaps there is no need to worry about regulatory conditions.

But administrative edicts are very dangerous. And regulatory conditions are even more troubling, for much more than administrative commands, they privatize government power. Although this privatization has already been mentioned, it now can be seen that, in three ways, it differentiates conditions from administrative power.

First, regulatory conditions take effect not through public consent in Congress, nor even through public commands by administrative agencies, but through private consent. Whether the details of a regulatory condition are stipulated by Congress or an administrative agency, the regulation ultimately takes effect through a private transaction.

Second, as a result of being imposed through private arrangements, such regulation also tends to be private in the sense that it is largely hidden from public view or at least difficult for the public to discern. For example, though agencies can impose regulatory conditions through rules, which they adopt in the same way as more directly binding administrative rules, agencies can also impose the details of regulatory conditions in mere contracts, assurances, and even conversations—thus regulating through relatively inaccessible transactions. And even when Congress specifies the full details of a condition, one often cannot discern exactly how and to whom it applies, as this remains a matter of private consent. The real effect and reach of regulatory conditions therefore typically cannot be discerned merely from public enactments or rules.

Third, the government often subsidizes or privileges private institutions on the condition that they regulate their personnel—thereby turning such institutions into agents for carrying out federal regulatory policy (as will be explored in Chapter 15). In devolving governance to private entities, regulatory conditions most fully privatize regulation and adjudication.

Thus, as bad as administrative power may be, regulatory conditions are even worse. Both are unconstitutional pathways for governance, which divest legislative power from Congress and judicial power from the courts and vest such powers in agencies. But regulatory conditions go much further, for in various ways they privatize the legislative and judicial powers.

The Constitution carefully protects the freedom of Americans to be governed only under laws made by their elected legislators and their freedom to be brought to account only through judgments of the courts. Nonetheless, the government increasingly regulates along other pathways—by means of administrative edicts and, of particular interest here, by means of conditions. The effect is to escape government by law, to divest Congress and the courts of their powers, and even to privatize such powers. All of this is unconstitutional.

6

Short-Circuiting Politics

The divestiture of legislative power is not merely unconstitutional; it also has political costs. In circumventing congressional lawmaking, regulatory conditions short-circuit the Constitution's system of political accountability and participation.

And once again the evasion of constitutional process has predictable consequences for policy. Precisely because government can work through the subterranean conduits offered by regulatory conditions, it can impose policies that, if pursued through the Constitution's regular political processes, might not have survived the light of day.

Escaping Political Consent

At the very least, regulatory conditions sideline the political consent that comes through the Constitution's political process. Consider, for example, the Department of Health and Human Services' conditions regulating human subjects research. Leaving aside whether such conditions violate the First Amendment and other constitutional rights, they are disturbing for a more basic reason: they are a mode of regulation that relies on private consent to circumvent the Constitution's public political consent.

This loss of political consent is serious. Even when, atypically, Congress fully specifies the conditions, the resulting regulation is not given legal obligation by publicly elected legislators. Rather, it takes effect through the narrower consent of those who accept the funding. Private acquiescence thus displaces political self-government.

Private Concordats and a Loss of Public Accountability

By means of conditions, the government regulates with the consent of mere segments of the nation, thereby escaping the accountability that comes through the Constitution's system of politics.

The government makes one sort of bargain with the poor (restricting domestic privacy). It makes another sort of arrangement with academic institutions (restricting professors and students in much of their inquiry, speech, and publication). It makes yet other arrangements with idealistic organizations such as churches (confining their political speech). And it makes yet further agreements with businesses—varying its conditions industry by industry, often even company by company. And it makes yet other agreements with the states, often imposing different conditions on different states, depending on what it can get away with.[1]

Conditions, in short, revive the medieval system of concordats. Rather than regulate through law and public consent, the government makes different deals with various parts of society.

States and others are so eager for the money that they often agree to conditions with which they cannot comply, and the federal government deals with the ensuing grumbling by selectively offering waivers. The government, in other words, not only makes separate deals with different constituencies but also makes separate compromises when the initial deals are so tough as to be impracticable. Although this relaxation of federal standards is often welcomed as a form of deregulation, it is actually just another disturbing element of a broader system of regulating piecemeal.

Of course, congressional legislation can also fragment policy and reflect underlying deals with different groups, but it does so in public laws, for which legislators are publicly accountable. In contrast, regulatory conditions take effect through private transactions and very nearly privatize governance, with a concomitant loss of public debate and accountability.[2] When Congress debates and votes on a statute directly regulating industrial pollution, Congress itself imposes the regulations, making it accountable to the public. But when Congress votes to support or give other privileges to an industry on the condition that it comply with conditions regulating pollution, accountability becomes obscure. If only because companies consent, they cannot easily rouse the public to feel that anything was really imposed, thus leaving Congress off the hook. And Congress typically goes further in evading accountability by relegating the specification of conditions to agencies. In such ways, regulation through private consent short-circuits public accountability.

Buying Off Political Opposition

Even worse, by regulating through conditions on subsidies, and by offering different conditions to different parties, the government can make a separate peace with its critics. Private deals allow the government to buy off political opposition.

At the very least, government purchases the acquiescence of many who might have publicly resisted the direct imposition of a regulation. But the problem is more acute. Much regulation that is imposed through conditions could not easily have acquired enough political support to have been adopted in a statute or even an agency rule. The government therefore imposes such regulation in the form of conditions, getting private consent for what could not get public consent.

Even when the government imposes uniform conditions, its ability to buy off opponents one by one enables it to get around political resistance. And when it can make different arrangements with different parties, its capacity to get around opposition is all the greater. Each group has its price, and for each, the government can call a distinctive tune.

The overall effect (as noted by scholars as different as Robert Cover and Richard Epstein) is to divide and conquer. Cover explains that the "politics of spending" gives the federal government opportunities that go far beyond the "politics of national regulation," for "through the unfettered exercise of the spending power, the national government could co-opt local opposition, purchase acquiescence."[3]

In buying off some of the potential opponents of a regulation, the government deprives other opponents of the allies they would need to mount successful political resistance. For example, if the government had directly required the equal time rule, or if it had directly required licensing of human subjects research and its publication, there would have been relatively united resistance from the affected groups. But when it regulates broadcasters and academic institutions through a series of private deals, those who do not submit tend to find themselves facing insuperable odds.

Most seriously, conditions allow the government to buy off public opposition to its violations of constitutional rights. James Madison (in *Federalist Number Ten*) imagined that America's extended republic offered a solution to the danger of faction—that is, the threat from groups seeking unjust or oppressive ends. Whereas factions would have difficulty uniting to oppress minorities, the oppressed could successfully unite, among themselves and with allies, to resist the demands of factions. But nowadays the government, perhaps in the hands of a faction, can make a separate peace with some of those who might have resisted, leaving the others with little political hope.

These dangers—of short-circuiting public accountability and buying off opposition—remain serious even when Congress details the conditions. Regardless of congressional specification, the conditions take effect through private transactions rather than publicly debated decisions, and they subdue many potential opponents, leaving others in the lurch. Thus, even when, on rare occasion, Congress fully specifies regulatory conditions, this irregular path of governance short-circuits the Constitution's vision of politics.

Structural Costs of Inequality

In using private concordats to impose different terms on different Americans, the government has created profound inequalities—most basically for the poor but ultimately for the full range of Americans. And this inequality has structural consequences.

Equality is a key structural protection for liberty, as it enables Americans to feel a shared interest in protecting their freedoms, thereby uniting the society behind what is assured by law. This is why (as suggested in the Introduction) it is so significant that the Constitution recognizes the egalitarian status of at least all citizens and typically all persons. Even narrowly as to rights, equality is structurally essential, as it allows all to share an interest in protecting the rights of each. Of course, not every individual and institution will recognize this shared interest, but equality tends to secure the broadest possible societal commitment to the rights of others.

The threat to this structural role of equality can be illustrated by the current reality that churches, universities, and businesses must comply with different conditions on their speech, and that these speech conditions can even vary from one university to another or one business to another. Speech rights thus differ between individuals and institutions, and even among individuals and among institutions. This is sobering because individuals cannot protect their speech rights without the support of institutions, and institutions cannot defend their speech rights without the support of individuals and, indeed, other institutions. For example, when churches, universities, and businesses have different speech rights, each group can be deprived of its full freedom of speech, without provoking much anxiety among the others. The result is to divide the nation, leaving

Americans and their institutions without the shared interest in speech rights that is so valuable for their preservation—indeed, for the preservation of all freedoms.

Conditions imposing unequal restrictions on constitutional freedoms are thus very dangerous. Equality takes such freedoms beyond the Constitution's formal protection, giving them a depth and breadth of social support. It is therefore very worrisome that by rendering such freedoms unequal, conditions deprive Americans of a shared interest in preserving these liberties.[4]

Alienation

One of the more sobering consequences of control through conditions is a loss of public attachment to the government. Of course, by ruling through conditions rather than direct constraint, government can enjoy all of the advantages of using carrots rather than sticks. From this perspective, conditions turn fears of force into hopes for largess, thereby creating a soft power, which being consensual, is less likely to provoke political opposition. The purchase of submission can thus seem an appealing mechanism for avoiding resentment against constraint.[5]

But are subsidized Americans really less resentful? Generosity often spurs disappointment and hostility, and such results are all the more probable when the largess comes from a distant government, when its benefits are understood as rights or "entitlements," and when its generosity is limited to avoid countervailing resentments about taxes.

Even if government could pay off any resentment among the recipients of its largess, it cannot thereby satisfy other Americans. In fact, its generosity to some is apt to make the others all the more resentful—perhaps most immediately about not being included in the deal, secondarily about paying for it, and more generally about purchase as a mode of governance. A system of making deals one constituency at a time necessarily leaves others in the cold, both financially and politically.

Although conditions may sometimes seem to avoid temporary resentment about particular rules, government by subsidy is apt eventually to cause a deeper and more enduring alienation. The Constitution's system of representative government allows Americans to feel attached to their legal system, even if not to all of its decisions, for they can directly participate in choosing their lawmakers and so can feel themselves to have some role in the lawmaking process. In contrast, when government regulates by having agencies purchase submission, Americans are apt to feel a loss of political agency. This is profoundly demoralizing and is probably one of the reasons ever more Americans feel estranged from their government.

One might suppose that the hidden character of governance through conditions can preserve its legitimacy and avoid alienation. But is it to be supposed that Americans live in a *Wizard of Oz* world, in which they will remain content while being manipulated from above, behind a mere screen of constitutional governance? Even in Oz, the manipulation was eventually exposed. Here, in the real world, though the erosion of constitutional process is not yet fully understood, Americans sense that something is awry—that they have lost their political agency and are suffering under misbegotten policies. It is therefore a mistake to rely on conditions for constitutional deception. Exposure is inevitable and will lead to profound discontent.

The very legitimacy and acceptance of American government rests on a series of constitutional ideals. These principles include constitutional rights, independent and unbiased judges, trial by jury, federalism, and most centrally for this chapter, self-governance through laws made by the people's representatives. Not merely a matter of high theory, these ideals are prudent protections, which bar governance by private concordats and preclude the prostituted policies apt to result from such arrangements. It is therefore unsurprising that the abandonment of these ideals leaves Americans feeling alienated. The purchase of submission deprives Americans of the valuable freedoms that unite them with their government.

Like administrative power, the purchase of submission is a means of controlling Americans that evades the Constitution's avenue for lawmaking. But even more than administrative power, it deprives Americans of political self-government, escapes political consent and public accountability, buys off political opposition, and alienates Americans from their system of government.

7

Denying Procedural Rights

Just as the displacement of legislative power comes with political costs, so the relocation of judicial power comes with procedural costs. Conditions allow agencies to adjudicate for themselves and thereby sidestep the procedural rights available in the courts. Thus, even when not imposing restrictions that violate constitutional rights, conditions, as a method of control, can be procedurally unconstitutional.

When an agency adjudicates violations of its conditions, it can (as seen in Chapter 5) pursue formal administrative proceedings or can act informally. But either way the agency adjudicates the noncompliance for itself—without going to court, without persuading a judge or jury, without satisfying due process and associated burdens of proof, and without fulfilling any of the Constitution's other procedural rights. Indeed, because agencies usually adjudicate conditions informally, they ordinarily serve as judges of their own conditions without even offering the much-diminished rights available in administrative proceedings.

This loss of procedural rights can be troubling even when conditions are not regulatory and do not impose unconstitutional restrictions—for example, when agencies end up displacing the courts in adjudicating breaches of their own mundane nonregulatory conditions. The problem, however, is distinctively severe and interesting when the conditions are a means of regulation or impose unconstitutional restrictions; then it is especially clear that agencies displace the courts and their procedural rights.[1]

Procedural Rights

One might think that procedural rights constrain the courts, not other parts of government. But procedural rights do more than shape court proceedings; they also bar government from proceeding against Americans outside the courts.

Guarantees of the due process of law developed precisely to bar any binding adjudication outside the courts. The principle of due process became prominent already when, in the fourteenth century, Edward III brought Englishmen to account in his council and other prerogative or administrative bodies. Parliament responded with due process statutes, which barred binding adjudications outside the courts. The principle (as stated at the head of the 1368 statute) was that "none shall be put to answer without due process of law."[2] The English revived this principle in the seventeenth century against the High Commission and the Star Chamber, and Americans in 1791 guaranteed it in the Fifth Amendment.

One of the earliest academic commentators on the US Bill of Rights recognized the implications. When lecturing on the Constitution at William and Mary in the mid-1790s, St. George Tucker quoted the Fifth Amendment's Due Process Clause and concluded, "Due process of law must then be had before a judicial court, or a judicial magistrate."[3] Chancellor James Kent likewise explained that the due process of law "means law, in its regular course of administration, through courts of law."[4] And Justice Joseph Story echoed both Tucker and Kent.[5] Evidently, the due process of law can be enjoyed only in the courts, and binding adjudication outside the courts violates due process.

Similarly, juries are available only in the courts, and the right to a jury thus precludes binding adjudications in other tribunals. This was recognized by some of the earliest state cases to hold statutes unconstitutional. In 1780 in *Holmes & Ketcham v. Walton*, the New Jersey Supreme Court held a state statute unconstitutional for authorizing forfeiture proceedings before a justice of the peace with only a six-person jury. In 1786 in the *Ten Pound Cases*, the New Hampshire Inferior Courts repeatedly held that a statute could not authorize justices of the peace to hear cases for more than forty shillings without a jury—notwithstanding that the statute allowed defendants a jury on appeal to the regular courts. Although the forty shillings may nowadays seem to have been a financial limit on jury rights, it actually was the old jurisdictional floor for common law courts in civil actions. The *Ten Pound Cases* thus generally found a constitutional right to a jury, in a real court, and thereby recognized that the right to a jury bars out-of-court proceedings.[6]

In fact, almost all procedural rights bar adjudication outside the courts. The Constitution makes this clear through its drafting—for one thing, by stating most of its procedural rights in the passive voice, thereby limiting not merely the courts but all three branches of government. In addition, the amendments reciting procedural rights are located mostly at the end of the Constitution. Although the drafters of the Bill of Rights initially planned to rewrite articles within the body of the Constitution, this would have been inadequate. For example, a modification to Article III would have confined only the courts. The drafters therefore ultimately added their amendments at the end of the document, where the procedural rights could confine all three branches. These two drafting techniques—the passive voice and amendments at the end—give the procedural rights their breadth in limiting all parts of government.

The effect is to bar not only the courts but also the legislature and the executive from denying procedural rights. These rights, in other words, are violated not only when a court truncates them but also when an agency sidesteps the courts and their procedural rights by substituting agency adjudications. And this makes sense, for if government could avoid due process, juries, and other procedural rights simply by instituting executive branch adjudications, there would be little point in having procedural rights.

Violating Procedural Rights

Nonetheless, government agencies repeatedly displace the courts—most commonly, by adjudicating regulatory conditions for themselves—and they thereby violate the Constitution's procedural rights. Under the Constitution, Congress can leave the distribution of money and other privileges to the executive branch, but when conditions on such things are regulatory, they enable the executive agencies to substitute their decisions not only for those of the legislature but also for those of the courts. This initially happens when agencies measure compliance for purposes of making or denying a grant, and again when they decide whether a violation of a condition justifies withdrawing (or threatening to withdraw) the grant. At both stages, their adjudications deny procedural rights.[7]

When the government acted exclusively through statutes to regulate Americans, it could enforce its regulations only in the courts—with judges, juries, and the full due process of law. Nowadays, however, it frequently regulates through administrative rules and enforces them with its administrative faux process—at best, an administrative "hearing," subject to very limited judicial review.[8]

Yet when the government regulates through conditions, its agencies need not provide even this administrative process. Agency adjudications about conditions are not always subject to the Administrative Procedure Act. And though agencies can resort to formal administrative proceedings to enforce conditions, they usually handle such violations informally. Their adjudications thus typically come without even the weak process employed by administrative law judges.

Indeed, agency adjudications about regulatory conditions escape almost all constitutionally protected procedural rights. Courts sometimes violate procedural rights piecemeal by taking a confined view of one right or another. But agencies altogether displace court proceedings and thereby tend to violate such rights wholesale, including juries, due process, confrontation, warrants, reasonable searches, and so forth. By working through conditions, the government need not bother with such niceties.

Adding to the violation of procedural rights are conditions imposing controls that render defendants vulnerable to the government, such as conditions requiring inspections, warrantless searches, and self-monitoring. Some conditions even require the filing of compliance reports that function as modes of self-condemnation.[9]

In the compliance reports, organizations and individuals must recite that they have complied with their regulatory conditions. Some agencies even require reports about noncompliance—from organizations as varied as banks and universities. For example, in its conditions imposing institutional review boards (IRBs), the Department of Health and Human Services (HHS) requires research institutions to ensure "prompt reporting to the IRB, appropriate institutional officials, and the department or agency head" about "any instance of serious or continuing noncompliance with the applicable HHS and/or FDA regulations, or the requirements or determinations of the IRB."[10] A researcher's failure promptly to volunteer his violations can lead to government-established sanctions—whether by HHS at the top of the food chain, the funded academic institution, or its IRB.

Many conditions requiring noncompliance reports are more subtle. Rather than formally require such reports, some agencies simply hint that they expect reporting of any substantial noncompliance, and regulated entities recognize that it is unwise to resist. Other agencies reach settlements in consent orders or decrees, or in non- or deferred-prosecution agreements, on the condition that defendants share information and file compliance or noncompliance reports, thereby perverting the judicial process to enforce disclosure and self-incrimination.

The demands for compliance and noncompliance reports sweep aside the need for judicial or even administrative warrants or subpoenas. They erase the constitutional and even administrative burdens of proof and persuasion. They even press the reporting parties to incriminate themselves—sometimes at risk of criminal prosecutions and often in matters that, notwithstanding their civil form, are criminal in reality.[11]

Overall, the courts have scarcely acknowledged the loss of procedural rights. In one old case, *Speiser v. Randall* (1958), the Supreme Court rose to the occasion by rejecting a reversed burden of proof.[12] But on the whole, conditions are a nearly unchecked means of denying the due process of law, juries, and other procedural rights, and they create an atmosphere in which self-denunciation is cultivated.

Alas, it gets worse, for in their informal adjudications about conditions, agencies tend to evade judicial review. If an agency informally decides that a grant recipient has violated a condition, and if it then informally asks the recipient to cure the violation and submit to further conditions, the agency's conduct is not ordinarily considered final agency action. The recipient therefore does not have standing to challenge the agency's decision in court, and the agency's action is not ordinarily reviewable.

The nonlegal obstacles to review are even greater. Businesses and other institutions dissatisfied with agency decisions often must tread carefully—if only because of the risk of increased agency scrutiny. Indeed, some agencies carefully dole out their money or licenses in installments, so as to keep recipients anxious about the next payment or grant of permission. And some (such as HHS) have deliberately threatened agency intervention in order to make recipients more pliable.

The underlying reality is that those who contemplate challenging agency decisions must fear regulatory retaliation. Agencies typically wield all governmental powers—legislative, executive, and judicial—and so have multiple opportunities for retaliation against institutions and individuals who complain or seek judicial review. Agencies sometimes use their licensing conditions to attack and even close businesses that dare to push back.[13] (The New York State Department of Health shut down the Beechwood Restorative Care Center—among the very best such centers in the state—because its owner challenged the agency. Though he eventually established this wrongdoing in court, it took more than a decade of litigation and cost a fortune.[14]) The risk of agency retaliation is well known in private but is so threatening that few businesses or other institutions are willing to discuss their concerns publicly. In some industries, corporate counsel will quietly admit that because of the danger of agency retaliation, they would never even consider challenging their regulators, leaving many regulatory conditions nearly unreviewable.

The loss of procedural rights can be illustrated by the regulatory conditions imposed through licensing. When federal agencies impose and enforce conditions through licensing decisions, they only sometimes must provide the limited administrative process specified by the Administrative Procedure Act.[15] And even when this inadequate process is required for an agency's formal licensing decisions, the agency can often substitute informal pressures, which avoid the statute's process requirements. The Administrative Procedure Act, moreover, applies only to federal agencies. Accordingly, some agencies pass along their licensing decisions to states and private institutions, which then can adjudicate agency conditions as directed by the relevant federal agency.

The use of conditions to shift federal adjudicatory decisions to state and private bodies is exceedingly dangerous.[16] By this means, federal agencies can almost completely deny procedural rights and can even abridge First Amendment rights. HHS uses its conditions to get educational institutions to subject researchers to prior IRB licensing of their plans to read, take notes, ask questions, publish, and so forth—all without providing them a hearing, allowing them to present evidence, or letting them be represented by a lawyer. To top it off, there is not even an administrative appeal.

In a range of ways, therefore, much agency adjudication about conditions—not least about regulatory conditions—sidesteps the courts and thereby violates the Constitution's procedural rights.[17] The typical result is a process without much process. Indeed, agency and agency-authorized decisions about conditions are frequently so informal as to scarcely even resemble adjudication.

Ambidextrous Enforcement and the Changed Nature of Procedural Rights

Accentuating the loss of procedural rights is the government's opportunity for ambidextrous enforcement. Agency adjudications, both about administrative edicts and about conditions, give the government a pathway for judicial power that escapes the Constitution's court system and procedural rights. The government can thus choose whether or not to respect such rights.

Consider the government's pathways. The government once could engage in binding adjudication against Americans only through the courts and their judges. Now, instead, by acting through administrative rules or conditions, it can choose agency adjudication. In some instances, Congress alone makes this choice; in other instances, it authorizes an agency to make the selection. One way or another, the government can act ambidextrously—either through the courts, with their judges, juries, and due process, or through agency adjudication and its faux process or nonprocess.[18]

The result is a change in the very nature of procedural rights. Such rights traditionally were assurances against the government. Now they are merely one of the choices for government in its exercise of power. Though the government must respect these rights when it proceeds against Americans in court, it has the freedom to escape the rights by acting either administratively or through conditions.[19]

Procedural rights, in other words, are no longer guarantees but mere government options. Agency adjudications—whether about administrative edicts or about conditions—thus alter the very nature of procedural rights, depriving Americans of basic protections.

Title IX Kangaroo Courts

The threat to procedural rights from conditions has become painfully evident from Title IX proceedings against students and faculty. Title IX of the Education Amendments Act of 1972 (as amended in 1988) bars discrimination on the basis of sex in any academic institution receiving federal financial assistance.

As already noted (in Chapter 3), Title IX's anti-discrimination conditions were expanded from federally funded programs and activities to apply throughout funded institutions, and because they extend beyond the funded programs or activities, they are regulatory. This regulatory character of Title IX's conditions should be enough to question their constitutionality—or at least, to question the constitutionality of their expanded reach. But even more interesting are the implications for rights.

By means of Title IX, the Department of Education took aim at speech. In its infamous "Dear Colleague" letters, the department interpreted Title IX's condition to require educational institutions to prohibit much sexual and political conversation—to bar "unwelcome conduct of a sexual nature," including merely "verbal" conduct.[20]

Title IX thus illustrates, at the very least, the danger of conditions for the First Amendment.

Of particular interest in this chapter on procedural rights, Title IX is also a threat to procedural rights. The Department of Education used Title IX to subject student speech to adjudications by little academic tribunals, which combine investigatory and adjudicatory functions, adopt minimal burdens of proof, and otherwise displace due process with inquisitorial process.[21] Though the Department of Education recently sought to reduce these procedural harms—for example, by requiring these tribunals to permit cross-examination of witnesses—the Title IX conditions still shift adjudication to academic tribunals, which continue to offer far less than the courts' due process of law.

The Constitution guarantees Americans adjudication in the courts, with real judges, jurors, due process, civil or criminal burdens of proof, and so forth. In contrast, when government regulates through conditions, as under Title IX, it pushes Americans into petty kangaroo courts, in which these rights are denied.

Procedural rights suffer enough when federal agencies replace courts. The danger is even worse when agencies shove adjudication off into state or even private institutions. Of course, attendance or employment at a state university is a government privilege rather than a right, and when a private university disciplines a student or teacher, there is no state action. One might therefore conclude that all academic institutions may suspend or dismiss students and faculty as they see fit—without judge, jury, or the due process of law. But the Title IX tribunals in state and private institutions are the result of federal manipulation. The government uses its regulatory conditions to shift adjudication not merely from the courts to agencies but even from agencies to state and private institutions, whose inquisitorial committees systematically violate procedural rights.

One might protest that administrative rules also usually get adjudicated by petty diminutive tribunals—by administrative "judges" of one sort or another, who are not really judges, who act without juries or full due process, and who often are biased (as recently documented at the Securities and Exchange Commission).[22] Yet the tribunals that adjudicate Title IX violations, hidden away in state and private institutions, have tended to be much worse. Many still resist cross-examination and both investigate and judge in true inquisitorial style. It makes administrative adjudications seem almost wholesome.

Had Congress or the Department of Education directly required any of this, they would have encountered both political and constitutional obstacles, including the First Amendment's freedom of speech and the Fifth Amendment's due process of law. By using conditions, however, the department massively regulated sexual conduct and speech without having to bother with the courts and their due process. And to make sure of this, the department relegated adjudication to shabby little inquisitorial tribunals in state and private institutions. Title IX is a painful reminder that even when used for high-minded purposes, regulatory conditions come with profound costs for procedural rights.

Feasible to Leave All Such Decisions to the Courts?

Even once one recognizes the displacement of judicial decisions to agencies and the loss of procedural rights, one still might wonder whether the courts could really handle all of the adjudications currently done by agencies under regulatory conditions. If agencies did not make such decisions, wouldn't one need a vastly larger judiciary?

Certainly, if existing regulatory conditions were simply enacted as binding statutes and if all adjudications about violations had to be resolved in federal court, the judicial system would be overwhelmed. But it is a mistake to assume that the burdens of agency adjudication would simply be replicated in the courts.

First, if regulatory conditions were replaced by direct requirements in binding statutes, the drafting would change. Regulatory conditions typically are very open-ended—so as to leave the relevant agencies with vast policy, enforcement, and adjudicatory discretion.[23] If such regulations were imposed as binding statutory duties, however, there would be very different drafting incentives. There would be no reason to create such expansive discretion, and the statutes would thus tend to present the courts with a much tighter range of questions for adjudication.

Second, the availability of jury rights would affect judicial decisions. Without the right to a jury trial (as revealed by the English experience in almost completely abandoning juries), judges tend to blur the law with the facts and make the law inordinately complex. In America by contrast—even in an era in which most cases are settled before they go to a jury—judges anticipate that future cases will come before juries. Judges therefore tend to distinguish the law from the facts and often keep the law simple enough to be explained to a jury. Accordingly, it is difficult to believe that if the federal government were to enact its regulatory conditions as binding laws and were to leave their adjudication to the courts, decisions in court would simply imitate agency decisions. On the contrary, judicial decisions would likely develop a body of clarifying precedent, distinct from the narrow facts of particular disputes, thus enabling more disputes to settle.

These two differences—in drafting and adjudication—suggest that if regulatory conditions were replaced by direct statutory regulation, the courts would not face the same range or amount of adjudication as is currently undertaken by agencies. Although the Constitution's avenues for regulation and adjudication come with additional expenses, they also come with distinctive efficiencies.

It is thus misleading—indeed, an utter distraction—to claim that agency decisions cannot be replicated in the courts. To be sure, a repudiation of regulatory conditions would entail adjudicatory complications, but it is not evident that these difficulties would be insurmountable, let alone that they would outweigh the value of juries and other procedural rights. If the Constitution's courts and procedural rights are to be thrown aside as impracticable, it will have to rest on better reasoning than this.

Conditions—most clearly, regulatory conditions—enable agencies to escape the Constitution's procedural rights. The vast majority of regulatory conditions are not "unconstitutional conditions"—meaning that most of them do not substantively violate rights or other constitutional limits. Nonetheless, regulatory conditions typically do violate constitutional rights, for they enable agencies to adjudicate without judges, juries, due process, and so forth. By means of regulatory conditions, agencies sidestep the courts and thereby gut almost all of the Constitution's procedural rights.

8

Federalism

Federalism is the system by which Americans govern themselves in layers. Rather than have a single central government, which directs subordinate geographic departments—as in France—Americans share a federal government for some national issues and have fifty state governments for other matters. And to police the boundary between federal and state power, the Constitution elevates federal statutes above state law.

The federal government, however, no longer confines itself to using its statutes to trump state laws in areas of federal power; more ambitiously, it uses mere conditions to control the states—even in matters that the Constitution reserves to them. As a result, quite apart from the expansion of the federal government's substantive powers, the purchase of state submission threatens to defeat much federalism.

In colloquial terms, the "layer cake" of federalism has become a more vertically amalgamated "marble cake," in which federal money and conditions run down into the states and localities. Put more academically, states have become "integrated" into national policymaking.[1] Though they can negotiate some wiggle room within the federal chokehold, they feel little choice but to adopt and carry out federal policies. It is thus a relationship in which the federal government is the "aggressive" actor and the states are on the "defensive."[2] In almost comic euphemism, this is called "cooperative federalism."[3]

Yet rather than mean that Americans must give up on federalism, these developments suggest federalism's continued significance. It has never been more important to recognize the value of the Constitution's federalism and the unconstitutionality of subverting it by purchase.

Federalism's Value

Federalism is not as popular a feature of American government as are constitutional rights, but it, too, is essential.

Structurally, state power counterbalances centralized power. Just as the federal government can limit narrow local interests and prejudices in the states, so the states can sometimes push back against the centralized interests and prejudices that flourish in Washington.

Even more profoundly, federalism structurally secures Americans from a combination of general and centralized power—a peculiarly dangerous amalgam that is apt to intrude deeply while cutting off exit. At the same time that the generality of such power permits it to encroach into the most private spheres of life, its centralization precludes any relief through emigration to another state. Federalism protects Americans from this totalizing possibility by allowing only specialized federal power. Americans thus are subject to general power only in their own states and can escape local oppression by moving to another state. Put sociologically, the division of power among many governments is a valuable "obstacle in the way of accumulation of power by a single class or group, even a majority class or group."[4]

In multiple ways, therefore, as put by the Supreme Court, "the Constitution divides authority between federal and state governments for the protection of individuals."[5] Though federalism operates structurally, it secures personal freedom.

Theoretically, federalism leaves room for policy experimentation in the states. There is some truth to this—to which one might add another, less optimistic truth: that federalism disperses the costs of policy errors. One way or another, federalism is valuable for its recognition of the limits of human understanding.

Federalism is also a foundation of financial prudence. Although federal funding is often assumed to enrich the states and the lives of their peoples, it more clearly has moved many states toward fiscal irresponsibility. Many federal grants come with conditions requiring states to provide matching funds or at least to maintain their own spending. So it is not state profligacy alone that has led numerous states to slide into debt and near bankruptcy.

Federalism limits competing demands on the federal government's energy and resources. It creates a specialized federal government, which has different functions than the states. If this specialization were maintained, the federal government would not have to compromise on its specialized roles—for example, military preparedness—in order to satisfy demands for federal funding of other activities. In other words, federalism protects the federal government's specialized goals from competing demands to support general governmental ends.

Even in what is said to be an age of individualism, many Americans still want a sense of community, and federalism allows Americans to govern themselves in communities small enough that individuals can feel connected to each other. In many states, local connectedness, knowledge, and identity remain profoundly important, and the resulting communal strength is advantageous not only personally but also politically, as it enables locals to hold their government to account.

Federalism, moreover, goes far in solving the problem of geographic diversity. States have different characters. By way of illustration, Connecticut and California, Vermont and Texas, South Dakota and Florida, South Carolina and Massachusetts are not merely different places; they also are different states of mind; they offer different policies and visions of life, which appeal to different people. And when Americans are on the move, they sometimes cluster with others of similar tastes, making location an expression of elective affinities. For such reasons, geographic difference cannot be understood in merely geographic terms; it is also a manifestation of personal and political preferences, different visions of community, and other sorts of diversity. Federalism is therefore essential for reconciling diverging tastes and identities—whether on matters of religion, sex, taxes, guns, farm policy, industrial policy, or the environment.

Even at the federal level, federalism is baked into the very method of making law. Acts of Congress are the choices of both national and state communities. On the one hand, statutes are enacted by legislators directly chosen by the peoples of the states, and congressional legislation thus must satisfy lawmakers who are keenly attuned to the distinctive preferences of their different jurisdictions. On the other hand, being enacted by a body of lawmakers drawn from across the nation, federal statutes are the choices of the entire nation—of all the people and all the nation's territory, including all the states. This solution, which takes account of layered preferences, is crucial if Americans are to govern themselves both nationally and through a mechanism that reflects their diversity.

For all of these reasons, it is deeply troubling that conditions slice through federalism. And as will now become apparent, their threat to federalism is unconstitutional for multiple reasons.

Co-opting State Opposition

Although the danger of buying off political opposition has already been discussed (in Chapter 6), it becomes especially serious for federalism when the federal government gives grants in aid to the states. Ordinarily, the federal government spends directly for its own programs. But increasingly it also spends to support state programs, and then its money subverts the political independence of the states.

Robert Cover eloquently explains how the states are compromised:

If the exercise of the spending power can, in general, disarm and diffuse political opposition by compensating those subject to regulation, it can have more complex and potentially more dangerous consequences when federal funds are employed in cooperative schemes, in which the federal government provides grants-in-aid to state and local governments. Intrusive federal programs that establish independent federal bases for patronage and impinge on areas of traditional state and local concern will normally be opposed by local elites, which tend to benefit from the control of their own affairs. Cooperative programs, in contrast, co-opt this potential opposition. They actually increase the patronage exercised by local elites and retain local elite domination over beneficiary groups. As a result, state and local political figures and party organizations are "bought off," co-opted from pursuing opposition to national governmental programs.

By debilitating, if not disarming, the alternative sources of political power in our federal structure, "cooperative federalism" undermines the only viable restraint on the congressional exercise of enumerated powers: the political process. Thus, cooperative ventures should be considered of dubious constitutionality.

"Combative federalism," under which federal programs are exclusively federal, presents a desirable alternative, fully consistent with [Chief Justice John] Marshall's theory of enumerated powers. To protect the feedback mechanism that permits states to react to federal actions, the federal government ought to do more itself; it ought to provide funds directly, and be responsible for the administration of the programs it funds. Only the ensuing combat, prompted by the reactions of the states, can guarantee an effective political check on the exercise of national power.[6]

The federal government, in short, can often purchase its way out of state opposition.

Of course, as Cover recognized, states occasionally refuse to be bought off—as when fourteen states flatly declined federal funding tied to Medicaid expansion. But most federal efforts to purchase compliance do not encounter such impediments. Lubricated with federal funds, "cooperative federalism" tends to avoid substantial friction.[7]

Supremacy

A second threat to federalism is that conditions on states are assumed to come with the supremacy of federal law—an assumption reinforced by judicial doctrine.[8] For example, when the Department of Health and Human Services uses conditions on funding to require state universities to establish institutional review boards (IRBs), it is taken for granted that the federal conditions defeat state constitutional guarantees of speech and the press, which otherwise would bar such universities from licensing inquiry and publication. But can federal conditions really nullify contrary state laws?

Tellingly, the Constitution's Supremacy Clause says nothing about conditions. Laws have long been understood to have legal obligation—the binding force of law—because they come with the consent of the people. On this principle, laws made by the elected legislature of a state are binding in that state, and laws made by Congress are binding across the United States. Moreover, because federal laws come from a legislature drawn from across the nation, they are of higher legal obligation than state laws.[9] The Supremacy Clause recognizes this when it elevates three types of federal enactments as the supreme law of the land: "This Constitution, and the Laws of the United States which shall be made in Pursuance thereof; and all Treaties made, or which shall be made, under the Authority of the United States, shall be the supreme Law of the Land." The Constitution, statutes enacted by Congress, and treaties ratified by the Senate are the supreme law of the land and so render contrary state laws unlawful and void.

But what about federal conditions—at least those that are not also legal requirements? Do they defeat state laws? First, consider the special problems with conditions enunciated by federal agencies.

Although a higher law can render a lesser law unlawful and void, this is not true of things that are not law, for only laws (and court orders carrying out the laws) have legal obligation. The Constitution accordingly recognizes acts of Congress, not conditions adopted by agencies, as the supreme law of the land. It follows that federal statutes, rather than federal agency conditions, are the measure of when state law is unlawful and void. A federal agency condition cannot defeat state law.

Reinforcing this conclusion is that statutes traditionally enjoy the obligation of law precisely because they have been adopted by a legislative body representative of the people. Without such consent, such enactments would not bind the people or their states. It is therefore difficult to understand how mere agency conditions can defeat state law.

Moreover, agency conditions purport to defeat state laws without complying with what Bradford Clark has called the "procedural safeguards of federalism."[10] The Constitution establishes the supremacy of not just any laws, but those "made in Pursuance thereof"—that is, by Congress—thereby ensuring that state laws can be defeated only by such federal enactments as are adopted by representatives elected from the states. In contrast, when state law is trumped by agency conditions, this mechanism for safeguarding the concerns of the states gets pushed aside.[11]

In defense of the trumping effect of federal agency conditions, one might imagine that what defeats state law is not any condition set by an agency but rather the federal statute that authorized the agency to specify the condition. From this perspective, everything important has already been said by the statute, and the condition is of little significance, being merely the execution of the statute and thus a matter of executive power. Accordingly, where a state law conflicts with a federal condition, what voids the state statute is really the underlying authorizing statute, not the condition.

This, however, is a notorious fiction. When a similar argument was made on behalf of administrative power, it provoked James Landis (a prominent advocate of such power) to say that "it is obvious that the resort to the administrative process is not, as some suppose, simply an extension of executive power" and those who "have sought to liken this development to a pervasive use of executive power" are "confused."[12] Similarly, it is fictitious and confused to say that an agency's elaboration of a condition is merely an executive specification of the underlying statute and that the statute is what really defeats state laws. A legal sham is a poor excuse for erasing federalism.

Having considered the conditions spelled out by agencies, now let's turn, second, to an even more basic obstacle to permitting federal conditions to trump state statutes—an impediment that affects all such conditions, even those fully specified by Congress. No federal condition, by whatever means adopted, should be understood to defeat the obligation of contrary state law, because conditions do not purport to bind, let alone in the manner of law. In other words, regardless of whether a condition is specified by an agency or Congress, it does not profess to bind and so should not render state law void.

To understand this point, one should keep in mind that not everything in a statute is legally binding. For example, when a federal statute merely suggests a deadline or a process, without requiring it, such things are not binding as law and so do not defeat state law. Similarly, where a federal statute does not directly require compliance with, say, the equal time rule, but merely makes it a condition, that provision is not binding as law—it does not have legal obligation—and so should not be understood to deprive state law of its obligation.

Put succinctly, when federal conditions are not also legal requirements, they do not even purport to bind and therefore should not be
said to bind the states. What is not binding federal law should not
be understood to overthrow or void state law.

Of course, in some instances, a federal statute may propose the
terms of a contractual promise, which, if accepted, will be binding
as a promise to the federal government. But promissory obligation is
not legal obligation. Contract law has the obligation of law, but under
that law, contractual promises have only a lesser sort of commitment
or obligation. Accordingly, when a federal statute does not directly require adherence to its provisions, but instead proposes them as the
terms of a contractual promise, it is not giving them the obligation of
law. Such proposals for contractual promises therefore cannot defeat
state law.

Indeed, far from claiming the obligation of law for its conditions,
the federal government usually insists that its conditions are not even
contracts but rather are mere assurances. That is, most federal conditions are not even binding in the manner of enforceable promises;
on the contrary, as noted above, they are merely the circumstances
that the federal government requires to be in existence if it is to give,
or not withdraw, its support. From this point of view, federal conditions do not legally or even contractually oblige anyone to do anything. Instead, they merely stipulate what the government expects
from recipients if it is to pay them or, later, not withhold further payment and demand its money back. It thus is all the more clear that
even when fully recited in statutes, federal conditions do not come
with legal obligation and should not be thought to defeat the obligation of state law.

In fact, the federal government tends to act through conditions precisely to avoid the constitutional restrictions that would come into
play if it worked through binding laws or rules. The government thus
finds itself in a contradiction. For purposes of trumping state laws,

the government says that its conditions are legally binding or constraining, but for purposes of avoiding charges that it is abridging the Bill of Rights and other constitutional limits, it says that its conditions are merely consensual and so not binding or constraining.

The government cannot have it both ways—that conditions are both legally binding and not legally binding. Either conditions are binding as a matter of law and are therefore often clearly in violation of various constitutional freedoms, or they are not binding as law and consequently do not render contrary state laws unlawful and void.

Commandeering

A third constitutional problem is commandeering. According to the Supreme Court, the federal government may not commandeer the states. Yet all too often, federal conditions do precisely this.

Although the anti-commandeering doctrine is often said to have been created by the Supreme Court, it arises more fundamentally from the Constitution, which does not displace the states' sovereign character. States are independent governments, which draw their authority from below, from their own peoples, and in this sense, they are sovereign. Of course, they are only partly sovereign, for the people of all the states have granted some sovereign powers to the government of the United States, which thus enjoys a superior sovereignty in these spheres—such as war and peace and the regulation of interstate commerce. But where federal sovereignty ends, the states remain sovereign.

And underlying state sovereignty is the freedom of Americans to govern themselves through these lesser jurisdictions—a freedom of localized self-government that individuals enjoy through the election of state lawmakers in republican forms of government. Commandeering doctrine thus reflects fundamental structural elements of the US Constitution, including not only the limited but independent sovereignty of the states but also, underlying this, the freedom of Americans to govern themselves in these relatively intimate jurisdictions.

Indeed, the doctrine would seem to have a textual foundation in the Constitution's requirement that "the United States shall guarantee to every State in this Union a Republican Form of Government." When the federal government, directly or by conditions, dictates policy to the states, it is interfering with their republican self-government. This chapter will later return to the guarantee of a republican form of government, but already here it suggests the depth of constitutional authority for the anti-commandeering doctrine.

Commandeering is especially dangerous because it undermines accountability. The Supreme Court in 1992 in *New York v. United States* explained: "Where the federal government compels states to regulate, the accountability of both state and federal officials is diminished." This is obvious enough for state officials, but it would also appear to be true at the federal level, for "where the federal government directs the states to regulate, . . . the federal officials who devised the regulatory program may remain insulated from the electoral ramifications of their decision."[13]

The court in *New York* concluded that Congress cannot direct states in their governance. It cannot require them to carry out specific federal regulations; nor can it "require the States to govern according to Congress' instructions." Indeed, "the Constitution simply does not give Congress the authority to require the States to regulate."[14] Although the acts of Congress, within its constitutional authority, are binding throughout the United States and are therefore binding on the states, the federal government lacks a power to direct or command the states to adopt regulatory, spending, or other policies. Put generally, whether the federal government proceeds by statute or administrative edict, it cannot direct the states in their governmental policy decisions—be they legislative or executive.

But what about when the federal government acts through conditions on benefits and other privileges? Long ago, in *Steward Machine Co. v. Davis* (1937), the Supreme Court said that the key consideration was whether the federal government "by suit or other means" can "supervise or control" the states. On this basis, the court held that although a federal contract could impair state sovereignty, a mere condition could not.[15]

Whether conditions were really less controlling than contracts in the 1930s, they certainly nowadays encroach on state sovereignty and localized self-government. They drive much state policy, including regulatory and spending policy. Federal conditions have these effects, moreover, almost across the full range of state governance—in matters of health, education, policing, housing, welfare, the environment, and so forth. The reality of federal conditions is that they repeatedly turn states into French-style instruments for carrying out centralized policy, thus depriving Americans of a significant element of their freedom to govern themselves.

Acknowledging that conditions nowadays regularly deprive states of their sovereignty, Chief Justice Roberts in *National Federation of Independent Business v. Sebelius* echoed the line (in *New York*) that "the Constitution simply does not give Congress the authority to require the states to regulate," and then added: "That is true whether Congress directly commands a state to regulate or indirectly coerces a state to adopt a federal regulatory system as its own."[16]

Elaborating how conditions defeat state sovereignty, Roberts explained that when conditions threaten to "terminate other significant independent grants"—that is, when they are cross collateralized— they "cannot be justified" as mere spending. Instead, they "are properly viewed as a means of pressuring the states to accept policy changes."[17]

These conclusions should be no surprise, for the Constitution protects federalism. The judges therefore must "ensur[e]" that any condition "does not undermine the status of the states as independent sovereigns in our federal system."[18] Indeed, the judges must ensure that federal conditions do not deprive Americans of their freedom of self-government through the states.

Force Required for Commandeering?

In analyzing federal conditions that commandeer the states and thus threaten their sovereignty, the Supreme Court has suggested that a showing of something like force is necessary. The underlying assumption is that consent and force are mutually exclusive. In *Sebelius*, for example, Chief Justice Roberts contrasted a mere "inducement" (where a state has a "legitimate choice" whether to accept a federal condition) and a "gun to the head" (where the state has "no choice").[19]

All of this fails to recognize (as will be seen in Chapter 11) that the question is not merely one of force, but of constitutionally significant federal action, which can run the gamut from coercion and the obligation of law to mere economic pressure and sometimes not even such pressure. It also fails to understand (as explained in Chapter 12) that there can be force or other significant pressure amid consent—both in the inducement and in enforcement. It further does not perceive (as detailed in Chapter 13) that questions of force and pressure are altogether irrelevant for determining whether a condition is void and unenforceable for undue influence and contradicting public policy. All of this means that a "gun to the head" and similar ideas of coercion, let alone compulsion, dramatically misunderstand what can constitute legally significant federal action.

More specifically, it must be doubted whether a showing of any degree of force is necessary for commandeering. The label *commandeering* suggests coercion, but the underlying concern is the structural integrity of the Constitution's federal system, in which states enjoy sovereignty derived from their own peoples, and underlying this sovereignty is the freedom of Americans to enjoy localized self-government. The term *commandeering* is therefore a distraction and its suggestion of force must be put aside.

If the question were about a constitutional right, then some sort of force would ordinarily matter—at least in any initial analysis—because force is prototypically necessary for a violation of a right. The question here, however, is not about rights. Nor even is it about the enumerated federal powers as limits on the federal government. Instead, it is more broadly about how those powers are being employed. Is the federal government using them to direct states in ways that undermine state sovereignty and the nation's layered federal system of self-government? If so, force is not necessarily relevant.

Chapter 13 will show that all conditions against public policy (including those that commandeer the states) should be considered void without regard to questions of force or other pressures. But for now the point is simply that force is not as central to commandeering as may be thought. "Commandeering" is ultimately a question about state sovereignty and localized self-government, and the Constitution's federal structure can be as much undermined by federal conditions as by federal force.

Chief Justice Roberts was therefore correct in *Sebelius* when he urged that judges must ensure that conditions do "not undermine the status of the states as independent sovereigns in our federal system."[20] At stake is federalism itself—one of the most basic elements of the Constitution's form of government. Judges thus cannot ignore the reality of what many federal conditions do to state sovereignty and the freedom of Americans to govern themselves through their states.

State Consent to Commandeering and an Abnegation of Judicial Duty

Currently, when faced with commandeering, the Supreme Court tends to be satisfied with consent. As summarized in *Sebelius*, "we look to the states to defend their prerogatives by adopting 'the simple expedient of not yielding' to federal blandishments when they do not want to embrace the federal policies as their own."[21]

But can a state's consent relieve the federal government of its constitutional limitations? A full answer must await Chapter 9, but already here it must be anticipated. Money can undermine state sovereignty and self-government as much as overt force, and if the federal government has no authority to direct the states in their policies, it makes no difference that the states have consented. As put by the Supreme Court in *New York*, "Where Congress exceeds its authority relative to the states, . . . the departure from the constitutional plan cannot be ratified by the 'consent' of state officials."[22]

In leaving the states to defend themselves, moreover, the court is failing to do its duty of enforcing the Constitution's limits on the federal government. Those limits are the barriers that define and protect state power, and the states have as much of a right to have constitutional limits enforced in court as anyone else.

When the Supreme Court refuses to protect states from federal commandeering, it is not only the states who suffer. The people of the United States enjoy a freedom under the Constitution to govern themselves through their states. They have a constitutional freedom not to be subject to power that violates the Constitution's structures, and the consent of their state does not cure the damage to the freedom that is guaranteed to *them* by the Constitution.

The harm to individuals and other private parties becomes especially clear when Congress funds states (as will be seen in Chapter 15) on the condition that they regulate or control individuals—often, indeed, at the cost of their constitutional rights of speech, juries, due process, and so forth. For example, when the federal government in its funding of state universities requires IRBs or Title IX tribunals, it is dangerously violating the rights of individuals. It thus is irrelevant that the states have decided to cooperate with the federal government.

No amount of agreement between the federal government and the states can justify the federal government in commandeering the states in violation of the Constitution, let alone in ways that deny individuals their rights. The court's suggestion that "we look to the states to defend their prerogatives" is therefore a shocking abnegation of judicial duty.

The Reality of Commandeering

To understand the failures of current doctrine on commandeering, one need only examine the reality of federal-state relations. The federal government regularly uses conditions to direct state and local governments in their regulatory and spending policies.

Its conditions do this both by barring and by mandating state policies. The Clean Air Act, for example, uses federal highway funding to impose conditions on state environmental policies—limiting and mandating how states regulate.[23] Such conditions are at the very least regulatory. But quite apart from that, the conditions also direct or commandeer the states in their environmental policies.

When the federal government makes grants to states on the condition that they spend the money in pursuit of a federally favored policy, this looks generous. And one might assume that the conditions do not actually direct state policy, as the states agree to follow the federal policy and in some instances are already pursuing a version of it. But for at least half a century, there have been few illusions about the federal government's use of conditions. Martha Derthick writes: "A whole new perception of the state governments as subordinates of the national government, properly subject to command, had taken root, laying the basis for the regulation that spread like kudzu through the garden of American federalism in the 1970s."[24] As explained by Jessica Bulman-Pozen—a defender of the new "federalism"—states have been reduced to "component parts of the national administrative apparatus."[25]

The federal government is quite candid that it aims to direct the states. According to a 2013 Congressional Budget Office (CBO) report, federal grants "provide a mechanism for federal policymakers to promote their priorities at the state and local levels."[26] The result is a "grant system"—a mode of control distinct from binding laws—with which the federal government can shape state and local policies.[27]

The CBO acknowledges that "less federal control" would be advantageous. If the federal government lightened up its conditions, this "would produce efficiency gains" from local knowledge and flexibility. Without the homogenizing effect of controlling federal conditions, moreover, people could "vote with their feet" by moving to the states that "offer the combination of programs that best suits their circumstances and preferences."[28] The federal government, however, is more interested in imposing "federal policymakers' goals."[29]

States usually prefer their own policies, but the federal government has gradually made the states financially dependent. They therefore often go along with policies they would otherwise reject.[30]

Federal conditions distort state and local policy not only in regulation but also in spending. As cautiously put by the CBO, they "may cause state and local governments to spend more on a program than they otherwise would," which in turn "may constrain their ability to spend their own revenues according to their own policy priorities."[31] Recognizing the depth of the distorting effects, the CBO observes that when federal conditions require multiple state contributions, "the cumulative effect of those requirements on a state's budget may be substantial, constraining the state's ability to use its funds in a manner that addresses its own current priorities."[32] No kidding.

Notwithstanding the realities of federal commandeering, one might protest that some states, especially in the past decade, have occasionally refused federal funding or at least have successfully litigated against the associated conditions. What is unlawful, however, is the federal action in directing or commandeering the states, and a refusal to follow a command does not mean there was no unlawful federal command.

State rejection of federal funding, moreover, is by far the exception, not the rule. Though states can sometimes negotiate flexibility within federal conditions, they rarely reject funding on account of the associated conditions. Moreover, as aptly observed by Heather Gerken and Jessica Bulman-Pozen, the states' occasional pushback is often more akin to the noncooperation of a "servant" than the power of a sovereign.[33] Overall, notwithstanding sporadic repudiations of federal funds, commandeering is the overwhelming reality.

Although the Supreme Court has shut its eyes to this, a wide range of scholars over the past half century have not been so blind. It is recognized that "the priorities and programs of state and local governments have increasingly come to reflect federal decisions."[34] Martha Derthick more pungently observes that states have become "service stations" of federal policy.[35] Recognizing the implications, Jessica Bulman-Pozen generalizes that the states are now "disaggregated sites of national governance, not separate sovereigns."[36] This is the reality of commandeering.

Commandeering that Restructures State and Local Government

Even worse, federal conditions shape how Americans govern themselves in their states. As put by Martha Derthick, the conditions have consequences for "both policy making and administration."[37] Nor is this a surprise. It has long been a federal objective "to influence the structure of state decision-making processes in such a way as to produce results that will serve federal objectives."[38] This was already explicit in the 1960s, when Richard N. Goodwin—a leading assistant to President Lyndon Johnson—said that the federal government sought the "blended goal" of altering state "structure and policy alike."[39]

Underlying the federal intrusions on how states govern themselves have been conflicting visions of the nation. The America envisioned by the federal government, according to Derthick, is "bureaucratic and rationalistic. It values symmetry in the ordering of public institutions; universalism as the guiding principle of public programs . . . ; efficiency in the conduct of public business; and professionalism in public personnel." In contrast, state and local America has been "traditional rather than rationalistic." It "conducts public business in ways that vary from one locale to another, through institutions and processes that have developed largely through custom and habit and are nowhere highly systematic." And it places less value on "professionalism in personnel" than on "identification with the local community."[40]

The federal government has responded by reconfiguring the states in the image of federal agencies. It has used conditions to render state and local governance more administrative, more centralized in the states and therefore less local, and ultimately more responsive to federal policy. The effect has been to undercut elected political authority, and thus effective self-governance, at both the state and the local level.

The federal government sometimes very nearly sidesteps the states and their localities. By means of its funding conditions, the federal government has taken "a prime role" in getting states and localities to establish substate planning bodies to advance specialized federal policies.[41] Through such organizations, the Department of Housing and Urban Development has pursued metropolitan planning; the Department of Agriculture, resource conservation and development; the Department of Labor, cooperative area manpower planning; the Justice Department, law enforcement planning; and so forth.[42] Whatever the merits of what these substate institutions have done, they have had "adverse effects on state and local governments"—typically by shifting planning and the formation of policy out of elected local and state governments into bodies more responsive to federal goals.[43]

When federal agencies must work through the states themselves, the federal agencies often go around state governors and legislatures by offering money directly to state or local agencies. Federal agencies, in other words, circumvent elected state officials to make deals with fellow bureaucrats.[44] Nor is this an accident. Richard Cappalli observes that this approach to funding "may be a way of getting around local political opposition to federal policies," and in any case, state administrators often have interests and ideals roughly aligned with those of federal administrators.[45] The resulting conditions not merely commandeer states, but directly link the federal government to state and local agencies, thereby undermining the authority of elected branches and officers.

The federal government typically aims to funnel its money and control through a single local or state entity. From the perspective of a typical federal grant program, its provincial partner must be sufficiently consolidated to ensure consistency and easy auditing, must be powerful enough to carry out federal ambitions, and must be adequately aligned with the federal government to resist any possible pushback from elected political bodies. Federal agencies have therefore demanded that states or localities centralize the power relevant to a federal grant program in a single state agency—sometimes by expanding the jurisdiction and rulemaking power of an existing agency and sometimes even by creating a new agency.[46] Fortified with a combination of federal resources and exaggerated state or local authority, such agencies tend to become more or less independent of other state agencies and even of state legislatures and governors.[47]

By consolidating state power in state agencies, federal conditions have (in Derthick's words) "encourage[d] the formation of special-purpose units of government that are independent of general-purpose units and often of the local electorate."[48] Indeed, federal conditions have extended "merit" hiring and promotion to many state and local employees.[49] In such ways, the purchase of submission (like administrative power) shifts power from popularly accountable generalists in a legislature or governor's mansion to unelected specialists in mere agencies.

The empowering of bureaucrats in relation to elected officials has been intertwined with the expansion of state power in relation to local government. In Massachusetts, for example, federal conditions on public assistance in the mid-1960s shifted the distribution of public assistance from the towns to the state, and from elected selectmen to centrally appointed college-educated professional bureaucrats—a federal intervention that "permanently altered the structure of policymaking and administration" in Massachusetts.[50]

Of course, something may be gained when federal agencies use conditions to impose their centralizing administrative values on state and local agencies. But something is also lost—not least the power of states, localities, and their peoples to govern themselves and even to choose how they will be governed.

The federal commandeering that has restructured state and local government has not been unknowing. The point is not that there has been a coordinated federal policy, let alone conspiracy, to restructure the states and their localities. Rather, there has been a new ideal of federal dominance, which has animated much, even if not all, federal policy. As might be expected, this elevated vision of federal direction has thrived alongside a dismissive view of state and local decision-making—graphically expressed by the Advisory Commission on Intergovernmental Relations when it declared that part of the "agenda for the seventies" would be "civilizing the local government structural jungles."[51]

The reassuring euphemism for the new vision, positive and negative, has been "cooperative federalism." But the reality, as recognized already by Daniel P. Moynihan, has been "New Varieties of Government."[52]

The reconstruction of the states along federal lines was not without logic. When state legislatures could not be paid off, the federal government directly subsidized state agencies; when this was not adequate, it worked through localities; when more was needed, it supported the creation of substate and even nonstate organizations to effectuate federal policy. The overall effect was to transform American government—to recreate it in ways that profoundly undercut the independence of states, the power of their lawmakers and other elected officials, and the cohesion of their communities. And rather than a bug, this was a feature.[53]

The deliberate reconfiguration of state and local governments through federal conditions has not been sufficiently recognized, but once the reality is understood, it becomes painfully apparent how much the federal government has commandeered the states.[54] In a model of understatement, the Advisory Commission on Intergovernmental Relations described all of this in 1970 as an "intrusion into state organization and procedures."[55] More precisely, federal conditions have dictated a massive restructuring of state and local government, thereby commandeering the states not merely in their policies, but in their very modes of governance—the result being to move the states away from popular self-government and toward centralized control by agency specialists.

Republican Form of Government

The commandeering points to a fourth constitutional difficulty. It has already been suggested that the anti-commandeering doctrine has a textual foundation in the Constitution's guarantee of a republican form of government. Now it can be added that the threat to a republican form of government becomes especially acute when federal conditions induce states to shift their regulation and other policymaking from their legislatures to state administrative agencies. Even more than other commandeering, such conditions seem to violate the Constitution's provision that "the United States shall guarantee to every State in this Union a Republican Form of Government."

The leading case to interpret this clause is *Luther v. Borden* (1849). Many residents of Rhode Island had attempted in 1842 to displace the state's old 1663 charter with a new constitution, and Luther—an adherent of the new constitution—suggested that the old charter failed to establish a republican form of government. The Supreme Court held that this was a "political question"—meaning one that the Constitution left to the political branches of the federal government rather than the courts, so that the court could not hold against the old charter. But was the court really confronting a political question—one that had to be left to Congress? And are all Guarantee Clause claims nonjusticiable?

Far from simply securing a right, the guarantee of a republican form of government imposes a duty—a duty not merely on the political branches, but generally on the United States, including the courts. Moreover, the guarantee does not secure the states in any particular republican form of government. The court in *Luther* therefore had good reason, at least under this guarantee, to avoid choosing between two more-or-less republican forms of government—not because this was a political question reserved to Congress, but because both Rhode Island constitutions were republican in form, albeit not equally democratic. Last but not least, nothing in the guarantee of a republican form of government requires a court to order one of the political branches to act. This was not even an issue in *Luther*, and if there ever were a request for such an order, the court would ordinarily be bound by traditional equitable principles to refuse it. Accordingly, in one way or another, it may be doubted whether, as suggested in *Luther*, the question of republican government is really a political question or otherwise nonjusticiable. As noted by the Supreme Court in *New York v. United States* (1992), "perhaps not all claims under the Guarantee Clause present nonjusticiable political questions."[56]

This is especially clear when the federal government, which is bound by the clause, pressures states to abandon their republican forms of government. The clause imposes a duty on the United States, and violations of constitutional duties can be resolved by the courts—at least when the violations are sufficiently determinate.[57]

Of course, in many instances, the federal government's violation of the Guarantee Clause will be difficult to measure. At least in some instances, however, the question will not be so unclear. A republican form of government is an elective government—one in which officials are elected, and the people are governed by laws made by their elected legislature. A republican form of government, moreover, stands in contrast to absolutist or administrative forms of government. It is therefore difficult to avoid the conclusion that administrative governance, let alone the purchase of submission, deviates from a republican form of government. Even when imposed under statutory authorization, administrative power or the purchase of submission is not what traditionally was understood as a republican form of government.

This is not to say that the courts should necessarily hold Congress or the president accountable for their inaction—for their failure to secure a republican form of government in a state. Leaving aside the obstacles in equitable principles, it would often be difficult for the courts to ascertain exactly how and when the federal government should act under the Guarantee Clause. But when Congress or the executive branch actively interfere in the states' republican self-governance by directing them in their policies, it is another matter. Especially when federal conditions require a state to work through administrative power or through the purchase of submission, it is clear that the federal government is violating its duty to guarantee the states a republican form of government. In such circumstances, the courts do not face the usual objections to judicial enforcement of this duty.

Beyond Federal Powers

The threats to federalism discussed thus far—whether from co-opting state opposition, claiming supremacy for conditions, commandeering the states, or violating the Constitution's guarantee of a republican form of government—are sobering enough. And they are all the more

serious because of a fifth problem: the Supreme Court allows conditions to escape the Constitution's enumeration of federal powers.

The Constitution enumerates only limited federal powers for the
federal government, and it further confines that government by enu-
merating rights. Beyond these boundaries, it leaves power to the states.
Pressing this point home, the Tenth Amendment declares, "The
powers not delegated to the United States by the Constitution, nor
prohibited by it to the States, are reserved to the States respectively,
or to the people." Put another way, the powers that the Constitution
does not give to the federal government (and that the Constitution does
not take from the states) remain in the states or the people.

To be sure, the Supreme Court has so broadly interpreted federal
powers—notably, Congress's power over interstate commerce—that
the federal government nowadays enjoys a nearly general legislative
power, akin to that of the states. And this expansive vision of the
enumerated powers already severely threatens federalism. But that is
not all.

Recall that under Supreme Court doctrine, federal conditions are
not even confined to the federal government's judicially expanded
powers. As put by the court in *South Dakota v. Dole,* "We have . . .
held that a perceived Tenth Amendment limitation on congressional
regulation of state affairs did not concomitantly limit the range of conditions legitimately placed on federal grants."[58] Conditions are thus
not even theoretically limited by the federal government's enumerated powers.

Federal conditions can therefore carve through the full range of
state law. Although federal statutes and administrative commands are
nowadays only marginally limited by the Constitution's enumeration
of powers, conditions are even less confined. They can defeat almost
any state laws, without concern as to whether the conditions fit within
the Constitution's enumeration of federal powers.

This unconstrained reach of federal conditions makes them especially dangerous for federalism. In one of its more lucid moments, in

United States v. Butler (1936), the Supreme Court recognized the problem. Where Congress has "no power to enforce its commands," it "may not indirectly accomplish those ends by taxing and spending to purchase compliance." Moreover: "If, in lieu of compulsory [that is, binding] regulation of subjects within the states' reserved jurisdiction, which is prohibited, the Congress could invoke the taxing and spending power as a means to accomplish the same end, clause 1 of §8 of Article I [meaning the taxing power, including the alleged spending power] would become the instrument for total subversion of the governmental powers reserved to the individual states."[59] Nonetheless, the federal government now regularly uses conditions to regulate far beyond even the judicially expanded federal powers.

The threat is ultimately to freedom. Most basically, in cutting through constitutionally protected state power, federal conditions stifle the localized self-government protected by the Constitution's enumeration of federal powers. In addition, such conditions overturn lawful state constitutions and statutes that would ordinarily protect inquiry, science, speech, and so forth—a danger all too evident from the federal conditions imposing IRB censorship on human subjects research. By liberating federal conditions from the Constitution's enumeration of powers, the judges have made federal conditions a threat to the full range of freedom that federalism protects.

Federal conditions slash through the Constitution's foundations for federalism. They co-opt state opposition and thereby undermine a key structural limit on federal power; they violate the Supremacy Clause; they commandeer the states; they violate the guarantee of a republican form of government; indeed, they candidly eviscerate the enumeration of federal powers and the Tenth Amendment. The result is a dramatic erosion of federalism, including its structural limits on centralized power, its financial accountability, its dispersion of policy errors, its freedom for localized self-government and community, and its opportunities for Americans in different communities to pursue their diverse visions and identities.

More generally, Part II has shown that, even when conditions do not impose unconstitutional restrictions, they run afoul of the Constitution by creating an unconstitutional conduit for power. Conditions thereby often violate the government's authority to spend or otherwise distribute privileges. Moreover, regulatory conditions divest and privatize the government's legislative and judicial powers, short-circuit the political process, enable government to deny due process, jury, and other procedural rights, and frequently violate federalism. Conditions thus carve out a profoundly unconstitutional pathway.

PART III

Unconstitutional Restrictions

The most familiar constitutional problem with the purchase of submission is the danger of "unconstitutional conditions"—the conditions that impose unconstitutional restrictions, usually by abridging freedom of speech or other constitutional rights. In imposing unconstitutional restrictions through conditions, the government assumes it can largely avoid the Constitution's enumerated rights, and on the whole this strategy has succeeded.

The enumerated rights, in both the Constitution and its amendments, generally protect Americans from government constraint. A notable exception is the First Amendment's guarantee against an establishment of religion, which centrally limits government benefits and other privileges. But the Constitution's other rights, at their core, protect against various forms of government force.

Conditions have therefore seemed to offer the government a way to deny constitutional rights without constitutional accountability. When the government asks recipients of its money and other privileges to submit to conditions, it is understood to be offering benefits, not imposing constraints. On this assumption, conditions apparently can impose unconstitutional restrictions and yet not violate the Constitution.

For example, the Department of Health and Human Services requires licensing for the speech of academic researchers—not directly but through the department's conditions on its research grants. Federal Communications Commission licenses come with conditions limiting political speech. Churches lose much of their political speech under the Internal Revenue Code's conditions on tax exemption and deductibility. And so forth.

Many such conditions are already of dubious constitutionality because, being regulatory, they divest Congress and the courts of the powers vested in these bodies by the Constitution. But such conditions also collide with the Constitution by imposing unconstitutional restrictions, and this is a more focused reason for considering them void.

One view, espoused by Justice Joseph Bradley in 1876 when dissenting in *Doyle v. Continental Insurance Company*, is that government simply "has no power to impose unconstitutional conditions."[1] The opposite perspective, often attributed to Justice Oliver Wendell Holmes, is that if government may distribute a privilege, it may place almost any condition on it. Each of these generalities responds to serious concerns—respectively, about liberty and government—but they remain contrasting platitudes, which simplistically cut through the Gordian Knot without even trying to unravel it.

Unsurprisingly, greater care will be needed to answer the question as to whether conditions imposing apparently unconstitutional restrictions are, in fact, unconstitutional. The question will therefore be unpacked not all at once but layer by layer, over the next five chapters.

9

Consent No Relief from Constitutional Limits

Consent is sometimes assumed to be a jurisprudential solvent, which melts away the Constitution's limits, leaving the government free to do what it wishes, as long as it has the consent of those to whom it gives money or other privileges. As Chapter 10 will soon explain, the consent of states and private persons can do much for the government within the scope of the Constitution's powers and rights. But it first must be recognized, more basically, that such consent cannot enable the government to escape the Constitution's limits.

The Constitution Is a Law Based on Public Consent

The Constitution is a law publicly enacted by the people. It therefore cannot be altered or excused by the consent of states or private persons. For example, in the words of the Supreme Court in *Gonzales v. Raich*, "state acquiescence to federal regulation cannot expand the boundaries of the Commerce Clause."[1]

One might think that state or private consent has a place in shaping American constitutional law, but the history of such visions of constitutional governance do not inspire confidence. Prior to the adoption

of the Constitution in 1788, the United States was weakly bound together by the Articles of Confederation, which was nothing more than
a compact among the states. Although some lawyers sought to have
it treated as a law, this was an uphill struggle, for the Articles themselves recited that they merely formed a "league of friendship" among
the states. Afterward, in defense of slavery and other Southern interests,
many Southerners insisted that the Constitution was a compact among
the states—thus allowing Southerners to claim that when the Northern
states or the federal government violated the Constitution, a Southern
state could nullify it by declaring it void and of no effect.

Nowadays, it is not denied that the Constitution is a law, but it is
commonly assumed that individuals, institutions, and states, by their
consent, can relieve the federal government of its constitutional limits.
The Constitution's limits on government, however, are not merely
contractual terms.

The Constitution was designed to be a law, which would be binding
throughout the United States, and it was therefore formally enacted
by the people themselves. Hence, its preface: "We the People of the
United States, in Order to form a more perfect Union . . . do ordain
and establish this Constitution for the United States of America." To
"ordain and establish" was conventional language for enacting laws—
only in this instance, it was not a legislature, but more fundamentally the people who were legislating. The Constitution, in short, is
the people's law—a point confirmed by the Supremacy Clause when
it lists the Constitution as the preeminent element of the supreme law
of the land.

Even in most theories of unwritten constitutional change, constitutional alterations are said to have popular consent, not merely private or state consent. The constitutional change justified by such theories is not formally adopted by the people in amendments but is
nonetheless said to have the acquiescence or informal consent of the
people as a whole.

It is thus unclear how the consent of mere private persons or states can relieve the government of its constitutional limits. If the Constitution is a law made with the consent of the people, the government cannot escape its constitutional bounds by purchasing the consent of lesser bodies. An individual, a business, a university, a municipality, and even a state may consent to unconstitutional restrictions, but how can this alter the public constitutional limits imposed by the people of the United States?

Rights Not Merely Personal Claims, but Also Legal Limits

One reason consent has been so widely considered a constitutional solvent is that rights are often seen as merely personal spheres of freedom and thus tradable commodities. Frank Easterbrook summarizes:

> If people can obtain benefits from selling their rights, why should they be prevented from doing so? One aspect of the value of a right—whether a constitutional right or title to land—is that it can be sold and both parties to the bargain made better off. A right that cannot be sold is worth less than an otherwise-identical right that may be sold. Those who believe in the value of constitutional rights should endorse their exercise by sale as well as their exercise by other action.[2]

From this point of view, free speech and other constitutional rights are personal goods—no more or less than a used car or old rug, which individuals can bargain away as they please.

Of course, it is true that some constitutional rights, especially the free exercise of religion and the freedom of speech, are often justified in terms of personal commitments and expression. And such rights undoubtedly can be avenues for deeply personal satisfactions.

But constitutional rights are not merely personal claims; more broadly, they are legal limits on government. Indeed, constitutional rights secure private spheres of freedom, such as religion and speech, precisely by confining public power. And this is no surprise, for rights were adopted as structural limits on power. The Constitution initially sketches out the confined extent of federal authority with the broad brushstrokes of enumerated powers, and then it pencils in more detailed limits with rights. The rights, in other words, are further limits on the powers. As put by James Madison and Alexander Hamilton, rights are "exceptions" to the powers.[3] And being legal limits on power, they are more than personal possessions and cannot be sold as if at a garage sale.

Recall (from Chapter 6) that the equality of constitutional rights, unvaried by consent, allows these paper protections to rest on a depth and breadth of social support. In contrast, when these limits on government can, by means of consent, be rendered unequal, they lose the strength of widely shared communal commitments, and are apt to be eroded—with high costs even for those who did not consent. Also remember (from Chapter 6) that when government can make a separate peace with some Americans, the others cannot rely on their support against oppression. It is thus not merely the consenting parties who are affected when government uses consent to escape constitutional rights, and it is therefore all the more important to remember that constitutional rights are limits of law rather than private goods.

Being legal limits on government, constitutional rights cannot be bargained away. As with other restrictions on power, so with rights, consent cannot relieve the government of its constitutional boundaries.

The Constitution is a law enacted by the people and therefore is not variable with the consent of any state or private person. No such consent can relieve the federal government of the Constitution's limits.

10

Consent within and beyond
the Constitution

Although the Constitution's limits do not vary with the consent of states or private persons, the Constitution often authorizes the federal government to work through such consent. And this suggests that the Constitution itself has much to tell us about when a condition is constitutional or not.

Too often, commentators have thought that the Constitution's provisions have little to say about unconstitutional conditions—the conditions that impose unconstitutional restrictions. On this assumption, judges must evaluate such conditions in terms of abstract ideals that rise far above specific guarantees of rights. But much may turn on such specifics if different constitutional guarantees set different standards for what the government can do through consent.

Though some commentators (William Marshall and Cass Sunstein) question whether there is any general constitutional doctrine on unconstitutional conditions, there is no need to go to this extreme.[1] Instead, it is enough, as suggested by Mitchell Berman, to understand that different constitutional rights treat consent differently—that each right addresses the question of consent in its own terms.[2]

The conceptual point here is that consent has a role within some constitutional limits but can also exceed such limits. On this assumption, what remains to be done is to examine the Constitution's provisions to understand what government can do through consent and what it cannot.

Consent Candidly Acknowledged

Some constitutional limits, especially some rights, candidly leave room for the government to act with consent. The government, in such instances, can rely on consent to do what it otherwise could not:

- *Quartering Soldiers.* The Third Amendment bars the government, in peacetime, from quartering soldiers in any house "without the consent of the Owner" but does not otherwise prevent the peacetime quartering of soldiers.

- *Self-Incrimination.* Although the Fifth Amendment protects a person from being "compelled in any criminal case to be a witness against himself," it does not bar anyone from voluntarily testifying against himself.[3]

- *Takings.* The same amendment bars property from being "taken for public use, without just compensation." Such a taking is beyond the power of government, and thus even if there is subsequent consent, the taking was unconstitutional. It is a different matter, however, where the government purchases rather than takes the property. By focusing on takings, the Fifth Amendment practically acknowledges that it does not prevent the government from purchasing or otherwise securing property for public use with consent.

The government can do what would otherwise be prohibited by these rights, as long as it gets consent—not because private parties can relieve the government from complying with these constitutional provisions, but because the provisions themselves leave space for private waivers of what they guarantee.*

Of course, different constitutional provisions require different manifestations of consent. For some rights, such as that against self-incrimination, consent can be found when a defendant merely fails to assert the right. For other rights, such as that against takings, affected parties must more affirmatively consent. But the broader point is simply that some rights candidly open up opportunities for government to act with consent.

Consent Recognized

In other constitutional provisions, consent clearly can matter, even though it is not so directly acknowledged. At the same time, these provisions reveal limits on what consent can accomplish.

Consider the role of consent within federal powers, including the necessary and proper power:

- *Purchases.* By obtaining the consent of vendors, the government can purchase goods and services subject to conditions that define what it is acquiring.

---

* Incidentally, the word *waiver* is used here with an important caveat. It is commonly said that a defendant waives his right to a jury, his right against self-incrimination, and so on. For the sake of convenience, this book follows this colloquial path—that is, it usually speaks loosely about the waiver of rights. Readers should keep in mind, however, that no one can liberate the government from any right; instead, some rights themselves leave space for persons consensually not to exercise their rights. Thus, if one were to speak accurately, one would say that a defendant waives a jury, not the right to a jury.

- *Support*. Similarly, the government can tie consensual conditions to its financial aid—as when it requires that housing funds be used for housing and demands that student loans be used for education.

Thus, even when the Constitution does not directly acknowledge consent, federal powers leave much room for the government to act with consent.

Similarly, consent can matter—up to a point—for some of the rights that do not directly allude to consent:

- *Unreasonable Searches*. The Fifth Amendment's prohibition of "unreasonable searches" leaves much room for consensual searches—as long as the government does not secure the consent in ways that make the searches unreasonable.

- *Abridging the Freedom of Speech*. The First Amendment's bar against any act of Congress "abridging the freedom of speech, or of the press," leaves the government free to purchase speech and even in some instances to purchase silence—as long as the government does not thereby go so far as to abridge the freedom of speech or of the press. But when the government uses consent to impose restrictions that would not be constitutional if imposed directly, it evidently is abridging the freedom.

- *Juries*. The Constitution repeatedly guarantees juries but does not always require them, for historically that mode of trial was often elective. In civil cases, plaintiffs traditionally could secure different modes of trial (jury or wager of law) by pursuing different causes of action. In criminal cases, the defendants theoretically had a choice, as long remained evident in the practice of asking defendants at arraignment, "How will you be tried?"—followed by their answer: "By God and my country." Of course, in reality, there was little room for another answer, as noncompliant defendants were subject to *peine forte et dure*. At least in theory, however, the jury was a matter of choice. Against this background, the Constitution does not require a jury when both parties waive it. But though the parties can consent to trial without a jury, the Constitution does not permit the government to offer anything less than a full jury, such as a four-person jury or one preselected by the government.

Although these constitutional provisions do not directly say as much, they clearly permit the government to act, at least to some extent, on the basis of consent. But only within the limits established by the rights.

Consent Clearly Not Recognized

In contrast, some powers and rights leave little opportunity for the government to act on the basis of consent:

- *Subject Matter Jurisdiction.* A party can waive personal jurisdiction and thereby come within the power of a court that otherwise cannot reach him. But subject matter jurisdiction, established by the Constitution and federal statutes, is impervious to a party's consent. Even with the consent of the parties, courts cannot take jurisdiction beyond their subject matter limits.

- *Due Process.* Some of the Constitution's rights are similarly not variable with consent—an example being the Fifth and Fourteenth Amendments' guarantees of the due process of law. Whereas the consent of the parties can enable a court to hear their case without a jury, such consent cannot justify a court in denying due process.

  Of course, the Constitution's guarantees of due process do not prevent parties from choosing to opt in or out of the courts. Parties can stay out of court by agreeing to have a civil dispute decided by arbitrators; they can opt in by making an appearance and consenting to personal jurisdiction; and even once they are in court, they can settle with the approval of the judge. But their consent cannot enable a court to provide anything less than the due process of law.

The notion of due process of law developed in response to the lesser processes of prerogative or administrative tribunals—notably when Edward III in the 1300s forced his subjects to submit to the adjudications conducted by his council, and when Charles I in the 1600s tried to rule through the Star Chamber.[4] In contrast, the due process of law was most basically the legal process of the courts, and the principle of due process of law barred the government from imposing binding adjudications (those imposing legal obligation) except through the courts' legal process.

From this perspective, the due process clauses of the Fifth and Fourteenth Amendments not only guarantee the process of the courts but thereby also bar government from imposing legally obligatory adjudications outside the courts, for only in the courts can parties get the due process of law. The historical foundations and the blunt drafting of the due process guarantees leave no room for the government to evade the processes of the courts. And this invariant barrier makes much contemporary sense, for (as observed by Thomas Merrill) there is a public interest in the government's consistent adherence to due process.[5]*

---

* Incidentally, note the distinction between Article III courts and non–Article III courts, with judges sitting for terms of years, which the Constitution permits in the District of Columbia and the territories. Although the due process clauses in the Fifth and Fourteenth Amendments require the government to impose legally obligatory adjudications only through the courts, this does not mean Article III courts in locations where the Constitution permits non–Article III alternatives.

- *Equal Protection.* The Fourteenth Amendment's guarantee of the equal protection of the law is similarly closed to consent. The blunt drafting seems to bar government, even with consent, from providing unequal protection. The history confirms that the guarantee was designed to provide a floor of equality essential for all free persons.[6] And contemporary experience reinforces the importance of maintaining this baseline.

- *Voting Rights.* The Fifteenth Amendment guarantees that "the right of citizens of the United States to vote shall not be denied or abridged by the United States or by any State on account of race, color, or previous condition of servitude." Though this amendment does not require anyone to vote, it leaves no room for government to use payments or other privileges to suppress Black votes. Of course, bribery is a much broader problem, and a federal statute bars payments for voting or not voting. The point here is simply that the Fifteenth Amendment's prohibition on discriminatory interference with the right to vote is not adjustable with consent.

Such powers and rights do not allow much room for consensual variation.

Because these rights are so impervious to consent, one might consider them inalienable.[7] Certainly, it is widely assumed that some rights are so inherent in individuals that they cannot be relinquished. The argument here, however, rests not on abstract ideas about the inalienability of rights, but on the Constitution. That enactment leaves room for some rights to be waived and not others.

Open-Ended Rights

Whereas the rights discussed thus far are enumerated by the Constitution, some other constitutional rights—notably rights of contraception,

abortion, and sexual association—are not enumerated in the Constitution. It is therefore difficult to rely on the Constitution and its
phrasing, history, and traditional meaning to understand when
these rights can be waived with consent and when they cannot.

Imagine, for example, a state law benefiting private health organizations—a law offering them substantial funding to establish programs advising women about family planning, subject to the condition that whatever the organizations might say in their other activities,
the funded programs may not advise women about abortion. Does
this condition violate the right to an abortion? According to Supreme
Court doctrine, a state may not impose an "undue burden" on
abortion, but it is not obvious from either this doctrine or the Constitution whether the right to an abortion leaves room for the condition.[8] Put generally, it is often difficult to be confident about the
unconstitutionality of a condition when the US Constitution does
not enumerate the right or otherwise indicate its boundaries.

Welfare programs offer further examples. Recall that it was seriously proposed to condition aid for poor mothers on their taking a
contraceptive such as Norplant. Some states, moreover, distribute
such aid on the condition that the mothers be single, divorced, or sep-
arated.[9] Some states deny any increase in payments to parents who
have further children while on government support.[10] Though these
conditions may seem disturbing, it is not easy to evaluate whether they
violate rights of sexual association, as this depends on the scope of
the underlying sexual freedoms, which are unwritten and therefore
more than ordinarily unclear. Such conditions are as open to debate
as the underlying rights.

Running into the Future

By now, it should be clear that the Constitution allows the government to rely on consent in some instances but not others, depending
on what is required by each power and right. Yet some constitutional

limits cut across the full range of rights—one such limit being that conditions sacrificing rights cannot run into the future.

As seen in Chapter 3, conditions running into the future risk being regulatory, and when such conditions restrict constitutional rights, they are predictably regulatory. But there is more to be said about them, for such conditions reveal that the government is not merely seeking a waiver or limit on the exercise of a right, but is seeking a future relinquishment of the right and thus control over its exercise.

Many constitutional rights (as seen from those regarding speech, juries, self-incrimination, searches, and so forth) allow the government to rely on your consent. But even where a constitutional guarantee permits a condition limiting exercise of the right, it is another matter when the condition runs into the future. For example, if a condition asks you to commit that, even after the current transaction, you will limit your exercise of the freedom of speech, not ask for a jury, or not insist on just compensation, it is going beyond a permitted relinquishment of freedom. By controlling you into the future, it is attempting to restrict your exercise of the right.

Consider these examples:

- *Habeas.* The Constitution says: "The Privilege of the Writ of Habeas Corpus shall not be suspended, unless when in Cases of Rebellion or Invasion the public Safety may require it." This leaves little role for consent, other than a prisoner's decision not to seek habeas. But imagine that the government offered prisoners money or prison privileges on the condition that they not seek habeas for some period running into the future. The blunt phrasing of the right indicates that it is not variable with consent, and the history was all about making sure that habeas remained open as an avenue for redress. It thus becomes apparent that a condition cutting off habeas into the future is a forbidden suspension of habeas. The function of the right is also illuminating. More than merely a mode of liberating individuals,

habeas is a mechanism that can expose abuses of power, especially in prisons. Indeed, access to habeas is a foundation of the
legitimacy of the government. It is therefore difficult to see
how any government effort to purchase limits on habeas could
possibly be constitutional, and this is particularly clear when
the conditions run into the future to restrict the exercise of
the right.

* *Unreasonable Searches.* When an individual business proprietor
  is charged with violating laws, regulations, or even mere conditions, the government may enter a settlement with him on the
  condition that he allow government to search his records. It
  would be one thing for the defendant in the course of pending
  litigation to allow a current search, but can the government
  settle a case on the condition that the defendant consent to
  future searches, after the existing case is resolved? The government in such a case may offer to drop charges or accept a lower
  fine, but either way its condition stipulates future and thus
  unreasonable searches.[11] And if the government asks a defendant
  to accept delayed sentencing, so as to secure control over him
  and stretch out the opportunity for consensual searches, it again
  appears to be imposing unreasonable searches, if not denying a
  speedy trial.*

---

* Bail and parole are often subject to conditions permitting warrantless searches, and it
may be thought that these conditions run into the future and thereby unconstitutionally
restrict the right against such searches. One must pause, however, before reaching such
a conclusion. When a condition on bail permits warrantless searches, the condition relates to a continuing case against the defendant, and it therefore need not be viewed as
running into the future. And a parolee subject to such a condition has been convicted,
so he could be considered constructively still in custody, albeit of a relaxed sort. It thus
cannot be assumed that these conditions really run into the future.

All the same, the condition on bail may be problematic on other grounds. A person
released on bail has merely been charged with a crime, and when the circumstances

Similarly, when you arrive at the boarding area of an airport, the government has many potential justifications for searching your body and luggage—one potential justification being your consent. But it cannot ask you to consent to searches in the future, because any such later search based on a prior commitment would be unreasonable.* Once again, conditions running into the future are unconstitutional.

- *Juries.* A prosecutor will frequently propose to reduce charges in exchange for a defendant's waiver of jury trial. But even when a prosecutor offers such a plea bargain long before trial, the defendant's waiver of a jury occurs only when he appears before the judge. At that point, the defendant is still free to reject the plea bargain and insist on a jury trial. In other words, the waiver or nonexercise of this constitutional right is on the spot; it cannot run into the future, lest it violate the defendant's right to a jury.[12]

- *Proprietary and Confidential Information.* Notwithstanding what has been said here, note that conditions restricting disclosure of the government's proprietary and confidential information by government employees can run far into the future—indeed, for the life of the consenting parties—without abridging their

---

permit it, he has a right under the Eighth Amendment to be released. Thus, even though a bail condition permitting warrantless searches relates to a continuing case—and so might be thought not to run into the future—it still could be considered unreasonable under the Fourth Amendment.

*The government's airport options are poorly understood. By statute, the government can directly impose an inspection requirement; by judicial warrant, an officer can search a particular individual identified therein; on the basis of individualized reasonable suspicion, an officer can search an individual; with consent, officers can search individuals without any such suspicion; and under the unfortunate doctrine on administrative searches, an agency can engage in sweeping searches without really complying with the Fourth Amendment. Note that only one of these options depends on consent.

freedom of speech. These conditions usually do not go further than existing statutes or state common law, which generally bar disclosure of such information by such persons. Such laws are, on the whole, constitutional, and it therefore cannot be said that the corresponding conditions restrict government employees in their exercise of their freedom of speech.

> Put another way, there is an exception to the general point here about conditions running into the future. When a condition sacrificing a right runs into the future, it ordinarily would seem to limit the exercise of the right and thus be unconstitutional. But there is no such limit on the exercise of the right when the condition is not more restrictive than an existing, constitutional, and directly imposed legal requirement.*

Alas, as to some rights—such as the privilege against self-incrimination and the right against takings without just compensation—courts have accepted conditions that run into the future.[13] But these cases are surely mistaken. When conditions require a future sacrifice of a right, they demand more than merely the current nonexercise of the right; they give government a power to discourage and effectively prevent the exercise of a right—a sort of control forbidden by the Constitution's guarantees.

This point about commitments into the future is important enough that it is worth repeating what the Supreme Court said in *Home Insurance Company v. Morse* (1874). A person "may omit to exercise his

---

* Note that these conditions—which run into the future but without being more restrictive than existing legal requirements that are directly imposed and constitutional— overlap with the reinforcing regulatory conditions discussed in Chapter 3. In both instances, the existence of directly imposed requirements saves the conditions, but for different reasons—in Chapter 3 because there is no displacement of legislative power, here because the condition does not restrict the exercise of the affected right.

right . . . in each recurring case. In these aspects any citizen may no doubt waive the rights to which he may be entitled. He cannot, however, bind himself in advance by an agreement . . . thus to forfeit his rights at all times and on all occasions, whenever the case may be presented."[14]

Abridging the Freedom of Speech

This chapter closes by returning to the question of when a condition collides with the freedom of speech. The answer, as already noted, requires one to consider whether the condition is one *abridging* the freedom of speech. (To which it must be added that the regulatory analysis, discussed in Chapters 3 and 5, can fill in some gaps.)

When a law directly constrains speech, it can be difficult to sort out whether it violates the First Amendment, for this amendment does not specify the difference between a law that abridges the freedom of speech and one that does not. But when a *condition* restricts speech, the inquiry can be easier, for if the condition confines speech more severely than the government could do directly, then it is clear that the condition is *abridging* the freedom of speech.[15]

Of course, there may be additional circumstances in which a condition abridges the freedom of speech. But at least when a condition restricts speech more than could be done directly, it abridges the freedom of speech.

Not merely linguistically accurate, this understanding is very useful. All too often, the government assumes it can sidestep the freedom of speech by simply shifting its violations of this freedom to conditions, thus doing by condition what it could not do directly. But whenever it does this, it clearly is abridging the freedom. The word *abridging* prevents the use of conditions to evade the First Amendment.

The Supreme Court has at times come close to recognizing this understanding of the abridgment of speech—notably, when rejecting conditions that "deter" or "penalize" speech. In *Speiser v. Randall* (1958), for example, the court said: "To deny an exemption to claimants who engage in certain forms of speech is, in effect, to *penalize* them for such speech. Its *deterrent* effect is the same as if the state were to fine them for this speech."[16] Put more accurately, when a condition restricts speech more than is lawful through direct constraints, it abridges the freedom of speech.

Government can try to mask such First Amendment problems by stating a speech condition in positive rather than negative terms. For example, rather than deny employment to Republicans, a municipality or state college could simply offer positions to Democrats. In its defense, it would claim that this is not an unconstitutional suppression of speech, but merely patronage, which even if ugly, is not forbidden.

Of course, to favor one view is to disfavor others, and judges should recognize this reality. But such analysis does not hinge on doctrinal formalities, and it thus leaves judges on their own to figure out when the favoring of one view is really the suppression of others. Unsurprisingly, judges have not always been up to the task.

It therefore is valuable to recall that conditions favoring a viewpoint can be regulatory. Recall (from Chapters 3 and 5) that when conditions apply to numerous recipients or dominate a field, they should be understood as regulatory and so in violation of the Constitution. For example, when party affiliation matters for getting low-level positions in municipal government, or when ideological commitment matters for being accepted as a student or hired to teach in public schools, one must consider whether the condition is regulatory—that is, whether it is a mode of regulating the opinion and speech of administrators, students, or teachers. In short, even if it is difficult to discern whether a condition favoring a point of view is really a mode of stifling others, it can be much easier to make the more generic determination that the condition applies so broadly as to be regulatory.

Government can also try to mask constitutional difficulties by casting its conditions as mere considerations, and again, the regulatory analysis is a valuable stopgap. As an initial matter, it is important to remember that a law abridging the freedom of speech (or any other right) is unconstitutional regardless of whether it affects all Americans or only a single individual. As a result, it makes no difference whether a law abridging the freedom of speech predictably violates the rights of all or unpredictably violates the rights of a few. Either way, such a law is unconstitutional. Accordingly, if considerations are conditions, albeit unpredictable in their application, an unconstitutional consideration is unconstitutional in the same way as a more predictable condition. The Supreme Court in *National Endowment for the Arts v. Finley* said that a speech consideration cannot be held void as an unconstitutional condition, but under the First Amendment an unconstitutional speech restriction is no less unconstitutional merely because its application is less predictable.

Even more than in its conditions, the government in its considerations can easily avoid negative statements of the sort that would clearly violate the freedom of speech or other rights. Once again, therefore, it often is important to fall back on the regulatory analysis, for even if a consideration is not an abridgment of the freedom of speech, it still may be an unconstitutional pathway for regulating speech. For example, if the government, when awarding social security benefits, were to take into consideration the political views of the beneficiaries, it would be clear that the consideration, even if not always dispositive, is applicable to many individuals and thus regulatory. The point is that even if a judge, mistakenly, had difficulty concluding that such a consideration violates the First Amendment, she should have little difficulty in concluding that, being regulatory, it displaces the legislative power that Article I vests in Congress and the judicial power that Article III vests in the courts. To be sure, one cannot be certain in any one case that the consideration was determinative, but it is clear from the consideration's broad applicability that it is regulatory and should be held unconstitutional.

To understand these points about conditions abridging the freedom of speech, consider some examples:

- *Decency Limits on Grants.* (a) Suppose that the National Endowment for the Arts (NEA) commissioned artists to make paintings for government buildings on the condition that the pictures reflect a specified ideal of decency. Or, on the condition that the pictures celebrate the United States or promote the protection of wildlife and the environment. Or, put more negatively, on the condition that the pictures not celebrate communism or not promote anti-environmental views. Would such conditions abridge the freedom of speech? Well, imagine that Congress adopted a statute that not only authorized these art grants but also prohibited and penalized the diversion or use of any such grant money for purposes contrary to the conditions. Such a statute probably would not abridge the recipients' freedom of speech. Nor, consequently, would the NEA's conditions.*

  (b) Suppose the NEA offered grants to artists to support their work for one year, on the condition that, during that year, they only make art celebrating the United States or reflecting a specified standard of decency. Or, negatively, that they make no art denigrating the United States or violating the decency standard. A statute directly restricting not merely the use of the grants but all of the art produced by grantees, even in their spare time, would clearly abridge their freedom of speech and so, therefore, would a similar condition.

  (c) What if Congress required the NEA, when awarding grants to artists, to take into consideration "general standards of

---

* Similarly, there was no abridgment of the First Amendment when the Children's Internet Protection Act (2000) required public libraries receiving federal funds for computers to install filters on their computers to block pornographic content—a conclusion recognized, albeit on other grounds, in *United States v. American Library Association* (2003). There remains, however, the question of whether the condition was regulatory or a mode of commandeering.

decency and respect for the diverse beliefs and values of the American public"? Congress adopted such a statute, and recall that the Supreme Court upheld it in *Finley* on the ground that such standards were only "considerations," not a "categorical requirement."[17] As seen above, this reasoning is mistaken—even if the result in the case was correct. What should the court have said? First, as in example (a), when government supports art espousing or not violating a government point of view, a law barring diversion of the funds does not ordinarily abridge the freedom of speech; accordingly, a consideration reflecting such a point of view is not an unconstitutional condition. Second, it is not evident that NEA grants and the associated considerations are applicable to many Americans or even most artists, and thus the considerations are not regulatory conditions. On such grounds, rather than those offered by the court, the NEA's decency consideration was lawful.

(d) Imagine that Congress instructed the NEA not merely to make awards to some especially deserving artists, but instead to subsidize a large percentage or number of artists on the condition that the supported art meet or not violate a specified decency standard. One might conclude—as in example (a) above—that because the condition applies only to funded work, it does not abridge the freedom of speech. The program in this example, however, encompasses a significant percentage or number of artists, and this breadth is consequential. A direct imposition of the decency standard on so many funded artists would surely be considered an abridgment of the freedom of speech. The similar condition therefore also abridges this freedom. Put generally, there is no safety for speech conditions that apply only to work done in a funded program where the program is too encompassing.

- *Lawyers and Public Relations Consultants.* (a) The government pays lawyers and public relations consultants for their services on the condition (express or implied) that they live up to their ordinary professional duties of confidentiality and representation. Although such professionals are limited in what they can say disparaging the government—both because of their professional duties and because of the conditions echoing them—their professional duties are not ordinarily an abridgment of their freedom of speech, and neither, therefore, are the conditions that echo such duties.

    (b) But suppose the government were to require the lawyers and public relations consultants, as a condition of their employment, to silence themselves in ways that go beyond their professional duties of confidentiality and representation—for example, not to express their views on legislation clearly outside the scope of such duties? If such a restraint were imposed directly—for example, in a statute imposing such silence and so forth—it would be unconstitutional. Accordingly, if the government were to impose such a restriction by means of a condition, the government would be limiting the freedom of speech more severely than it can do directly, and this would reveal that the condition abridges the freedom of speech.

    (c) What if the government did not state such restrictions in conditions, but rather merely tended to choose its lawyers and public relations consultants on the basis of whether they refrained from criticizing legislation desired by the government? This is a consideration or unpredictable condition, and if—as seen in example (b)—the restriction is unconstitutional in a regular condition, it is also unconstitutional in an unpredictable one. Of course, the government can easily mask any such unconstitutional condition by saying that it is merely considering which lawyers or public relations consultants will work effectively with the government. It is therefore worth noting that the consideration may also, perhaps, be unconstitutional as a regulatory condition. At least if it is applicable to many lawyers or public relations consultants, or otherwise dominates those fields, it would be unconstitutional because it was regulatory.

- *Rust v. Sullivan* (1991). In this case, the Department of Health and Human Services (HHS) funded family planning services on the condition that the funded providers not counsel or otherwise encourage abortion as a method of family planning.[18] The providers required their doctors to confine their speech along these lines, and when the doctors protested, the Supreme Court upheld the condition. If the federal condition in *Rust* merely barred the use of federal money within the funded program for a medical message different from what the government was funding, then—following the logic already seen in example (a) about the NEA—the condition did not abridge the freedom of speech of the funded organizations or of their doctors. But it would be a different matter if the federal condition restricted the speech of the organizations outside the funded program—or if it required the organizations to limit their employees' speech outside the funded program. Similarly, it would be a different matter if—along the lines of the NEA example (d)—the federal program were so broad that the condition ended up restricting the speech of large numbers of doctors. Direct versions of so far reaching a restriction would abridge the freedom of speech and therefore so would an equivalent condition.[19]

- *Proprietary, Confidential, and Classified Information.* Another example concerns government employees and contractors handling proprietary, confidential, or classified information. When such information is acquired by persons who serve as government employees or contractors and thus in a fiduciary capacity, they have a lifelong duty under federal statutes not to share it.[20] Being aimed at breaches of fiduciary duties, these statutes generally do not abridge the freedom of speech; nor, therefore, do the conditions imposing similar restrictions.

Of course, the nation's intelligence agencies may need to go further than such statutes in restricting the flow of secret information—for example, to protect information that is not narrowly proprietary or confidential or to limit former employees who still have informal access to secret information. For such reasons, the Central Intelligence Agency long ago conditioned employment on compliance with the agency's security regulations.[21] It has also sought promises from employees not to disclose any information relating to the agency or its intelligence activities, either during or after employment, unless they obtain agency permission. Though *Snepp v. United States* (1980) centered on Snepp's nondisclosure promise, it is suggestive of the sweeping extent of government nondisclosure conditions in intelligence agencies.

Such conditions have many constitutional vulnerabilities. The problems include the breadth of the speech restrictions beyond what ordinarily would be considered proprietary or confidential information, the imposition of prior licensing (to delineate the boundaries of such information and to enforce compliance), the regulatory character of the conditions, and their limits on the exercise of the freedom of speech by reaching into the future.

Accordingly, if the conditions are constitutionally justifiable, it can only be because, in the context of intelligence agencies, proprietary and confidential information can be understood more capaciously than in other circumstances. If this is true (certainly it is not unreasonable), then the conditions restricting the disclosure of such information are not regulatory and can be enforced through prior licensing. And to the extent the existing statutes already directly bar disclosure of proprietary and confidential information, the conditions can run into the future. The conditions thus do not obviously abridge the freedom of speech.

- *Other Speech Conditions on Government Employees.* Justice Oliver Wendell Holmes justified speech conditions on public employees by saying: "There are few employments for hire in which the servant does not agree to suspend his constitutional rights of free speech as well as of idleness by the implied terms of his contract." But most conditions limiting the speech of public employees cannot be considered abridgments of their freedom of speech, for it would not be such an abridgment for Congress directly to bar government employees, while at work, from speaking out of turn, from being rude, from discussing politics, and so forth. As so often, therefore, Holmes wrote with greater verve than accuracy.

  Although a range of cases have upheld speech conditions on public employees, there are limits.[22] For example, when in *Pickering v. Board of Education* (1968), a local board of education fired a public school teacher for his out-of-school political speech critical of the school board, the Supreme Court correctly held this to be an unconstitutional condition on employment.[23] Such a restriction, if imposed directly on public employees, would abridge the freedom of speech, and it thus abridged this freedom when imposed by condition.

- *Hatch Act.* By means of both a direct restriction and a condition on public employment, this federal statute bars federal employees from engaging in politics, including much political speech, while at work. To the extent the statute focuses on what the employees do at work, the direct restriction does not abridge their freedom

of speech. Nor, therefore, does the condition. But to the extent
the statute also applies to what federal workers say on their own
time, the direct restriction and so, too, the condition would seem
to abridge the freedom of speech.[24]

One might protest that it is valuable to bar federal workers
from politics even on their own time, as this prevents
political cronyism and corruption—for example, when a
senior political appointee threatens to fire subordinates who
refuse to work on a political campaign. The law, however,
could directly prohibit such pressures without going so far as
to suppress the political speech of government employees.
A bar against out-of-office political speech is thus the
opposite of a narrowly tailored solution. Any such direct
Hatch-Act limit on political speech is consequently
an abridgment of the freedom of speech, and any similar
limit through conditions is therefore also such an
abridgment.

- *Prior Licensing of Speech.* The most disturbing speech conditions involve licensing. Of course, the government can license
its private rights—such as the use of its land and its proprietary
or confidential information—but it cannot impose regulatory
licensing of words, as this is a central example of what abridges
the freedom of speech or the press.

A small-scale example occurred when the National Heart,
Lung, and Blood Institute—part of the National Institutes
of Health—announced that it would award contracts for
research on an artificial heart, and that the contracts might
include a confidentiality clause requiring researchers to
get government approval before publishing or publicly
discussing their preliminary research results. In *Board of
Trustees of the Leland Stanford Jr. University v. Sullivan*
(1991), the US District Court for the District of Columbia

held that this condition abridged the freedom of speech and the press, and rightly so, as the direct imposition of the prior review would have been such an abridgment.[25]

On a larger scale, HHS conditions require prior institutional review board (IRB) permission for much research speech and publication, and the Internal Revenue Code conditions in sections 501(c)(3) and 170 enable the IRS to license churches and other idealistic organizations in their political speech. Being regulatory, these conditions are already of dubious constitutionality, but that is not all. Prior licensing of words was the central example of what the speech and press clauses of the First Amendment prohibited. One might add that such licensing inevitably delays and limits much innocent speech and is therefore not narrowly tailored or proportionate to any lawful government interest. The government consequently could never have imposed the IRB or IRS licensing directly; any such attempt would have been an outrageous abridgment of the freedom of speech. Accordingly, the government's conditions requiring such licensing also abridge this freedom.*

---

* One might wonder whether the HHS and Internal Revenue Code speech conditions could be justified because they apply only to what government has subsidized. The factual assumption, however, is mistaken. The HHS conditions usually apply not merely to federally funded research, but to all research at research institutions; and similarly the Internal Revenue Code conditions apply to vast numbers of churches and other nonprofits that have little or no benefit from the tax privileges.

Also incorrect is the legal assumption. The English government in the seventeenth century licensed printing indirectly through privileged agents such as the universities and the Stationers' Company, which in turn licensed privileged members and their publications. Thus, the central example of what the First Amendment barred was privatized licensing—licensing by privileged private institutions. The First Amendment recognizes that licensing of words (other than as to proprietary or confidential information) is a distinctively dangerous mode of control and flatly prohibits it, regardless of the subtleties by which it is imposed.

The word *abridging* is clarifying. It reveals that the government cannot employ conditions to get around the freedom of speech, for whenever the government uses a condition to confine speech more severely than it could do directly, it is abridging the freedom of speech.*

The Constitution itself thus sometimes leaves space for the government to act on the basis of consent and sometimes does not. And to resolve such questions, one must examine the relevant constitutional provisions.

This, however, is not the end of the matter, for there remains the question of force.

Additionally—as in the NEA example (d)—the far reach of the IRB and IRS "subsidies" enables the conditions to apply so broadly that, even if they did not work through licensing, they would be considered an abridgment of the freedom of speech. Put another way, most federally funded academic research cannot be considered part of a government research program, and the speech of churches and other nonprofits cannot be viewed as part of a government tax program. The programs are so broad as to abridge private speech.

* Incidentally, the same analysis applies to the Fourteenth Amendment's provision that "no state shall make or enforce any law which shall abridge the privileges or immunities of citizens of the United States." Article IV of the Constitution already stated that "the Citizens of each State shall be entitled to all Privileges and Immunities of Citizens in the several states"—a guarantee requiring each state to provide at least a basic level of freedom to citizens coming from out of state. But in the nineteenth century, states such as Missouri repeatedly denied the privileges and immunities of its citizens to free Blacks visiting from other states, and the Fourteenth Amendment therefore had to reinforce what the Constitution already provided. It did so by making clear the privileges or immunities it was securing were not merely the privileges and immunities of state citizens but also were the privileges or immunities of citizens of the United States. And because the Fourteenth Amendment was reinforcing a preexisting set of rights, it stated that they were not to be abridged. It thus is clear that, although states can ask out-of-state visitors to consent to many restrictions, it would be a violation of the Fourteenth Amendment for states to use conditions to accomplish what they could not do directly under the two clauses on privileges and immunities.

PART IV

Federal Action

It is widely assumed that conditions, being consensual, are ordinarily without force. And on the further assumption that violations of constitutional rights ordinarily must come with government force, in the sense of something like physical coercion, it is taken for granted that conditions cannot typically be held unlawful and void under the Constitution. These suppositions, however, cannot survive much scrutiny.

The initial step is to recognize the perversity of framing the question in terms of coercive force or even merely economic pressure. To be sure, in some circumstances, a range of force or lesser pressures can matter, but many constitutional violations do not depend on any showing of coercion, other force, or even mere pressure.

It is therefore essential to begin by recognizing that the opening question must be, more broadly, about federal action. Just as inquiries about state unconstitutionality must deal with the varieties of state action, so an investigation of federal unconstitutionality must concern the full range of federal action. On this foundation, it soon becomes evident that there are varieties of constitutionally significant federal action. Depending on the circumstances, they can include lawful or unlawful coercion, the force of law in the sense of its obligation, various lesser economic and other pressures, and sometimes even no pressure at all.

Moreover, even when some sort of force or lesser pressure is required in order to find a constitutional violation, it cannot be presumed that the presence of consent puts an end to inquiries about such constraints. On the contrary, consent and force are different questions, and thus even when a recipient consents to a condition, one still must ask about the role of force or other pressures.

Last but not least, it is necessary to observe that consensual arrangements are subject to the traditional doctrines on undue influence and public policy. Although binding laws cannot be held void for such reasons, conditions in consensual arrangements are another matter. If obtained by undue influence or if contrary to public policy, they are void and unenforceable.

11

Varieties of Federal Action

It frequently is assumed that a constitutional analysis of conditions must founder on the hard rock of compulsion, coercion, or other nearly physical force. Even when scholars do not go so far, they still assume the need to find at least economic pressures. All of this, however, ignores the degree to which force or even pressure is often not an element of a constitutional violation.

It thus is useful to step back from the narrow analysis in terms of force or even economic pressure and begin more generally with an inquiry about constitutionally significant federal action. Having done this, one can see that there is a variety of significant federal action, which can involve a range of force, lesser pressures, and sometimes not even mild pressure.

The Broad Significance of the Question about Force

The concern about force has the potential to sidetrack constitutional inquiry about all sorts of conditions. Of particular importance, an absence of force may seem to push aside inquiries about unconstitutional conditions, commandeering conditions, and regulatory conditions.

Force has long seemed a crucial question for unconstitutional conditions because it is widely believed that constitutional rights are not violated unless the government acts with force. For example, to make an unreasonable search or to abridge the freedom of speech, one might assume that the government ordinarily must act with force. So if consent makes force improbable, it may be wondered how conditions can ever violate constitutional rights.

Similarly, when conditions commandeer the states, it is often expected that they must do so forcefully. Certainly, the label *commandeering* seems to suggest something vigorous. As it happens, the label is misleading, for the actual question (as seen in Chapter 8) is about maintaining federalism—about preserving the limited but real sovereignty of the states and the freedom of Americans to govern themselves through these localized sovereignties. Commandeering is thus a structural problem, and the need to protect the federal structure is not confined to cases involving federal force. All the same, a showing of force is often assumed to be crucial.

And if judges and scholars were to focus on the threat from regulatory conditions—on how such conditions displace the Constitution's avenues for legislative and judicial power—such commentators might also mistakenly expect these conditions to be forceful before being held unenforceable.

In short, it is difficult in the minds of many commentators to consider a condition unlawful without a finding of force, and there consequently is a powerful presumption in favor of upholding conditions. This narrow focus on force, however, obscures more than it reveals, and it therefore needs to be reconsidered.

Blurred Distinction between Constraints and Benefits

As a preliminary matter, it is necessary to recognize that much legal theory over the past half century has repudiated the distinction between rights and privileges and, concomitantly, between government constraints and benefits. Whatever the merits of this perspective, one result is that it looks somewhat incongruous to insist that conditions cannot be held unconstitutional unless they come with force.

A few cases illustrate the trend. In *Speiser v. Randall* (1958), when California required recipients of a tax exemption to declare their loyalty to the state, the US Supreme Court held that although this was merely a condition on a privilege, it was unconstitutional. Similarly, the Supreme Court in *Sherbert v. Verner* (1963) held that South Carolina's denial of unemployment benefits to Mrs. Sherbert violated her free exercise of religion. Although the vision of the free exercise of religion enunciated in *Sherbert* has not survived unscathed, the court gave classic expression to the view that: "It is too late in the day to doubt that the liberties of religion and expression may be infringed by the denial of or placing of conditions upon a benefit or privilege."[1] This sort of rejection of any sharp distinction between rights and privileges was further endorsed in *Goldberg v. Kelly* (1970), *Board of Regents of State Colleges v. Roth* (1972), and a host of other cases acknowledging due process rights in some government benefits.[2]

It thus seems more than slightly odd to insist that conditions are sharply different from direct constraints and cannot be unconstitutional unless they come with force. If the court in so many cases has repudiated any rigid distinction between rights and privileges, or constraints and benefits, then surely the significance of force is at least an open question.

As it happens, the Supreme Court's pronouncements collapsing the distinction between constraints and benefits are at best overstated. Undoubtedly, a denial of benefits can sometimes function as a constraint, and from this point of view, it may, perhaps, be reasonable to treat some denials of benefits as constraints for purposes of preserving constitutional rights. But the distinction between constraints and benefits remains essential for most constitutional rights—for example, in criminal law. It is one thing to treat conditions on some benefits as constraints so as to preserve constitutional freedom, but quite another to diminish this freedom by treating constraints as if they were mere benefits.

Alas, this is what has happened. The court has treated the denial of benefits as constraints for purposes of securing some negligible due process for a limited range of government beneficiaries—as laid out in *Goldberg* and *Mathews v. Eldridge* (1976).[3] But the court has thereby more generally legitimized a minimal version of due process not only in benefits cases but also in constraints cases—notably, to justify administrative procedure.

The result has been to treat constraints like benefits—at least for purposes of due process. The peril is evident throughout administrative enforcement proceedings, but never more clearly than in *Hamdi v. Rumsfeld* (2004). The court in *Hamdi* relied on *Mathews v. Eldridge*—a benefits case—to uphold the administrative detention of an American who had become an enemy combatant. The effect was to deny him a jury and all the rights of a criminal defendant and, instead, subject him to imprisonment (an acute constraint) with only the minimal due process that the court had developed for benefits cases.[4] Although the blurring of the distinction between constraints and benefits secures a smidgeon of process in benefits cases, it evidently can eviscerate due process in constraint cases.[5]

This book therefore does not endorse or rely on the court's muddying of the distinction between constraints and benefits.[6] Instead, it merely observes that the court has often loosened up the Constitution's requirements of constraint or force. The willingness of the court to relax the Constitution's requirements—although not a source of gratification—should at least induce judges and commentators to be open-minded about this book's much more modest argument: that courts should not insist on a showing of force where the Constitution does not actually require it.

So let's turn to the question at hand: In what circumstances, even outside questions about conditions, does coercion and other force, even mere pressure, not matter for holding a restriction unlawful and void?

Coercion Not Required for the Force of Law

For one thing, not even the force of law requires coercion. The Supreme Court and many commentators allude to the centrality of coercion and even compulsion when evaluating conditions, and certainly coercion can matter. At the same time, the law itself has a measure of force—the force of law—which does not always depend on a showing of coercion, and this reveals that coercion is emphatically not the only possible sort of constitutionally significant force or pressure.

The noncoercive aspect of the force of law is its force in the sense of its obligation. Of course, the force of law in the sense of its obligation is ordinarily backed up with the force of law in the sense of its coercion. But the two are not the same, and the obligation involved in the first sort is constitutionally significant even without the coercion associated with the second. This is an important initial indication that force in the sense of physical coercion is neither a necessary nor even a prototypical element of constitutional violations.

From a positivist perspective, the force of law consists of the government's sanctions. Jeremy Bentham and John Austin defined law as a sovereign's coercive command, and on this foundation, it is commonly assumed that the force of law is any official coercion or credible threat of coercion.

Yet this narrow conception of the force of law as official coercion falls apart along fault lines famously delineated by H. L. A. Hart. A society's general rules of conduct are very different from its orders to particular persons to comply, and the official coercion theory is therefore unpersuasive when it conflates the two by understanding the rules as if they were orders. Moreover, much law, such as contract law and corporate law, largely authorizes or empowers and so cannot easily be understood as a matter of command, let alone coercion. Further, when public officials discern and apply the law, they are not responding to coercion, and if official enforcement were mere coercion, this would be little better than the conduct of a gunman who abandons any claim of legitimacy and declares, "Your money or your life." Of particular interest for constitutional law, the official coercion theory cannot without difficulty explain legal rules that confine government and its officials.[7]

It should therefore be no surprise that, traditionally, the force of law has not consisted narrowly of official coercion. Though such coercion can show the force of law, the force of law has most centrally been the obligation of law—its binding quality, which obliges persons to obey it—this being what is usually backed up with the law's coercion and what legitimizes that coercion. For example, even when a law barring drinking in public fails to state a penalty or is systematically unenforced, it still has the force or obligation of law. Though without physical force, it is obligatory and thus has another sort of force.[8]

In other words, the prototypical force of law—the obligation to obey—binds Americans even when it is clear that they have no need to fear enforcement. And many Americans understand this. For example, drivers who encounter a stop sign in the middle of a desert will often hit the brakes and pause. Similarly, even without worries about enforcement, vast numbers of Americans assiduously pay their taxes and avoid insider trading. They understand that the force of law is not narrowly a matter of coercion.

This force of law, consisting of its obligation, is enough to render a statute void for violating constitutional rights. For example, if a statute were to bar speech critical of the president, this would be an unconstitutional abridgment of the freedom of speech, even if it clearly would never be enforced. Actual harm is ordinarily necessary to establish standing to sue, but as hinted by the Supreme Court's overbreadth doctrine, the threat of enforcement is not essential to show the constitutional violation. On the contrary, an unenforced statute contrary to the Constitution is already unconstitutional because it has the force of law—in the sense that it binds or has legal obligation.

Thus, even if one were to elevate the significance of force, one should not assume that it requires coercion. The force of law is prototypically the law's obligation or binding quality, and therefore, whether one is thinking about direct legal constraints or mere conditions, one should not ordinarily expect something dramatic like judicial enforcement or physical coercion. Put another way, notwithstanding what is commonly taken for granted, coercion tends to be a distraction. It can matter but is unnecessary.

Sometimes Not Even Pressure Is Required

Indeed, at the opposite extreme, a wide range of constitutional limits can be violated without law's coercion, without its obligation, and even without mere economic or personal pressure.

To take a narrow example, government pressure is unnecessary for a violation of some rights, such as the First Amendment's prohibition of an establishment of religion. Most constitutional rights protect against government constraints on the persons claiming the rights— as when an individual claims that a statute violates her free exercise of religion. In contrast, the traditional freedom from an establishment of religion is a freedom from government privileges for someone else's religion—at least where the privileges are so substantial as to establish it.

Of course, Supreme Court doctrine has interpreted the freedom from an establishment of religion in varied ways—sometimes with suggestions that government coercion is necessary for an establishment. But the core example of an establishment has always been government financial support for churches on account of their

religion—that is, a benefit or other privilege—and the freedom
from an establishment is thus structurally different from most other
constitutional rights. When evaluating conditions for their violation of
this freedom, not only force but even mere pressure is unnecessary.*

More broadly, even mere pressure is irrelevant when one considers
whether a condition goes beyond the government's legislative powers,
including its authority to spend. Regardless of the source of the government authority to spend—whether in a distinct "spending power"
or in the enumerated powers—spending is not ordinarily a constraint,
which Americans seek to avoid, but a privilege, which they hope to
secure. Accordingly, when the government goes beyond its authority
to spend or otherwise distribute privileges, the constitutional problem
is not that it is acting forcefully or with pressure against anyone, but
rather that it is being generous in ways it should not.

Assume, for example, that federal spending is authorized by a general spending power. Then, if the federal government spends without
providing for the general welfare, this spending and any associated
conditions should be considered unconstitutional without any
showing of force or other pressure. And on similar assumptions, when
the government imposes conditions that do not specify how the funds
are to be used, the conditions are not really part of the spending and
should be viewed as unconstitutional, without regard to the question
of force or pressure. To be sure (as noted in Chapter 4), the courts are
not currently willing to draw any such lines limiting spending. But

---

* An even narrower example of a right that can be violated without force or pressure is
the Third Amendment's prohibition of quartering soldiers in time of war without consent. One might think that a violation would necessarily involve force or at least pressure. But consider the Third Amendment's implications for an officer who quarters his
troops in an unoccupied home, with a door left open, whose owner is unavailable. The
officer surely has quartered them without consent and yet also without coercion or even
pressure. The point is that many constitutional rights can, in some situations, be violated
without any force or even lesser pressure.

the point here is simply that, if they were to do so, they would not have to worry about force.

Most expansively, many of the Constitution's structural limits do not involve any force or other pressure. For example, the Emoluments Clause concerns privileges granted by other governments, not any government pressure. More significantly, the Constitution's congressional pathway for lawmaking, its judicial path for adjudication, its enumeration of congressional powers, and its barriers to what the Supreme Court calls *commandeering* are matters of structure, which are violated whenever the government departs from them, regardless of whether it acts with force or other pressure.

Of particular importance here, regulatory conditions are constitutionally problematic without concerns about government force or lesser pressures. Regulatory conditions raise constitutional questions for structural reasons—because they displace lawmaking in Congress and adjudication in the courts—and this deviation from the Constitution's structure can occur with or without government force or pressure in securing or carrying out the conditions. In short, the government can violate its structural limits without exerting any force or other pressure.

Range of Pressures Obscured by False Alternatives

Even when a degree of pressure matters—notably, for violations of many constitutional rights—the possibility that pressures less than force are constitutionally significant has been obscured by a tendency to frame the question in terms of false alternatives. In particular, judges and commentators tend to ask whether the recipients of funding are either free or unfree, and in thus overstating the possibilities, they miss more moderate and accurate conceptions of constitutionally relevant pressure.

Judges ask (as in *Frost & Frost Trucking v. Railroad Commission*) whether the recipients have a "choice" to reject the funding or have "no choice" but to accept the condition.[9] Or (as in *Dole*) they contrast a "small financial inducement" with economic pressure that amounts to "compulsion."[10] And similarly commentators distinguish between offers and threats, or between a refusal to support and the imposition of a penalty. The dominance of these false alternatives is such that even when the Supreme Court, in *United States v. Butler*, recognized the significance of a middle ground in economic pressure—saying that "the amount offered is intended to be sufficient to exert pressure on him to agree to the proposed regulation"—it strained to conclude that "the regulation is not, in fact, voluntary."[11]

But it is misleading to frame the question in such stark terms. Almost no one is free from financial pressures, and no one is physically forced to accept government conditions. Accordingly, the question (as observed by Mitchell Berman) cannot be accurately understood in terms of a sharp contrast between freedom and compulsion, and any attempt to analyze it in such extremes is apt to become a rather sterile inquiry, which reveals little about the realities.

Instead, one needs to recognize a complex spectrum of economic, personal, and other pressures to accept conditions, and an equally complex range of personal circumstances and psychology in which different persons feel the same pressures differently. Of course, these factual observations cannot provide a baseline—that is, they cannot answer the legal question as to when a condition comes with constitutionally meaningful pressure. All the same, it is useful to remember that the factual foundations are more complex than can be reduced to sharply demarcated alternatives, such as freedom and compulsion, or choice and coercion.

Pressures Illuminated by Shifting Sensibilities

Adding to such cautions are changing sensibilities about the degree and type of pressure that is legally significant. Over the past half century, the law has become profoundly sensitive to the complex pressures—including economic and informational imbalances—that can deprive apparently consensual arrangements of their voluntary character.

Although contract law historically paid little attention to such imbalances, notions of economic duress and informational disparities have gained much credence, even if not consistently, in the past half century.[12] Similarly, medical treatment is not considered truly voluntary unless doctors disclose enough information to their patients for them to exercise informed consent. Researchers are required to secure informed consent from their human subjects, and payments to impecunious volunteers, even payments as low as $20, prompt soul searching as to whether the resulting economic pressure renders their participation nonconsensual. Most recently, pressures less than coercion have come to the fore in sexual relations. In the context of employment or education, a range of economic and peer pressures for sex or for conformity to sexual stereotypes can be legally significant, and a wide variety of words can create a hostile work environment.

Admittedly, some of these developments can go too far. For example, the regulation of human subjects research endangers freedom and health by adopting conceptions of pressure or consent that are so sensitive as to stymie research and the freedom of speech. Similarly, this freedom is at risk when a mere difference of opinion is treated as intimidating or harmful.

But the underlying insight—that economic and personal pressures can compromise consent—is undeniable. Accordingly, it would be very odd for an analysis of conditions to ignore the past century of expanding legal sensitivity to the range of pressures less than coercion. When the law recognizes such threats to consent across the legal landscape, it does not make sense to pretend that such questions do not arise in conditions.

Pressures Need Not Be Coercive

The economic and personal pressures involved in conditions are frequently dismissed as insufficient to show a violation of constitutional rights, on the ground that they are not really coercive. It has clearly been seen, however, that for some constitutional violations, no force or pressure is necessary, and now it can be added that even when some pressure is expected, it often need not be so strong as to be coercive. Indeed, in some circumstances, the necessary pressures can be so slight as to be elusive.

When an errant agent of the Federal Bureau of Investigation surreptitiously and without permission makes an unreasonable search of an unlocked home, he is violating the owner's rights under the Fourth Amendment without coercion and with no more pressure than turning the door handle and quietly pushing open the door. When a prosecutor does not disclose exculpatory information to a criminal defendant, the withholding of information, by itself, may not be coercive, and yet it denies the defendant the due process of law. And when a state university admissions officer discriminates against applicants on grounds of race, her conduct may be coercive only in the sense of not granting, and thus barring admission, but this does not save her from violating the Constitution.

It therefore is mistaken to generalize that federal pressures, economic or personal, are insufficient to violate constitutional rights because they are not coercive. Of course, this leaves unanswered which pressures are constitutionally significant and which are not—more will be said about that in the next chapter—but already here it at least is clear that, although government coercion can violate constitutional rights, coercion is not always requisite to show such violations.

Fortunately, the Supreme Court has increasingly recognized the limited role of coercion in evaluating constitutionally significant pressures. This tendency to accept the relevance of noncoercive pressures can be observed across a wide range of rights—most saliently, the First Amendment freedoms of speech and religion. In *Trinity Lutheran Church v. Comer* (2017), to take a recent example, the state of Missouri offered grants for resurfacing playgrounds while barring any such funding to religious organizations. The denial of a playground resurfacing grant obviously imposed only mild economic pressure on the church; it is nearly inconceivable that any religious organization would thereby feel obliged to abandon its beliefs. Nonetheless, the court held that this condition violated the First Amendment's free exercise of religion—as applied to the states by the Fourteenth Amendment. The condition, according to the court, was incompatible with the free exercise of religion because it "inevitably deters or discourages the exercise of First Amendment rights." To be sure, the court spoke of this economic discouragement as "indirect coercion," thereby clinging to a theory of coercion. The case, however, adopted a standard of mildly discouraging pressure, which is a far cry from coercion.[13]

Just as this chapter began by noting that the force of law can exist without any coercion, so it now winds up by observing that mere pressures, economic or personal, can be constitutionally significant without coercion. Once again, coercion is a false standard.

Range of Federal Action

In closing, it is useful to ask, what federal action is constitutionally significant? The answer must come not in oversimplifications about force or coercion, but in a range of federal action, which may or may not be significant, depending on the circumstances.

At the mild end of the spectrum, no force or pressure is necessary for violations of the Constitution's structural limits. For example, as already noted, when the government imposes regulatory conditions, thereby displacing the Constitution's pathway for regulation, it makes no difference whether it did so with coercion, force, or other pressure.

Similarly, such considerations do not matter for determining whether the federal government has gone beyond its spending or other powers or has commandeered the states or otherwise violated federalism. Structural violations do not depend on any coercion, force, or even pressure.

At the most severe end of the spectrum is official coercion, which can be relevant for most violations of constitutional rights. This can be the lawful coercion employed in the sanctions that reinforce the obligation of law. Less legitimately, official coercion can be imposed without any underlying obligation of law. That is, even when the government acts lawlessly, it can act with constitutionally significant force—for example, when an FBI agent beats a defendant into confessing. Whether or not the government acts with the obligation of law, it can violate constitutional rights when it acts coercively.

Also at the severe end of the spectrum, but not by itself physically coercive, is the force of law in the sense of its obligation, which similarly can be relevant for most violations of constitutional rights. Although this sort of force is ordinarily associated with direct legal duties, it will become apparent (in the next chapter) that it can also underlie or reinforce many types of conditions.

Last but not least—somewhere in the middle of the spectrum—are the various economic and personal pressures that come with conditions. Coercion is not requisite for direct violations of constitutional rights; often merely burdensome or pressuring federal action is sufficient. It is therefore a mistake to insist that conditions must come with coercion if they are to violate constitutional rights. Inasmuch as burdens or pressures less than coercion frequently suffice to show direct federal violations of constitutional rights, they surely are also adequate to show that conditions violate such rights.

Evidently, there is no single degree or sort of federal action that is unconstitutional. Instead, depending on the constitutional limitation, one must consider a range of actions, including not only coercive force but also the force of law in the sense of its obligation, a variety of pressures less than coercion, and sometimes even government action without any force or even pressure.

The constitutional analysis of conditions thus does not grind to a halt because of protests about the need for compulsion, coercion, or even pressure. Although these hard-edged concerns sound merely realistic about the elements of constitutional violations, they actually are caricatures, which grossly overstate the need for force. In fact, even outside the realm of conditions, constitutional violations can come with a wide range of federal action, not all of which is coercive, obligatory, or even a matter of pressure.

12

Force and Other Pressure amid Consent

Whendern government force of some sort, or at least substantial pressure, is necessary to render a condition constitutionally vulnerable, it may be asked how consensual conditions can ever come with such constraints. Put simply, how can voluntary conditions come with force? This question has long seemed profoundly difficult, but only because there has been a failure to recognize that force can exist amid consent. Once this is understood, it can be seen how conditions in conflict with the Constitution can come with constitutionally significant force or other pressure.

This is of particular importance for evaluating conditions that conflict with constitutional rights. As noted in the last chapter, force or other pressure is not necessary for violations of the Constitution's structures, but such things can be important for violations of its rights. At least for these purposes, therefore, it is important to understand how force or at least pressure can coexist with consent.

Force and Consent

It is commonly assumed that where there is consent, there cannot be force—as if the one were the measure of the other. Certainly, when consent and force are presented, in the abstract, as opposites, the existence of consent seems to settle the question of force. Accordingly, where the government secures consent to its conditions, one might assume that there cannot be force.

But consent to a condition does not really answer the question about force. Both in reality and in law, it is well recognized that consent can be accompanied by force, either concurrently or later—that is, either in the inducement or the enforcement.

Consent can thus easily become a distraction, which obscures the inquiry about force, let alone lesser pressures. Just as consent cannot relieve government of its constitutional limits, so too it is not the last word on whether there is force or other pressure. Even when the Constitution gives significance to consent—for example, when the Constitution allows the government to seek a waiver of jury trial— the existence of consent does not settle whether or not there has been constitutionally significant government force or other pressure. That must be a separate investigation.

Force or Pressure in the Inducement

When the government secures consent, one often must consider whether it obtained acquiescence by force or other pressure. That is, one must ask about force or pressure in the inducement.*

---

*Although force in the inducement can matter for all sorts of government conditions restricting rights, this sort of force is especially significant for conditions that require an immediate sacrifice of liberty—that require a current relinquishment of rights rather than a loss that will occur in the future. For example, suppose that the government asks you to plead guilty to lesser charges on the condition that you do not insist on a jury trial, or it asks you to testify and waive your right against self-incrimination. In such instances, where the government is asking you to relinquish your rights on the spot, it will usually have no need afterward to force your compliance with its conditions, and the question of force therefore comes to rest on the force used by the government to induce consent.

In private contracts, this danger is known as *duress*, and the Supreme Court has echoed standard premodern ideas of duress in its commandeering and unconstitutional conditions cases—for example, by speaking of *coercion, compulsion,* and a *gun to the head*. But as already hinted, twentieth-century doctrine has been open to less forceful ideas of duress including, in contract law, economic duress. Moreover, the constitutional measure of force is different from that which vitiates private arrangements. Whereas the traditional model of duress in contract law is, indeed, a gun to the head, it has been seen (in the last chapter) that significant federal action in constitutional law includes a wide range of things, including not only coercive force but also the force of law in the sense of its obligation and mere pressures— even sometimes (notably in structural questions) actions that involve no pressure at all.

In other words, the court has repeatedly confused the issue. It has focused on "coercion" and "compulsion"—as if it were considering a question of duress in contract law. In fact, it should have recognized that contract law and constitutional law deal with different problems and thus set different standards for force or pressure in the inducement.

Force in the Inducement: Regulatory Licensing

Force in the inducement often comes through the force of law. This may seem improbable, as conditions are not ordinarily binding, but the conditions imposed through regulatory licensing are an important exception. They reveal how even supposedly consensual conditions frequently come with the force of law in the sense of both its obligation and its coercion.

A license is a grant of permission. In some licensing schemes, the government is merely distributing a benefit or other privilege—as when the government licenses the use of its land or proprietary rights or licenses access to its classified or otherwise confidential information. In contrast, other government licensing takes place against a background prohibition, and this licensing is regulatory, for although the grant of permission is formally a privilege, it is in reality demarcating the boundaries of a binding regulatory prohibition. For example, the federal government licenses stockbrokers, investment advisers, and broadcasters; states license morticians, barbers, doctors, and lawyers; and local zoning boards license building and other land use.*

The privilege to build and so forth offered by this regulatory licensing typically comes with conditions, which usually are also regulatory—inasmuch as they regulate the stockbrokers, broadcasters, and so forth. There consequently are at least two layers of regulation. The licensing is regulatory because it offers relief from a general prohibition, and the conditions on which licenses are granted are regulatory because they are a means of regulating those who are allowed to escape the general prohibition. Often, the underlying prohibition is statutory, and the conditions are specified by the licensing agency. The overall effect is to offer the public a choice between two levels of regulation: a complete statutory prohibition for unlicensed persons or more moderate agency restrictions for those who get a license.

Of particular interest in this chapter, the conditions imposed by regulatory licensing often violate rights. It therefore is important to recognize that regulatory licensing always takes place against a background prohibition with the force of law—both in the sense of legal obligation and in the sense that it is backed up with the threat of legal coercion. In two ways, therefore, the resulting unconstitutional conditions are induced by the force of law.

---

* The point about broadcasters may require explanation. As seen in Chapter 2, the airwaves are not actually government property, but common property, and the Federal Communications Commission therefore is not licensing government property, but rather is licensing against a background prohibition—in this case, a prohibition on using the airwaves. The licensing of the airwaves is thus a mode of regulation.

One might think at first glance that such licensing merely involves the mundane distribution of a privilege in exchange for a condition, without any force of law. But the underlying statutory prohibition—for example, barring anyone from building without permission—comes with the force of law, and relief from this binding prohibition is what induces acceptance of the associated conditions. Consent to any unconstitutional condition in this context is thus induced by the force of law.

A particularly interesting example can be observed in section 501(c)(3), which offers tax exemption to nonprofits on the condition that these organizations suppress much of their speech in politics. The section, in other words, authorizes the Internal Revenue Service to license nonprofits for exemption from the income tax on the condition that they suppress some of their speech. This is regulatory licensing subject to regulatory conditions, and the background prohibition—that one must pay income tax at the marginal rate—is what induces compliance with the condition.

Imagine that the government simply offered churches cash—say, $10,000 per congregation—for tamping down their political speech. This would clearly be unconstitutional, even though the inducement would consist merely of economic pressure. Now consider section 501(c)(3)'s offer of a choice of tax rates (ranging from zero to the marginal rate) depending on whether a church submits to the section's speech conditions. Here, compliance is induced by the force of law— to be precise, by the obligation to pay the higher tax rate. Whereas the offer of cash would at least leave churches the choice between not getting cash or giving up their speech, the tax code as it exists threatens a higher rate, with the obligation of law, unless the churches quiet themselves down. Thus, in contrast to a cash offer, section 501(c)(3) relies on a background restriction with the force of law to induce acceptance of the speech conditions.

All regulatory licensing rests on a binding background prohibition— that is, a constraint with legal obligation and backed by legal coercion. Accordingly, when such licensing comes with an unconstitutional condition, there is force in the inducement. Consent to the condition is induced by the force of law.

Pressure in the Inducement: Nongermane or Disproportionate

Even more common than force is pressure in the inducement. And one consideration when focusing on such pressure is whether the subsidy or other privilege inducing consent is nongermane or disproportionately large in relation to the condition. In such instances, the pressure to accept the condition is apt to be disproportionate.

For example, when the Federal Communications Commission licenses the use of the airwaves on the condition that broadcasters conform to the equal time rule, the cost of not getting a slice of the airwaves is disproportionately large compared to the speech restriction. The restriction should therefore be understood to come with pressure in the inducement. That is, notwithstanding the consent, it may come with constitutionally significant pressure.

Another example of disproportionate pressure in the inducement can be found in the Affordable Care Act (2010). The federal government had already funded state Medicaid programs, and it had tied this funding to a condition specifying the medical coverage states had to offer. The Affordable Care Act offered expanded Medicaid funding, tied to a condition requiring states to expand their Medicaid coverage. But not content with this, the act threatened to withdraw preexisting funding unless the states complied with the new condition. According to Chief Justice Roberts in *National Federation of Independent Business v. Sebelius*, this new condition went astray by "surprising" states with "postacceptance" or "retroactive" conditions.[1] Many commentators wondered why an expansion of funding could not be accompanied by expanded conditions, but the court's conclusion about unconstitutionality (even if not exactly Roberts's reasoning) is less puzzling when one considers the weight of the funding in relation to the condition. By tying the new condition to the full amount of federal aid—not only the expanded funding but also the prior level of funding—the government left states at risk of losing all Medicaid funding if they rejected the new condition. The subsidy was thus disproportionately large, and this amounted to undue pressure in the inducement.

One might protest that where a subsidy is disproportionately large, the corresponding condition is disproportionately small, which should not be considered objectionable. Put another way, getting a good deal should not be viewed as undue pressure!

But governmental relations are not consumer contracts, and the federal government cannot purchase relief from its constitutional limits. So when the federal government persuades Americans to relinquish their constitutional rights, and states to sacrifice their sovereignty, by offering them overly large inducements, it is not really giving them a good deal. Rather, it is creating financial pressures for them to accept departures from the Constitution.

When government offers money to a poor woman on the condition she give up her freedom to have children or to marry, or when it offers her housing on the condition that she accept government intrusions into her home, the inducement or pressure is usually more than can reasonably be refused. Thus, to the extent there is an assault on constitutional rights, it is not a bargain, but a matter of excessive pressure. And as will be seen, the same is true when states, universities, and business corporations are subsidized. If they typically cannot afford to refuse the money, there is economic pressure.

Of course, the point is not that economic pressure by itself is constitutionally problematic, for even when a subsidy is nongermane or disproportionately large, the condition is not necessarily unlawful. Only when the condition is constitutionally dubious for another reason (such as that it abridges the freedom of speech) does one need to consider whether the inducement is disproportionately large or nongermane.

This is not, moreover, the sole measure of undue pressure. Even when subsidies or privileges are entirely proportionate and germane, they can come with overwhelming pressures because of the competitive relationship among the potential recipients of government funding or privileges. After some cooperate with the government, there is ever less chance for the holdouts to organize political resistance to the conditions. And when government support for cooperating recipients becomes a competitive advantage, the pressure for others to accept the aid with its concomitant conditions can be overwhelming. Indeed, because of the danger of government support for competitors, any significant subsidy for businesses and other institutions is widely assumed to come with the grim message: comply or die. Even the most temperate and relevant subsidies can thus come with profound pressure—a pressure not so distant from physical coercion.[2]

Overall, one must be open to the possibility that even amid consent, there can be constitutionally significant force and other pressure in the inducement. As put by the Supreme Court in *South Dakota v. Dole*, "Our decisions have recognized that, in some circumstances, the financial inducement offered by Congress might be so coercive as to pass the point at which pressure turns into compulsion."[3] Of course, terms such as *coercion*—let alone *compulsion* or *gun to the head*—set the bar too high. But the broader point, that there can be constitutionally significant force and other pressure in the inducement, is obviously correct.

Force in Enforcement

When a condition requires not merely an immediate sacrifice of liberty, but a loss that will continue or occur in the future, the condition will often be enforceable—sometimes in a court or other tribunal and sometimes in other ways. This is significant because where government can bring or take legal action for noncompliance—for example, to recover funds that were subject to the condition—the condition is backed by the force of law.

Most conditions by themselves are not legally obligatory. Instead, the conditions that carry into the future are merely triggers, which indicate when the government can deny future funding or demand repayment. But when the breach of a condition is subject to a legally binding duty, such as the return or setoff of funds, the government can take action against the defaulting party.[4] Thus, many conditions, though not themselves legally obligatory, are backed by the direct force of law, including both its obligation and its coercion.[*]

This force is apparent even when the government cannot demand the return of funds, for it can often bring the force of law to bear in other ways, which are not widely recognized:

- *Penalties.* If an agency finds that a grant recipient intentionally violated one of its conditions, it sometimes can administratively recover a "penalty"—usually taken out of subsequent grant allocations.[5]

- *Cease-and-Desist Orders.* An agency such as the Department of Education can obtain administrative cease-and-desist orders directing recipients of its grants to stop violating associated conditions.[6]

- *Injunctions.* The federal government can at times go to court for injunctions against grant recipients, ordering them not to violate

---

[*] Note the difference between the arguments about force in this chapter and in Chapter 8. That chapter observed that conditions do not have the force of law and therefore cannot trump state law. This chapter, in contrast, points out that although conditions themselves ordinarily do not have the force of law, they can be accompanied by force or pressure and thus can be unconstitutional—either because they are induced by force or other significant pressure or because they are backed by force or significant pressure in their enforcement.

conditions. (Even third-party beneficiaries of grants have occasionally secured such injunctions.)[7]

- *False Claims Act.* Under the False Claims Act, the federal government (or a plaintiff acting for the government in a qui tam action) can obtain civil penalties and triple damages from persons who recklessly make false assurances that they are in compliance with federal conditions.[8] And when the assurances are made knowingly, the federal government can even impose criminal penalties under an equivalent criminal statute.[9]

Federal law piles on legal remedies. Accordingly, though conditions standing alone do not have the force of law, they frequently are backed by the force of law.

To be sure, the federal government does not resort to defunding or its other legal remedies as often as might be expected, but this is no surprise. After gently hinting at its capacity to use the force of law, the government can usually get much of what it needs without any such unpleasantness. Defunding and other formal remedies, in other words, typically lay the foundation for understated threats, informal sanctions, and quiet resolution.[10] But this is hardly to say that federal conditions are not backed by the force of law. On the contrary, recipients of federal funds usually bend over backward to avoid displeasing their federal paymasters precisely because they understand the federal government's overwhelming legal remedies. And recipients therefore often acquiesce in severe remedial demands—such as for certifications, representations, and additional conditions.

The force of law in the enforcement of conditions is particularly severe in criminal law. Consider, for example, the parole conditions that are backed with the threat of returning a parolee to prison or the conditions in deferred prosecution agreements that are backed with the threat of reinstituting prosecution.

Of course, the force of law only matters if the condition itself is at odds with the Constitution. For example, imagine a government employment contract stipulating, as a condition, that the employee may not engage in partisan political speech while at the office (a narrow version of the Hatch Act), and imagine that the government can recover past payments for any breach of the condition. This condition requires no more than the government could require directly by law, and it thus does not abridge the freedom of speech. And because it is not substantively unconstitutional, it makes no difference that the government could recover the money it has paid to the employee or bring other proceedings against him. In contrast, imagine government research grants to a university with conditions requiring prior review of any such research and any publication of it and providing that the government can recover past payments for any breach. This condition does abridge the freedom of speech, for it imposes prior licensing, which the government could not have required directly, and it consequently is significant that it is backed by the force of law.

Admittedly, when a condition appears merely in a transaction between two private parties, the fact that it can give rise to a lawsuit does not ordinarily suggest that it comes with the force of law. But where the government both imposes the condition and can sue for breach, it is difficult to avoid the conclusion that the condition is supported with government force.[11]

Force in the enforcement is not as elusive as may be imagined. Conditions themselves are not legally binding. But when the government has the potential to secure a repayment, a penalty, a cease-and-desist order, or an injunction, the condition is backed by the force of law, including at least the law's obligation and ultimately its coercion. Conditions that run into the future thus usually come with more than enough force to be unconstitutional.

The Not-Contractual Excuse

Many agencies emphasize that their conditions do not appear in contracts. These agencies seem to think that if they can avoid seeking legally obligatory promises, they can avoid any suggestion of the force of law and so can avoid constitutional challenges.

The notion that the government can sidestep questions of force by not using contracts acquired legitimacy in 1936 in *United States v. Butler*. The Supreme Court in that case distinguished "between a statute stating the conditions upon which moneys shall be expended" and a statute "effective only upon assumption of a contractual obligation to submit to a regulation which otherwise could not be enforced."[12] And the court echoed this distinction the next year in *Steward Machine*.[13] In line with such reasoning, an agency will often state that it will not give a grant until it has received an "assurance" from the grantee—the assurance being the grantee's statement that it is in compliance with the agency's conditions. From this perspective, the recipient makes no enforceable contract or other commitment, but merely states a factual condition. The federal agency thus can claim that there is no force of law.

But this is odd, even merely as a matter of contract law. Although specific performance is more widely available than in the past, it has been emphasized for about a century that contract law does not ordinarily oblige one to keep one's promises, but rather merely requires one to pay compensation for damages, if there are any. From this perspective, a contractual promise is backed by the force of law, but it itself does not come with any legal obligation—the only exception being contracts that are specifically enforceable in equity.

Putting this in rather sharp terms, Oliver Wendell Holmes famously wrote: "Nowhere is the confusion between legal and moral ideas more manifest than in the law of contract," for "the duty to keep a contract at common law means a prediction that you must pay damages if you do not keep it—and nothing else."[14] Holmes may have been overstating the matter, as contractual promises are personal commitments into the future and so, in contrast to conditions, have a sort of moral obligation. But even if a contract comes with some personal obligation to keep one's promise, this falls short of the force of law—the more public obligation to obey the law.

Therefore, regardless of one's theory of contract—whether Holmesian or not—it does not make much sense to distinguish (as in *Butler*) between the legal obligation of contractual promises and the lack of legal obligation for conditions. Both contracts and conditions are generally without legal obligation, but each type of transaction (in its own way) can be backed by the force of law. Consequently, *Butler*'s effort to excuse unconstitutional conditions on the ground that they are not contractual duties is very nearly comic. It distinguishes conditions from contracts on the basis of a claim about contracts that is largely denied by contract law.

For purposes of understanding force in the enforcement, it thus makes no difference whether a restriction is stated as a contractual promise or as a condition of a grant. Regardless, the restriction will typically be without the obligation of law and yet will often be backed by the force of law—thereby rendering it void to the extent it conflicts with the Constitution.

Butler's distinction between a contract and condition is misleading. With or without a contract, conditions can be backed by the force of law. The federal government, accordingly, cannot find a safe (or safer) harbor by avoiding putting its conditions in contracts.

Pressure in Enforcement

Even when conditions are not subject to legal action to recover the money and so forth, and so are not backed by the force of law, they can be backed by constitutionally significant pressure.

For example, suppose the government carefully structured its conditions to avoid the force of law and thereby escape constitutional scrutiny. For example, it could make its conditions merely the preconditions of recurring annual grants—so that its conditions would not run into the future and would avoid any force in the enforcement.

Such conditions would not be subject to any legal action to recover the money and so forth and thus would not be backed by the force of law. All the same, recipients would always fear that they might not be refunded if they did not repeatedly live up to the conditions. And if their competitors also received such grants, the pressures for compliance would be all the greater. Thus, even without force in enforcement, such conditions would come with strong enforcement pressures.

Especially worrisome are cross-collateralized conditions. Their effect is to threaten grant recipients with the loss of multiple grants—sometimes all federal grants—for even a single breach of a single condition. Cross-collateralized conditions thereby magnify the severity of any one condition on any one grant. When conditions are backed by the force of law, be it coercive or obligatory, the cross collateralization accentuates the force. But even when the conditions are not backed by the force of law, there remains the economic and other pressure, and the pressure created by the cross collateralization is utterly overbearing. This threat of losing other funding is surely constitutionally significant.

Even amid consent, conditions can come with the force of law or other constitutionally significant pressure—sometimes in the inducement and sometimes in enforcement. Accordingly, many conditions that restrict constitutional rights should be considered unlawful and void.

13

Irrelevance of Force and
Other Pressure

It is widely taken for granted that the force of law or some other government pressure is necessary for constitutional violations. This book has narrowed the scope of this assumption, pointing out that force or pressure is unnecessary for violations of the Constitution's structures. But the book does not dispute that, at least for most violations of rights, some sort of force or at least pressure is necessary. Thus, for example, a statutory condition abridging the freedom of speech cannot be held void unless induced or enforced with some constitutionally significant force or pressure.

There are, however, multiple reasons for holding conditions void, and two have yet to be considered: undue influence and public policy. Quite apart from whether a statute stating a condition is void under the Constitution, there is another question about whether the conditions in any resulting consensual arrangements should be held void and unenforceable under traditional doctrines governing consensual transactions. Of particular importance are the doctrines on undue influence and public policy. Even when a statute's recitation of an otherwise unconstitutional condition survives constitutional analysis because it does not come with force or other pressure, there remains a question under these doctrines on consensual agreements as to whether the same condition in a grant arrangement is void and unenforceable.

This chapter may therefore be a surprise. Although the prior chapter showed the prevalence of force and other significant pressures underlying conditions, this chapter goes a step further. It points out that force or other pressure is largely irrelevant.

Undue Influence

Quite apart from the well-known question as to when a law is unconstitutional, there is the very different question of when a contract, trust, or other consensual arrangement is void and thus unenforceable for other reasons. Some arrangements—for example, contracts for prostitution—are void for being contrary to law. Others are not so directly unlawful but are void on other grounds—for example, on account of undue influence.[1]

The problem of undue influence is familiar from the law on consensual arrangements, and though undue influence is notoriously difficult to reduce to a simple rule, some conclusions are fairly clear. Such influence tends to be found where one party takes advantage of its fiduciary or confidential relation to another—a confidential relationship being not quite a fiduciary relationship, but a factual situation in which one party has superior knowledge, skill, or other resources, and the other is accustomed to relying on that superiority being used in a way that does not take advantage of the imbalance. Similarly, undue influence is apt to be found where one party is overbearing in relation to another, who is necessitous and susceptible to suggestion.

Such grounds for holding conditions void are relevant when the federal government asserts that it has special expertise, beyond what is easily accessible to private parties or the states, and when the public or the states depend on the federal government for accurate information and advice. For example, if the federal government takes advantage of its apparent expertise on health care to get states or individuals to consent to conditions that are not really in their interest, the conditions could be considered the result of undue influence and thus void.

Undue influence is also relevant where the federal government supports states and private institutions on the condition that they control others—for example, on the condition that academic institutions, including private universities, regulate the speech of their researchers. Although such conditions ultimately control third parties, they are often justified on the theory that the restricted individuals have consented, and this is where undue influence comes in. The universities purport to speak with expertise about the ethics and regulation of research, and teachers and students rely on this institutional expertise. They also rely on their universities to protect their interests. At the same time, they are easily intimidated by their institutions—as when the universities simultaneously declare their attachment to academic freedom and announce that everyone must submit to federal speech conditions or face a range of internal and legal consequences. The universities thus get faculty and student "consent" to the suppression of their speech and due process in circumstances that often amount to a sort of undue influence.

Public Policy

Even more broadly, the force of law and other government pressure is apt to be irrelevant where the terms of consensual arrangements violate public policy. Agreements in violation of public policy, just as much as those in violation of law, are void and unenforceable. Although this may initially seem surprising, it is long-standing doctrine. Indeed, it is "firmly rooted in precedents accumulated over centuries."[2]

The potential breadth of this doctrine may seem worrisome. Certainly, judges have long been conscious that the doctrine is "liable to be misunderstood, and extended beyond its proper dimensions."[3] But instead of displacing the doctrine, this realization has tended to confine the doctrine in ways that limit its misuse. One traditional solution was to cabin the relevant public policy to "the policy of the law, or public policy in relation to the administration of the law."[4] The Restatement of Contracts suggests in more contemporary terms that judges should consider the weight of the public policy and the strength of the authority underlying it.[5] As a practical matter, judges do not use the doctrine whenever a contractual provision seems loosely against public policy, but rather tend to limit its application to clear, concrete, and serious threats to distinctively important and well-established public policies.

A nineteenth-century commentator gave this example: "A gives a bond to secure B, a creditor of C, in the payment by C of a sum agreed to be paid B in consideration of his withdrawing opposition to C's discharge in bankruptcy." Even if not unlawful, the bond was void.[6]

The usual remedy, as put by Justice Joseph Story, has been to "leave the parties to their own good pleasure in regard to such agreements."[7] That is, as with contracts contrary to law, so with those against public policy, a court will typically not undo the arrangement but rather will simply refuse to enforce the contract or, at least, the wayward provision—thus allowing an adversely affected party to keep its consideration or benefit.

And far from merely affecting private parties, this doctrine has long been understood to be applicable against government. A nineteenth-century treatise explained, "The defense that a contract is void as against public policy may be raised against the state as well as against its citizens."[8] In *Frost & Frost Trucking*, the Supreme Court opined that "even generally lawful acts or conditions may become unlawful when done or imposed to accomplish an unlawful end" and that this "applied to acts of the legislature as well as to the doings of private parties."[9] As summarized by a commentator, John French: "The law will prohibit the recovery of damages or restitution for the breach of a contract unenforceable as against public policy. It is not difficult to bring this chain of inference to bear on our problem. For the concept of 'public policy' in contract law, we merely substitute the term 'constitutional policy' to obtain a major premise applicable to the debate over unconstitutional conditions."[10]

It is therefore typically unnecessary to worry whether conditions are imposed with force or other pressure. When the government gives tax exemption to churches on the condition that they sacrifice much of their political speech, or when it supports universities on the condition that they license the research speech of their personnel, the question of force or even pressure is a red herring. The conditions are consensual arrangements against public policy. And because the conditions are thus unenforceable, the recipients can keep the money without complying with the conditions.

The government may protest that because its conditions enunciate public policy, they cannot be void for violating public policy.[11] But the Constitution is a public policy that rises above mere conditions, whether stipulated by Congress or agencies.[12] The Constitution establishes the government's power to regulate and adjudicate—respectively, through acts of Congress and judgments of the courts—and it is against the Constitution's public policy for government, by means of regulatory conditions, to create alternative mechanisms for binding regulation and adjudication. The Constitution, moreover, establishes a federal system, and it is against the Constitution's public policy for the federal government to impose conditions that commandeer the states, defeat their laws, or otherwise undermine their separate sovereignty and their people's freedom of self-government. Of particular importance in this chapter, the Constitution protects rights such as the freedom of speech, and it is against the Constitution's public policy for the government to use conditions to impose restrictions that abridge the freedom of speech or other constitutional rights. Regardless of questions about the force of law and other government pressures, such conditions violate public policy.

This application of a doctrine drawn from the law on consensual arrangements is all the more compelling because the government systematically uses such arrangements to evade the Constitution's pathways for power, its federalism, and its guarantees of rights. On the theory that conditions are merely consensual arrangements, the government has gone far in unraveling much of the Constitution's structures and its protections for freedom, including its rights. This is a profound danger, and it is therefore essential to recognize that the law itself addresses this threat from consensual transactions.

When the government employs private consensual arrangements to evade the Constitution's limits on public power, the government should at least be subject to the law regarding consensual arrangements.

Government force and other pressures matter less than is usually assumed. As shown in the two previous chapters, many conditions come with the force of law or other constitutionally significant pressure, and many (especially conditions contrary to the Constitution's structures) are unconstitutional even without such force or pressure.

This chapter adds that even in the absence of such force or pressure, conditions contrary to public policy or obtained by undue influence are void and unenforceable. That is, even if not void as a matter of constitutional law, they are void under the law on consensual arrangements. And few conditions are more clearly against public policy than those at stake in this book—those that evade the Constitution's modes of lawmaking and adjudication, that undercut federalism, or that impose restrictions in violation of constitutional rights.

PART V

Beyond Consent

What has been seen thus far may seem disturbing enough. But there is more, because numerous conditions go beyond the conventional vision of conditions. Although it is commonly assumed that conditions are more or less consensual, many do not entirely fit this model.

14

Regulatory Extortion

Rather than offer money or some other privilege in exchange for a condition, agencies sometimes threaten regulatory hassle until they get acquiescence. The government in this way often imposes conditions in ways that are difficult to distinguish from extortion.

Bad as this is, the extortion is even worse when the government threatens regulatory hassle to secure consent to regulatory conditions. The resulting extortion is doubly regulatory—both in the pressure to submit and in the resulting acquiescence to further regulation.

Extortion

What distinguishes regulatory extortion is that the conditions begin not with contracts or purchases, nor even with government funding or benefits, but with government regulation. Agencies threaten to adjust regulation or how it is enforced or adjudicated in order to secure acquiescence to extra conditions—often conditions that impose further regulation.[1]

For example, an agency might threaten to amend its rules, inspect, demand documents, bring enforcement proceedings, adjudicate, or otherwise use its powers with severity—unless a regulated party agrees to a condition not required by law. And all too frequently, such threats are employed to secure consent to regulatory conditions. Making it worse, the resulting regulation is often of a sort that agencies could not otherwise adopt without facing legal or political obstacles.

Of course, when an agency uses its powers—whether legislative, executive, or judicial—to threaten regulation or its application, and then relaxes this threat in exchange for consent to an extra condition (sometimes even a regulatory condition), this could often be understood as an offer of a privilege, subject to a condition. But this is not the ordinary offer of a privilege, for when an agency uses regulatory harassment to secure consent to an extra condition, the condition has been extorted. Rather than extortion in the sense of a bribe, which involves a payment for specially favorable treatment, this is extortion in the sense of a government demand imposed under threat of specially unfavorable treatment.[2]

Such demands, it should be noted, will not always meet the legal definition of extortion, as the definition varies across jurisdictions. In some states, for example, there is considerable tolerance for demands made in furtherance of the public interest. All the same, demands for extra conditions under a threat of special severity are essentially a type of extortion.

For example, the Federal Trade Commission (FTC) often brings administrative proceedings against telecommunications firms for breaches of data security—even when the firms are not in violation of any statutory or common law standard for data security. Relying on the threat of such proceedings, the FTC then typically forces the firms to accede to consent decrees that specify data security standards. The FTC thereby uses the threat of administrative enforcement and adjudication to secure consent to data security standards not set by law and even to impose different standards on different companies, depending on what it thinks it can get away with and on what it thinks of the companies. In the last two decades, the FTC has entered into more than sixty such consent decrees.

Although these FTC settlements are bad enough for divesting Congress of legislative power (as seen in Chapter 5), they also illustrate the danger of the doubly regulatory extortion. Instead of offering money or other privileges for a regulatory condition, the FTC uses the threat of regulatory power to secure consent to additional regulatory conditions, which are not required by law. As put by one of the agency's commissioners, J. Thomas Rosch, in 2011, there is reason for "concern" when "the agreed-upon remedies" are "more than what the Commission would have been able to obtain, had it been forced to litigate."[3]

The FTC is all the more confident that it can get away with this regulatory extortion because the FTC requires parties who settle with it to waive judicial review.[4] Consequently, as noted by the same commissioner, "a petition for review of an FTC consent decree is virtually unheard of."[5] There is thus repeated extortion. The agency first extorts submission to regulation it could not otherwise impose and then protects this illegality by also extorting a waiver of accountability in the courts. In 1876, when dissenting in *Doyle v. Continental Insurance Company*, Justice Joseph Bradley expressed concern for the "constitutional right" of individuals and organizations of all kinds "to resort to the courts of the United States." As he explained, "any agreement, stipulation, or state law precluding them from this right is absolutely void—just as void as would be . . . a city ordinance prohibiting an appeal to the state courts from municipal prosecutions."[6]

The basic danger of extortion is familiar from prosecutors. They frequently overstate charges, and then offer accommodations, allowing the defendants to escape further litigation and the risk of a high fine—as long as they agree to conditions, including regulatory limits not required by law. Indeed, prosecutors often ensconce these extorted restrictions in consent decrees. But prosecutors thereby usually abuse only their prosecutorial power.

The danger is much greater when prosecutors and especially agencies acquire multiple governmental powers. Prosecutors have secured the power to demand information in subpoenas or "civil investigative demands"—a power that once belonged exclusively to the judiciary—and they therefore have more than prosecutorial opportunities for extortion.[7] And agencies have even more power than prosecutors. They can exploit the full range of government powers—a combination of legislative, executive, and judicial powers—to extort conditions.

Legislatively, agencies can threaten severity in administrative regulations or regulatory conditions. Executively, they can overcharge defendants. Judicially, they can demand information, impose inspections, and be severe in adjudicating conditions. Agencies can thus threaten the full extent of governmental powers to demand acquiescence to their extra conditions, sometimes even additional regulatory conditions.

Good Regulatory Results?

Of course, the extortion can be used for what may seem appealing regulatory purposes. For example, when a zoning board threatens to withhold zoning permission in order to secure public access to a beach or the preservation of a historical building, it may be that the conditions are extorted, but they still may be very valuable for the public.

Do the valuable ends justify the unlawful means? Perhaps in extremis—for example, during a war threatening the very existence of the nation. Even then, however, the government should acknowledge the unlawfulness and seek indemnification. In contrast, more mundane public ends, such as beach access or historic preservation, do not justify unlawful means, let alone covering up the unlawfulness.

For these quotidian policy goals, it surely is not too much to ask government to enact a binding statute and avoid extorting conditions.

A federal example of extortion used for good ends can be found in a strategy employed by the Occupational Safety and Health Administration (OSHA). OSHA does not have enough employees to inspect all of the workplaces subject to its regulations, and it therefore made an offer to the 200 employers in Maine with the state's most workplace injuries and illnesses. OSHA assured these employers a much-reduced chance of inspection as long as the companies voluntarily adopted a higher standard of safety than required by statute or OSHA rules. Of course, after a substantial number of companies accepted this condition, OSHA would have plenty of employees to engage in severe inspections of the noncompliant companies, and unsurprisingly 198 of the 200 companies submitted. Overall, the higher standard seems to have been beneficial for workers.[8] Nonetheless, the higher standard was imposed through a regulatory condition, and OSHA extorted compliance with it by offering reduced inspection and concomitantly subjecting noncomplying companies to especially severe inspection. However valuable the higher standard of safety, it should have been imposed directly rather than through regulatory extortion.

Extortion through Regulatory Licensing

The extortion is especially common in regulatory licensing. As noted earlier (in Chapter 12), a license is a grant of permission. Some government licensing merely distributes benefits or other privileges—such as the use of government or common property—but other government licensing, which offers relief from a background prohibition, is regulatory—as when the federal government licenses broadcasters, states license hair braiders, and local zoning boards license construction.

Ordinarily, agencies simply grant licenses to persons who meet the legal qualifications to build a house or operate a business, and there is already a risk in this, for the agencies thereby often impose regulatory conditions, which divest Congress and the courts of their powers. More to the point in this chapter, agencies sometimes use their regulatory licensing not merely to impose regulatory conditions, but to engage in regulatory extortion. That is, they occasionally threaten to adjust their licensing decision to secure acquiescence in extra conditions—conditions that do not merely bar or limit a harm defined by law, but that impose additional regulation, that require a transfer from the licensee to the government or the "public," or that are otherwise irregular. Sometimes agencies candidly insist on these extra conditions; sometimes they simply delay a licensing decision until the licensee volunteers what the agency wants.[9] And whether such extra conditions press the licensee to submit to further regulation, transfers, or other irregular conditions, they are extortionate.*

Such practices are notorious in zoning. For example, in *Nollan v. California Coastal Commission* (1987) and *Dolan v. City of Tigard* (1994), the landholders were told that they could have permission to build as long as they gave up some of their land rights—in *Nollan* for a public easement across a beach and in *Dolan* for a public greenway and public pathway. Improvements of this sort serve the public interest in some sense, but this cannot justify the use of extortion to secure them from private owners.

None of this is to say that a state cannot directly secure the public interest. It can legislate limits on land use, and it even can legislate

---

* Note the distinction between regulatory *licensing*, regulatory *conditions*, and regulatory *extortion*. Here, the focus is on regulatory licensing—the licensing that regulates by offering relief from a background prohibition. Regulatory licensing is only one mechanism for imposing regulatory conditions—the conditions that regulate. It also is but one mechanism for regulatory extortion—the use of regulatory harassment to secure acquiescence in conditions.

takings of private property for public use as long as it compensates the owners. The problem is that it cannot extort such takings or other limits.

Although the Supreme Court used the word *extortion* in *Nollan* and *Dolan*, it did not really recognize extortion and takings as distinct problems, but rather merely held that the conditions in those cases were unconstitutional on the ground that they were takings.[10] Even in this regard, the court was not troubled that the landholders (the licensees) were being asked to give up some of their property to secure zoning permission. Instead, the court developed the view that a zoning condition becomes an unconstitutional taking when it is unconnected to, or much larger than, the harmful land use. As it summarized in *Dolan*, there must be an "essential nexus" and a "rough proportionality" between the condition and the harmful land use—otherwise the condition amounts to an unconstitutional taking.[11]

A taking, however, does not occur only when a zoning or other licensing board asks for too much or something too far afield. On the contrary, it also happens when the board asks for something relevant and equivalent in value to the harms it is regulating. The Constitution forbids all takings without compensation, not merely unrelated or excessive takings. Thus, when a board delays declaring a landowner's conduct lawful until he makes a transfer, it does not matter if it is merely extracting something that corresponds in substance and size to the permitted activity; this is still a taking.*

---

* It might be responded the condition determines a sort of compensation for the harm. But legally cognizable harms should be predetermined by law and government should seek redress for such harms in regular courts. In contrast, when harms are not defined by law and their adjudication comes in licensing proceedings, not to mention when such proceedings involve extortion, it is difficult to avoid the conclusion that there is a denial of the due process of law.

It might also be said that a board's license or permit is, in effect, compensation for the taking. But zoning and other licensing against a background prohibition is a form of

More centrally for this book, all *Nollan-* and *Dolan*-style licensing conditions are a form of extortion. *Nollan* and *Dolan* began with threats of constraint and therefore cannot be fully understood within the consensual framework associated with conditions. Instead of offering government money or benefits for the conditions sought from the landowners, the local governments threatened to deny permission under regulatory licensing schemes unless the regulated parties agreed to give up some of their property. The threats alone made the conditions a mode of extortion. Far from being the simple purchase of submission, this was the use of threats to secure submission to transfers.

Some regulatory licensing agencies have tried to evade the Supreme Court's rulings in *Nollan* and *Dolan*. For example, in *Koontz v. St. Johns River Water Management District* (2013), when a landowner sought permission from the local water management district to build on wetlands, the district attempted to avoid the Constitution's barrier to takings of property by seeking only the landowner's money, not restrictions on his land—as if the Constitution's limit on taking property protected only real property, not personal property. And to avoid even a taking of his money, the district described its request as remedial, saying that it was merely asking him to compensate for the loss of wetlands on his property by having him pay for "off-site mitigation" restoring other land in a nearby nature preserve—as if a theory of compensation could alter the underlying reality of a taking. Indeed, to avoid claims of coercion or pressure, the district did not ask for any

---

regulation, not of compensation. And if the government's relaxation of a prohibition on the development of land is understood in the same way as a distribution of compensatory money, then the government can take property simply by prohibiting development and offering a permit in exchange for the rights it wants in the regulated land. Put briefly, relief from a prohibition is not compensation, let alone the just compensation that could justify a taking. Accordingly, all *Nollan-* and *Dolan*-style licensing conditions remain takings, and they cannot be saved by any "nexus" or "proportionality."

particular payment in relation to any particular land, but rather merely hinted that Koontz should make a proposal for "off-site mitigation" if he wanted the district's approval—as if by forcing him to speak first, the district could avoid any sense of threat. Notwithstanding these games, the district's use of delay to extract a payment remained a mode of extortion.[12]

Although the Supreme Court considered the extortion unconstitutional, it did so by holding that there had been a violation of the Takings Clause: "Extortionate demands for property in the land-use permitting context run afoul of the Takings Clause not because they take property but because they impermissibly burden the right not to have property taken without just compensation."[13] This was a valuable recognition of the extortion. All the same, the court might have added that such extortion is unlawful even without a violation of the Takings Clause. From this alternative point of view, the Takings Clause reveals that when the water management district sought a payment, it was going beyond its lawful regulatory authority. That is, it was using regulatory hassle to obtain something extra—in this instance, to secure a transfer of money or other property. On this basis, it is clear that the district engaged in regulatory extortion. *Koontz* thus involved not only a taking; it also was a case in which a regulatory licensing board sought something extra (be it additional regulation, a transfer, or something else) through delay or other regulatory hassle.

Consider an example outside the realm of zoning—in the provision of services. Lawyers typically are prohibited from practicing law unless they are licensed by their state's bar association. The bar associations sometimes require lawyers, if they are to maintain their licenses, to do pro bono work, thereby making them give up some of their own professional time and work. This is not a taking of property, and the condition is thus not unconstitutional on that account. Nor is it necessarily extorted, for to the extent the bar associations are merely enforcing legal or judicial requirements, they are not asking for anything extra. But what if an association threatened hassle in renewing some or all lawyers' licenses unless they agreed to do things not required by law or the courts—such as extra pro bono work or caring for the elderly in nearby nursing homes? The goal might be worthy, but the condition would be extorted.

Whenever government officials threaten or even merely hint that they will adjust regulatory decisions in exchange for something extra—for example, when they hint that they will alter regulatory licensing decisions depending on compliance with additional regulatory conditions or private transfers—there is an abuse of office and regulatory extortion. And this extortion should be considered unlawful regardless of whether the demand violates the Takings Clause or other protected rights. To be sure, the extortion is all the worse when it is used to force a sacrifice of rights, whether ordinary legal rights or constitutional rights. The essential point, however, is the unlawfulness of the regulatory extortion.

Unconstitutionality

Quite apart from the unlawfulness of the extortion and the unconstitutionality of forcing a sacrifice of constitutional rights, there are further reasons for considering regulatory extortion unconstitutional.

To the extent that agencies extort conditions through determinations that are judicial in character, they are displacing the Article III power of the courts. Moreover, they are violating the due process of law. Recall that the Constitution's due process of law "must . . . be had before a judicial court, or a judicial magistrate"—in other words, due process "means law, in its regular course of administration, through courts of law."[14] But licensing boards are not courts. And even if one accepts the Supreme Court's watered-down administrative version of due process—consisting of "all the process that is due"—that at least means one must get a "neutral" adjudicator and a "fair" process. Under a regulatory licensing scheme, when a licensing board threatens to adjust its decisions depending on compliance with its extra conditions—conditions that sometimes impose additional regulation or even takings—it is difficult to conclude that the board is neutral or that the process is fair. By any standard, whether the Constitution's due process or the court's faux process, the perversion of licensing and other agency adjudication for purposes of regulatory extortion grossly violates the due process of law.

An additional problem arises from the assumption of legislative powers. Like any other regulatory conditions, those secured through regulatory extortion displace legislative power from the legislature, and thus violate the Constitution's vesting of all legislative powers in Congress. Put another way, the resulting regulatory conditions deprive Americans of their constitutional freedom to be bound only by laws enacted by their legislature.

Some extorted conditions also run afoul of federalism—most dramatically when a federal statute authorizes a federal agency, such as the Environmental Protection Agency, to impose a severe federal regulatory scheme in states unless they adopt their own regulations, which of course must be approved by the federal agency. In other words, with the threat of very severe direct commandeering, the federal government extorts state consent to impose regulations that, for political or legal reasons, the federal government may not have been able to impose directly. The condition that a state accepts, requiring it to regulate, is itself regulatory and a mode of commandeering. Yet it is also a product of regulatory extortion on a grand scale, in which the federal government uses the threat of direct and severe commandeering to extort acquiescence to slightly less onerous regulatory and commandeering conditions, which require states to regulate as approved by the federal government.[15]

Consensual conditions are only part of the problem. Often confused with them are the demands secured through regulatory extortion—

through agency threats to adjust regulation or its enforcement or adjudication in order to secure acquiescence in additional conditions.

The full extent of government extortion is beyond the scope of this book, for it includes not only extorted conditions but also, for example, regulation "by raised eyebrow" and hinting at retaliation for seeking judicial review. Such practices constitute a form of government unanticipated by classical political theorists: not monarchy or aristocracy, nor republic or democracy, but thugocracy under color of law. Whether or not it involves conditions, it is government under the outward show of a republic and its laws, but conducted through mere bullying.

15

Regulatory Agents

This book has saved the worst for last. Not content to use conditions to control those from whom it secures consent, the government asks consenting states and private institutions to control others. The federal government thereby employs conditions to turn the states and private institutions into agents for regulating Americans—often even for imposing unconstitutional restrictions.

Of course, the federal government sometimes directly requires states or private institutions to regulate others, and this is already dangerous. But more typically, and more central in a book on the purchase of submission, the government uses its financial support to get states or institutions to control their populations or personnel.

The point is not that the co-opted states and private institutions are federal agencies, for they do not become part of the federal government. The observation, instead, is that even while standing outside the government, they become its agents, carrying out its regulatory and otherwise unconstitutional policies.

The result is a dual constitutional threat—initially to institutions and then to individuals. No other mechanism reaches so far into American life, suppressing both institutional and individual freedom.

Examples

How exactly does the federal government turn states and private institutions into agents for the regulation of others? Here are some illustrations.

- Recall (from Chapters 2 and 3) that in *South Dakota v. Dole*, the federal government funded state highway construction on the condition that the states impose a federally determined drinking age. This condition not only commandeered the states but also made them agents for carrying out federally demanded regulation of their populaces.

- The Department of Health and Human Services (HHS) uses conditions on its research grants (as seen in Chapter 2) to turn academic institutions into agents for regulating human subjects research. The conditions require universities to establish institutional review boards (IRBs), which in turn license speech in and about human subjects research conducted by students, faculty, and other personnel.

- The Department of Education also relies on educational institutions as agents. Recall (from Chapter 7) that Title IX makes it a condition of federal funding that educational institutions must not discriminate on the basis of sex, and that because this requirement applies to entire institutions rather than merely the funded programs or activities, it is regulatory. To this, it now must be added that Title IX turns the educational institutions into agents for regulating their students, teachers, and other personnel.

- A further example can be found in §501(c)(3)'s conditions on tax-exempt organizations. Not only are the organizations themselves asked to satisfy the speech conditions, but to avoid falling out of compliance, many such organizations feel obliged to direct their ministers and other personnel to be careful what they say.[1] Even churches thus become regulatory agents for the control of political speech.

These examples and myriad others illustrate how the federal government works through regulatory agents. Colleges and universities, churches and charities, have all become agents, who for the sake of money and other privileges, assist the federal government in regulating others.

The federal government has thereby been all the more effective in evading the Constitution's avenues for regulation and adjudication and even in imposing unconstitutional restrictions. By using conditions to devolve regulation to agents, the federal government now exercises a power over inquiry, science, religion, speech, and politics that the Constitution does not entrust to it, that the First Amendment denies to it, and that judges would never tolerate in direct congressional regulation.

Attenuated Consent and Exaggerated Severity

Before exploring the constitutional problems, one must note the worrisome combination of diminished consent and increased severity. This perverse blend gives urgency to the constitutional arguments, and the severity confirms that the federal conditions are disproportionate and thus regulatory.

Attenuated consent is pervasive where the federal government regulates and adjudicates through agents. When acting through prototypical conditions, the federal government obtains the consent of the persons with whom it deals and who ultimately are restricted. But when the government uses conditions to get agents to impose restrictions, the government more clearly obtains consent from these intermediary bodies than from those restricted by them. Such conditions (as put succinctly by Richard Epstein) affect third parties.[2]

Undoubtedly, some acquiescence by these third parties can be presumed from their remaining with their employer, church, or other institution. But this is not the active and considered consent one would expect for a mode of control that repeatedly cuts off constitutional freedoms. And the consent looks especially insignificant when the federal conditions are pervasive—that is, when they apply to almost all academic institutions or almost all churches—thereby leaving individuals with few realistic alternatives.*

The presumption of consent collapses entirely when the federal government asks states to impose restrictions on the public. Persons lawfully within a state have a right to be there and cannot be understood to have relinquished any of their constitutional freedoms merely by remaining within the jurisdiction. It is difficult enough to conclude that employees who remain in their jobs thereby consent to a sacrifice of their constitutional freedoms, as dictated by federal conditions on their employer. And it is even more strained to suggest that individuals consent to such a loss merely by continuing to live in a state that has consented to carry out a federal condition depriving them of their freedoms.

Agent-imposed regulation, moreover, often combines this attenuated consent with exaggerated severity. The danger begins with the government's exaggerated enforcement power against funded institutions. A single breach of a federal condition can allow the government to stop further funding or even take back past funding. Federal conditions, moreover, are often so confining that many institutions

---

* Recognizing the danger of attenuated consent, some universities ask their students and faculty to acknowledge that they are subject to the human subjects research rules imposed in layers of conditions by HHS, the universities, and their IRBs. But the pressure on teachers and students to sign is profound, as they can otherwise lose their employment, even their freedom to publish.

are always in noncompliance. Under HHS's research conditions, for example, there is always at least one individual at a university who is out of compliance with HHS's conditions, and this means that universities are almost always out of compliance.

A department such as HHS can therefore, at almost any time, declare almost any university out of compliance, and because the conditions are cross collateralized, the department can demand the return of all of its funding. HHS can even, largely at its discretion, demand that a university shut down all human subjects research by all of its personnel—stopping all human subjects research, including the associated inquiry and publication, merely because one research project is not in compliance. This is a formidable power with high risks for funded institutions, and after HHS for a brief period ostentatiously used it and threatened to use it, institutions have bent over backward not to incur the department's wrath.[3] HHS thus no longer needs to make such threats overt. All it has to do is have a conversation with university officers, and the university will grovel.

To avoid the severity of federal enforcement, academic institutions have ratcheted up their own severity. Fearful of losing all of their funding on account of a minor slip-up by a single person, institutions often carry out their role as regulatory agents with such vigilance as to demand more from their personnel than the federal government actually requires.[4] And individual administrators tend to protect themselves by further ratcheting up the severity—all in the name of enforcing federal conditions. As a result, individuals in federally funded institutions (notably academic institutions) are usually subject to restrictions that exceed what is stated in the government's conditions. Indeed, the federal government has often encouraged these additional layers of severity.[5]

Not all of this severity, to be sure, appears in the federal conditions; much of it is conveniently left for the agents to impose on their personnel. But the harshness is the natural and often deliberate consequence of the federal conditions and thus is attributable to them.

The combination of attenuated consent and exaggerated severity offers an initial hint as to how much is awry with the use of regulatory agents. The severity, moreover, confirms that the federal conditions are regulatory. And this is just a foretaste of the constitutional difficulties.

Defederalizing and Privatizing Federal Power

The federal conditions that turn other institutions into regulatory agents shift federal power to the states and private bodies. Such conditions, in other words, not only divest Congress and the courts of their powers but also defederalize and even privatize federal powers.

The Constitution vests federal legislative powers exclusively in Congress and vests federal judicial power exclusively in the federal courts. In contrast, when federal conditions turn states into regulatory agents, requiring them to regulate under federal auspices, the states and their institutions (such as state universities) end up exercising the federal government's legislative and judicial powers. This is a defederalization of powers that the Constitution vested in branches of the federal government.

Even when federal conditions merely ask states and private institutions to carry out regulatory policies entirely specified by the federal government, the conditions defederalize the federal government's judicial power by leaving the states and private institutions to adjudicate breaches of the conditions. Usually, moreover, the states and private institutions enjoy some discretion in deciding the exact contours and application of the federal policies. Often, in fact, they are overtly expected to develop or expand upon the federal policies. As a result, when federal conditions turn states and private institutions into regulatory agents, the conditions defederalize both the legislative and the judicial power of the federal government.

The problem is not merely defederalization but even an exaggerated privatization by which the federal government uses conditions to hand off its lawmaking and adjudication to private bodies. To be sure, the executive can privatize much of its power without constitutional difficulty—as when it hires outside consultants to develop policy ideas, to train federal employees, or to run prisons. In fact, executive privatization can go much further. Domestically, lawsuits on behalf of the government can be brought by private plaintiffs (in qui tam actions), and militarily, public force can be exercised by private ships (privateers). But the Constitution places federal legislative powers exclusively in Congress, and federal judicial power exclusively in the federal courts, and such powers therefore cannot be shunted off to private organizations.

The contrast with administrative power is illuminating. Nowadays, many executive and semi-independent agencies, acting under congressional authorization, administratively exercise binding legislative and judicial power. And their administrative power could be understood to mean that the Constitution nowadays permits legislative power to be exercised outside Congress, and judicial power to be exercised outside the courts. On the whole, however, the federal government at least exercises its own administrative power. In contrast, the federal government regularly uses conditions to turn private organizations into regulatory agents, and in thereby shifting federal legislative and judicial powers out of the federal government, it defederalizes and even privatizes them.

Violating Rights

The use of regulatory agents has consequences not only for powers but also for rights. By working through states and private institutions, the federal government has found an especially effective mechanism for depriving Americans of their constitutional rights.

The Supreme Court's current doctrine on unconstitutional conditions is weak enough when applied to conditions that merely restrict the recipients of federal aid; it is even weaker when applied to conditions that turn states and private institutions into agents for regulating others. For example, although judges occasionally slap down conditions limiting the speech of funded organizations, they have been much less willing to interfere when the government subsidizes other institutions to deny rights to their personnel. The federal government therefore assumes that, with conditions, it can rely on other institutions to do what it cannot.

Why has there been so much judicial acceptance of the conditions asking agents to deprive Americans of their rights? One reason is the confusion about consent and force.

It is often assumed (as noted in Chapter 11) that conditions can be unconstitutional only if they come with force and that consent precludes force. The necessary force seems doubly missing when the federal government works through layers of conditions—imposing its conditions on states and private institutions, which then carry out the federal conditions by imposing their own conditions on their people or personnel. In these circumstances, it has appeared to be difficult to find any federal force in the conditions that most immediately restrict teachers, students, and other personnel. Especially when the institutions are private, what chance is there of finding government force or equivalent government action?

But (as evident from Chapter 11) the relevant question is not about force but about federal action. And (as explained in Chapter 12) even when force or other pressure is requisite, it can exist amid consent. Moreover, where *states* serve as regulatory agents for the federal government, their own force or other state action is constitutionally significant—under their own constitutions and under the Fourteenth Amendment. Further (as noted in Chapter 13), conditions can be void even without force or pressure if they are contrary to public policy—

something that is clear whenever the federal government regulates through agents and, moreover, whenever it uses those agents to deprive Americans of their constitutional rights. Such conditions are, if not always unlawful, then at least void and unenforceable for violating public policy.

A second reason why the violation of rights has not been fully recognized is that by working through agents, the federal government seems to displace its responsibility. But a foundational maxim of agency law recites, *qui facit per alium facit per se*—meaning that "what a man does by another, he does by himself." As restated in another maxim, *nam qui facit per alium, facit per se*, "he who acts through another does the act himself." For purposes of constitutional law, this means that when government is barred from abridging or denying rights, it cannot avoid its constitutional limits by asking someone else to do the prohibited act.

The logic of *qui facit* is based on causation. In other words, the constitutional point rests not merely on an old Latin phrase, but on the underlying reasoning. A person who uses a physical or electronic instrument to harm another in his body or his freedom cannot claim that the act is not his. By the same token, when he uses another person to do the act, he cannot disown it. He cannot escape the legal obstacle by asking another to act in his stead; on the contrary, he is ordinarily understood to have acted unlawfully.

It thus becomes apparent that the federal government cannot escape its legal duties by asking others to do what it cannot. For example, if the secretary of the interior unlawfully takes and destroys an individual's trailer home, it does not matter whether the secretary drives the bulldozer with her own hands, orders a subordinate to do it, or hires someone outside the government. Similarly, if the federal government imposes licensing of speech and the press, it makes no difference whether it acts by itself or asks states or private institutions to carry out the licensing. The use of the agents is no cure.

Consent of Agents

Notwithstanding all of this, one may suppose that the consent of the agents can cure the federal government's departures from its constitutional limits. Merely to state this supposition is to expose its falsity, but it is worth spelling out why it is wrong.

The basic point (echoing Chapter 9) is that no amount of consent can relieve the government of its constitutional limits. Different constitutional provisions (as explained in Chapter 10) allow the government, to different degrees, to act with consent. But beyond that point, consent is of no help. For example, where the federal government works through states or private institutions to abridge the freedom of speech or to deny the due process of law, it makes no difference that such bodies have agreed to cooperate.

Consent of Agent's Personnel

One may, however, assume that the government can find solace in the consent of those controlled by its agents. If these individuals have consented to participate in their institutions, then perhaps it does not matter that the federal government is using such institutions to deprive them of their rights, for they have (at least unconsciously) relinquished their constitutional claims.

This sort of argument typically concerns employees—it being said that employees consent to the terms of their employment, including any restrictions on their constitutional rights that come with the federal funding of their employers. But even if this were true as to employees, it would not be very explanatory, as most of the people controlled by their states or institutions at the behest of the federal government are not employees. Most students are not employees of their academic institutions, most church members are not employees of their churches, most citizens are not employees of their states, and so forth. The government sometimes lumps such persons together with employees under the rubric of "personnel," but this is merely a way of obscuring the realities that they are not employees. They are therefore clearly outside of any doctrine regarding employees. The larger question, in fact, is not really about employment, but rather about the consent of the "personnel" of institutions (state or private) that serve as agents for federal regulation.

As already observed, an agent's consent cannot relieve the federal government of its constitutional limits, and by the same token, no amount of consent from the agent's adversely affected personnel can excuse the federal government's adventures beyond its constitutional bounds. It thus makes no difference that the federal government's unconstitutional schemes are carried out with the consent of those regulated by its agents.

Put another way, the primary constitutional problem with the suppression of rights through federal conditions on agents is not that the agents are selling other people's rights. Rather, the situation is simply another example of how the federal government goes beyond its constitutional limits. That the federal government does this through agents is particularly insidious but not constitutionally distinct from its use of its own officers. Whether acting through its own officers or subsidized agents, it is violating constitutional rights.

State Violations of Rights

When states serve as regulatory agents and deprive persons of their rights, not only the federal government but also the states are acting unconstitutionally. Consider, for example, a state university that, in compliance with HHS's conditions, imposes IRB censorship. The university and its IRB are enforcing a regulatory condition—indeed, one that abridges the freedom of speech. The university is thus in direct violation of its state constitution's guarantees of freedom of speech and of due process.

One might suppose that because HHS imposes its conditions under a federal statute, the state's protections for speech and due process are of no effect. But the federal government itself emphasizes that its conditions do not come with the force of law. It is therefore difficult (as seen in Chapter 8) to understand how they defeat a state constitution's guarantees of speech and due process.

In fact, a state that complies with an unconstitutional federal condition will often be in violation of the Fourteenth Amendment. This amendment bars states from denying the due process of law, and this has been interpreted not only to protect procedural due process but also to incorporate most of the federal Bill of Rights against the states—so that states must comply, for example, with the federal guarantee of freedom of speech in addition to any similar state provision. Thus, when a state university lives up to HHS's conditions by imposing IRB censorship on research speech and publication—in violation of procedural due process and the freedom of speech—the university cannot justify itself on the theory that it is acting under a federal condition or that the condition is authorized by a federal statute, for the Fourteenth Amendment trumps any such condition or statute, and the university is directly violating the US Constitution.

Put briefly, a state cannot rise above the Fourteenth Amendment, let alone by agreeing to a federal request. No amount of consent to a federal condition can relieve a state of its obligation to adhere to the federal constitution.[6]

Wholesale Control

Exacerbating the danger for rights is the wholesale control. Traditionally, the law could be enforced only in court proceedings, and this was especially important when constitutional rights were at stake. For example, to suppress speech, the government or a private party had to persuade a judge and jury, in accord with the rules of evidence, that the particular words of a particular defendant violated the law.

This was retail adjudication, and it was essential for the protection of speech and other rights.

But nowadays, the government relies on wholesale proceedings—most centrally, through licensing. By prohibiting conduct and then licensing it, the government can suppress conduct without taking action—by merely not making a decision. It thereby avoids the need to make a case against a particular defendant and his particular conduct. In fact, it can altogether sidestep the usual burdens of proof, the conventional rules of evidence, and even the bother of a judge and jury and other due process. Licensing streamlines wholesale control.

All of this is hazardous for speech, especially when the wholesale control is privatized. Americans are so numerous that, even with licensing, it would be difficult for federal agencies themselves to control what individuals say. In any case, a direct federal attempt at widespread censorship would face too much resistance. The government therefore uses conditions to corral previously independent states and private institutions into carrying out its wholesale control. By assigning its unlawful censorship to agents, the federal government can successfully suppress speech on a massive scale for which retail due process in the courts would be impracticable. This is the defederalization and even privatization of censorship.

For example, the Internal Revenue Service licenses churches for tax exemption on the condition that they not engage in campaign speech or too much speech about legislation, and the churches carry this out by asking their ministers to tone down such expression in their sermons.[7] Indeed, some federal conditions openly require recipient institutions to suppress the speech of their personnel. HHS distributes research grants on the condition that academic institutions establish IRBs to review and censor what scholars and students say and publish. The Department of Education distributes money to schools on the condition that they limit sexual speech, and although it does not require them to license such speech, it has pressured them to bear down on their personnel through inquisitorial tribunals and harsh sanctions that similarly enable wholesale control.

It is striking that even churches and universities—supposedly the most independent of private institutions, in which individuals allegedly enjoy the greatest freedom—have become agents for carrying out policies that stifle individual speech. The federal use of agents for licensing and other wholesale suppression of speech evidently reaches deep into American society and private life.

Already in seventeenth-century England, the government suppressed speech and printing by farming out the licensing to privileged institutions—the universities (Oxford and Cambridge) and a trade guild (the Stationers Company). This system of wholesale control, including its use of agents to do the licensing, was the most salient example of what the First Amendment forbade. Nonetheless, the government is once again asking universities and other agents to license and otherwise control speech and the press, thereby allowing the government to suppress speech without the accountability of retail proceedings in court.

This revival of wholesale suppression confirms the larger point here, that the use of regulatory agents multiplies the threat to rights. Through conditions, independent states and private institutions have become instruments for profoundly abridging the freedom of speech and other rights.

Control of Society

By acting through conditions that turn states and private institutions into regulatory agents, the federal government (as noted in Chapters 6 and 8) undermines the independence of bodies that traditionally were understood to counterbalance federal power. But that is not all, for it also transforms them into its own regulatory tentacles, which penetrate deep into American society.

Part of the danger arises from the leverage over third parties—from the use of institutional consent to secure power over individuals. By getting the consent of states and private institutions, the federal government can extend the reach of its regulatory and unconstitutional conditions to all whom its agents can control—leveraging the consent of a relatively small number of intermediaries to impose unlawful restrictions on vast numbers of Americans.

Not only the breadth of the intrusion but also its depth is worrisome, for it increasingly imposes unconstitutional speech constraints that severely limit private speech. Consider, just for example, the prior licensing and other regulation that restricts speech lest it cause mental discomfort. Ordinarily, this sort of harm is not legally cognizable—in the first instance because of standing requirements in federal courts, and more substantively because of the First Amendment obstacle to regulating words for being emotionally difficult. Nonetheless, by working through state and private bodies—including academic institutions and their IRBs and Title IX tribunals—the federal government has gone far in suppressing speech for its merely psychological consequences. The federal conditions thereby give legal effect to merely subjective reactions to speech, with utterly arbitrary and stifling consequences.

Adding to these incursions into society and private life is the alignment of policy across institutions. When the federal government acts through states and institutions, it subjects individuals to the coordinated effect of multiple layers of power—federal, state, and corporate. Such entities would ordinarily act independently, and the layered character of the American political and social system traditionally allowed individuals to find some refuge, for themselves and their liberty, in the different stances taken by their varied governments and private institutions. The federal government, however, increasingly uses its laws and especially its conditions to align federal, state, and private policy—creating a uniform phalanx of public and private power, often in pursuit of unconstitutional restrictions. Indeed, largely through conditions, the federal government increasingly creates an alignment of federal, state, local, educational, corporate, and other private bureaucracies. It is an unbroken wall of power that discourages legal and political resistance and renders private life vulnerable. By imposing aligned policies, it homogenizes institutions and eventually the people, ultimately consolidating government and society, so that little remains outside the federal imperium except in name.[8]

When the federal government pays state and private institutions to become agents for carrying out federal regulatory policy, the constitutional problems are numerous and severe. Even when carrying out otherwise lawful regulation, this mode of governance unconstitutionally defederalizes and privatizes federal lawmaking and adjudication. And most troubling, it has become a pathway for the federal government to violate freedom of speech and other constitutional rights with impunity—as if it could escape constitutional rights by simply paying others to do its dirty work.

Conditions thus reach far beyond consent. Not merely consensual arrangements between the federal government and the people, they are often instruments of even more dangerous modes of power: regulatory extortion and regulatory agents.

Conclusion

Money is power, but not always constitutional power. Although the federal government can constitutionally make purchases and provide support, it cannot lawfully circumvent the Constitution and its freedoms by purchasing submission. Therefore, the old saw that "he who pays the piper calls the tune" must be qualified: the government cannot call a tune out of harmony with the Constitution.

Too often, the problem is understood narrowly as a matter of unconstitutional conditions—those that impose unconstitutional restrictions, especially on rights. From this point of view, the problem with conditions is centrally about the substance of their restrictions. The threat, however, is much broader, for conditions serve as an irregular pathway for power, with profound consequences for both the Constitution's structures and its rights.

The most basic danger is that conditions sidestep the Constitution's regular avenues of power and other structural protections for freedom. By working through conditions, government can regulate and adjudicate outside the Constitution's mechanisms for legislative and judicial power, it can escape the limits on legislative power, it can deny procedural rights, and it can cut through the separation of powers and federalism—indeed, it can engage in extortion and can govern through agents.

The second and more familiar danger from conditions concerns the substance of their restrictions. They have become a pathway for government to impose unconstitutional limitations, especially on rights, without accountability under the Constitution—thus allowing the government to do what the Constitution expressly forbids.

It is useful to distinguish the two categories of conditions, as this allows one to move beyond a focus on unconstitutional conditions and the threat to rights. Serious as this danger is, there is no less a threat from conditions as a pathway that can escape the Constitution's regular avenues of governance and its other structural protections for freedom.

Overall, the threat is far reaching. With conditions, the federal government sidesteps the Constitution's avenues and institutions for lawmaking and adjudication; it candidly goes beyond its enumerated powers; it gets around judges, juries, due process, and other procedural rights; it defeats the constitutional limits that secure separation of powers and federalism; indeed, it not only commandeers states but also turns states and private institutions into its agents, thereby defederalizing and privatizing federal power; it abridges the freedom of speech and other constitutional rights; it even imposes wholesale suppression; and it ultimately centralizes and homogenizes American life in ways that deprive institutions of their independence and leave individuals profoundly constrained.

Although conditions empower the same agencies that exercise administrative power, they are a distinct and even more sobering constitutional problem. Federal agencies can announce regulatory conditions in administrative rules, but they ultimately impose the conditions in contracts, assurances, and other private arrangements— thereby shifting lawmaking from public rules to private transactions. Agencies, moreover, can adjudicate violations of conditions without even the mock judges and faux process that are familiar from administrative power. And by means of conditions, agencies can transfer regulation and adjudication from the federal government to states and private institutions, making them agents for carrying out federal policies, including policies that are utterly unconstitutional. Conditions thus exceed even administrative power as a threat to civil liberties.

Degradation of Law

Though the Constitution elevates law as the federal government's avenue of regulation, the government increasingly relies on other pathways for control. The result has been a substantial degradation of law.

For thousands of years—at least in the traditions that gave rise to the United States—law has seemed the central method of governance. And in the Anglo-American tradition, what has centrally distinguished law from other government rules has been the combination of the sovereign's coercive force with the people's consent, for only with such consent can rules have legal obligation. Of course, consent can be given in different ways, but it has long been understood that enactments must come with express consent—from the people or at least from their elected representatives. On these foundations, the US Constitution authorizes the federal government to regulate through statutes adopted by the nation's legislature. The Constitution's avenue for federal regulation is thus law—meaning enactments that bind because they are adopted by the nation's popularly elected lawmaking body. (The only and partial exception consists of treaties ratified by the Senate.)

The federal government, however, has not been content to regulate through statutes. One departure has been toward administrative power—a system of executive command. European monarchs claimed a power to bind their subjects with edicts that they simply announced in their councils or commissions, and already then these commands stood in sharp contrast to laws passed by legislatures. Drawing on this monarchical vision, the Prussians and other Europeans developed

administrative power—transforming the monarch's prerogative
power into the state's bureaucratic power. In England, Jeremy Bentham and John Austin echoed this continental tradition by defining
law as the coercive command of a sovereign. Americans eventually
imbibed administrative ideas, mainly from the Germans, and created their own administrative state.[1]

Not satisfied with administrative commands, the federal government increasingly goes a step further by purchasing submission—
seeking public power, even unconstitutional power, through consent
in private transactions. The government thereby creates a new pathway
of governance, which evades not only the Constitution's avenues for
lawmaking and adjudication but also the lesser pathways and processes offered by binding administrative power.

Even if one could swallow the administrative evasion of the Constitution's avenues for power, one should hesitate to accept the additional evasion through conditions. Whereas administrative power
comes primarily in promulgated agency commands, conditions take
a more subterranean pathway through private transactions. Whereas
administrative edicts ordinarily make clear what they require and to
whom they apply, conditions usually are fully known only to those
who privately consent, thus often leaving opaque who has submitted
and to what they have agreed. Whereas administrative power at least
recognizes public participation—albeit merely through notice and
comment—the purchase of submission often short-circuits even this
limited public political participation and accountability. Whereas administrative power is frequently adjudicated with at least the administrative pretense of due process, regulatory conditions tend to be adjudicated so informally as to be without even the pretense. Whereas
administrative edicts at least purport to bind in the manner of regularly adopted laws and adjudications, conditions on privileges (even
if adopted in administrative rules) circuitously induce compliance,
purportedly without the binding effect of law—thereby threatening

to defeat constitutional rights. Indeed, with conditions, even more than with administrative power, the federal government can turn state and private institutions into agents for the control of their personnel, including the wholesale suppression of their speech and other rights. Last but not least, conditions allow government to extort what it does not want to pay for. The purchase of submission is thus even worse than administrative power.

The overall result of the purchase of conditions is a soft tyranny—a gentle but enervating mode of governance of the sort feared by Alexis de Tocqueville, in which federal largess and private consensual arrangements often displace the need for laws and even for administrative command. Administrative command has reduced the need for public consent in Congress, and conditions have diminished the need for administrative command. The effect is to shunt regulation off the public rails of legislative consent, and even off the alternative rails of administrative command, so that the government can get its way along a private siding.

But this mode of regulation is not really very gentle. It exploits the financially vulnerable, it buys off political opposition and so deprives the stalwart of their political and legal allies, it dodges the Constitution's avenues of power and its rights, it often relies on extortionate threats to secure "consent," it turns states and private institutions into agents for the control of third parties, it evades legal accountability, and it reaches deep into society to subvert the independence of state and private institutions and ultimately to control individuals. This is not so much soft as sinister.

The grim reality is that America has acquired yet another irregular channel for control. No longer simply a republic governed by law, the United States has become a society increasingly governed along other paths: administrative command and even the purchase of submission.

Reducing the Constitution to a Contract

Conditions tend to reduce the Constitution to a sort of contract, which is renegotiated over time, and this is worrisome. Although the Constitution was conceived as a law enacted by the people, it now is widely understood as an evolving societal arrangement, and this already comes with risks. But conditions go even further, as they make the government itself a party to the arrangement and enable it to adjust constitutional freedoms on the basis of private consent.

The government was not a party to the Constitution. On the contrary, the people enacted the Constitution as a law and thereby established and limited the government to serve their needs. All the same, the government now, by means of conditions, renegotiates constitutional freedoms—both the structural freedoms and the enumerated rights—and thereby transforms constitutional law into a mere agreement.

In ordinary transactions, when parties are relatively equal or independent, it can be valuable for them to renegotiate a contract in response to their changing circumstances. But when one party is unequal and even dependent, renegotiation is apt to exaggerate existing inequalities. This matters for conditions because the government usually has vastly disproportionate power, and individuals and even private or state institutions tend to be highly dependent on it. Therefore, when the federal government renegotiates the Constitution by making private deals with different individuals and institutions, it usually can get much of what it wants. Enjoying the upper hand in such arrangements, it can repeatedly renegotiate constitutional limits, always increasing its power and diminishing liberty.

The result is dismal. By reducing the Constitution to a renegotiable contract, conditions defeat its character as a law. And by enabling the government to act as a party—the most powerful party in a series of private contracts—conditions enable the government recurringly to reduce the people's constitutional freedoms.

Unjustified by Regulatory Ends or Difficulties

One might hesitate to abandon the purchase of submission for fear that it is the only way to secure valuable regulatory goals or avoid regulatory difficulties. But such concerns are overstated.

The lawful regulatory ends achieved through regulatory conditions could just as well be imposed directly through binding statutes, let alone binding administrative edicts. Regulatory conditions are thus not the only or most direct pathway for securing regulatory goals, and the desirability of such ends therefore cannot justify regulating through conditions.

Of course, one might worry that some worthy regulatory policies are so politically or legally controversial that they are unlikely to be adopted by binding statute or even by binding administrative rule, thus making a more indirect pathway necessary. But however valuable they may be, regulatory policies are relatively mundane compared to the more profound policies underlying the Constitution, and they therefore cannot justify stretching, let alone breaching the Constitution. If the difficulty of adopting valuable regulatory policies really justifies departing from the Constitution's avenues for self-government and adjudication and its protections for procedural rights, then this should be openly asserted and debated in pursuit of a constitutional amendment, not hinted at quietly in justification of a surreptitious mode of control.

The alleged value of regulatory policies, moreover, cannot be assumed when they are pursued through a mechanism that avoids public debate and decision, evades political accountability, buys off political and legal opposition, slices through federalism, enables regulatory extortion, turns state and private institutions into agents for regulating individuals, and threatens a wide range of constitutional rights, including the freedom of speech. In such circumstances, the evasive regulatory process cuts off many of the opportunities to evaluate, refine, or reject regulatory policy. Good process is essential for good policy, and the policies produced by this process therefore cannot be assumed to justify it.

One might still worry that if regulation had to run through the regular avenue of binding statutes and court decisions, Congress and the courts would not be able to handle the resulting burdens. But this is far from clear. Congress would not face insuperable difficulties, because agencies could still draft the nation's regulatory policies and then send them to Congress for enactment. As for the courts, their decisions would be very different from those of agencies adjudicating conditions. Whereas regulatory conditions are usually designed to preserve the policy, enforcement, and adjudicatory discretion of agencies, there would be no similar incentive in the drafting of directly imposed regulations, which would therefore be less open-ended. And in contrast to agencies, the courts would have to anticipate the need, at least occasionally, to instruct juries. For both reasons—as explained in Chapter 7—the amount and character of the cases in need of adjudication under a regime of direct statutory regulation would be significantly less burdensome than under the current regime of regulatory conditions.

None of this is to say that a shift of regulation from conditions to binding enactments would be easy. And there may be advantages in gradually experimenting with such a move, agency by agency. However, it cannot casually be taken for granted that it would be insuperably difficult to follow the Constitution's avenues for regulation and adjudication.

The Failure of Judicial Doctrine

It is little comfort that the Supreme Court has occasionally spoken with vigor against the loss of liberty resulting from conditions. Even when merely addressing the most familiar aspect of the problem—the conditions that violate constitutional rights—judicial doctrine has failed to stem the tide.

In *Frost & Frost Trucking Co. v. Railroad Commission* (1926), the Supreme Court grandly declared that government "may not impose conditions which require the relinquishment of constitutional rights. If the state may compel the surrender of one constitutional right as a condition of its favor, it may, in a like manner, compel a surrender of all. It is inconceivable that guarantees embedded in the Constitution of the United States may thus be manipulated out of existence."[2] Decades later, in *Perry v. Sindermann* (1972), the court more modestly cautioned that government "may not deny a benefit to a person on a basis that infringes his constitutionally protected interests—especially, his interest in freedom of speech."[3] And after yet further decades, notwithstanding the court's words, the use of conditions to suppress speech and other freedoms has become commonplace—a matter of agency confidence and judicial indifference.

For example, although judicial doctrine declares that political speech is profoundly protected by the First Amendment, idealistic organizations (including churches, nonprofit schools, and charities) are subject to conditions that sweepingly deny them speech in elections and in advancing or opposing legislation. Judicial doctrine celebrates free speech as the foundation of free government, but broadcasters are still confined by the equal time rule. Doctrine emphasizes the importance of freedom in academic speech; all the same, academic researchers are subject to prior licensing of their speech and publication. These are massive deprivations of speech rights, all made possible by the purchase of submission, and the law seems none the wiser.

When it comes to regulatory conditions, which divest Congress of its legislative power and the courts of their judicial power, the courts are not merely unmoved; they are unaware. Rather than failing to live up to their doctrinal ideals, they do not even have doctrines that recognize the problem.

Checklist

How should conditions be analyzed? Here is a constitutional checklist—focusing on federal conditions, but largely also applicable to state and local conditions.

Spending and Other Privileges

- *Privileges within Enumerated Powers.* There is no general spending power. One therefore must ask whether the condition and the underlying expenditure, benefit, or other privilege is really within the enumerated powers of Congress.

- *Spending.* Nonetheless, if one thinks that Congress has a general spending power, is the condition really part of government spending—that is, does it specify how federal money or other benefits should be used?

- *Nonspending Privileges.* Even if one assumes there is a general spending power, where a condition is tied to a nonspending privilege (such as a plea bargain or a regulatory license), one still must ask whether the condition and underlying privilege really has a foundation in an enumerated federal power.

- *General Welfare.* Regardless of one's view of the constitutional authority for spending, one must inquire about general welfare. If one is relying on a general spending power, does the spending, including any associated condition, provide for the general welfare? And if one recognizes that there is no general spending power, one must ask if tax funds are being used to provide for the general welfare.

Evasion of Legislative and Judicial Pathways

- *Legislative Power.* Are the conditions regulatory? If so—regardless of whether they are specified by Congress or an agency—they divest legislative powers and vest them in private decisions, in violation of Article I of the Constitution. Of course, when agencies specify the conditions, there is an additional vesting of legislative powers in the agencies—also in violation of Article I.

- *Reinforcing Regulatory Conditions.* The only exception to the point about legislative powers occurs when regulatory conditions merely reinforce direct statutory duties. Then it usually is difficult to say that the conditions divest Congress of its legislative powers.

- *Judicial Power.* If regulatory conditions are enforced by agency decisions—as is usually true—then they divest the courts of judicial power and vest it in agencies in violation of Article III of the Constitution.

- *Procedural Rights.* Regulatory conditions typically leave agencies to decide whether there is noncompliance, and such conditions thereby enable agency violations of jury rights, the due process of law, and other procedural rights protected by the Constitution.

Federalism

- *Commandeering.* Do the conditions direct or commandeer the states in violation of the Constitution's division of sovereignty and the freedom of Americans to govern themselves through their states?

- *Supremacy.* Even if federal conditions conflict with state law, they cannot, under the Supremacy Clause, defeat state constitutions or other state law.

- *Defederalization and Privatization.* Do the conditions shift regulatory decisions to state or private agents, thereby defederalizing and sometimes even privatizing federal legislative and judicial power?

Conditions Imposing Unconstitutional Restrictions

- *Consent No Relief from Constitutional Limits.* Does the government rely on consent for relief from its constitutional limits? Consent cannot do this.

- *Consent within and beyond Different Constitutional Limits.* Does the applicable constitutional limit leave room for consent to the condition? If not, the condition imposes an unconstitutional restriction.

Federal Action

- *Not Coercion, but a Range of Federal Action.* Must conditions come with coercion to be held unlawful? Even outside the realm of conditions, constitutionally significant federal action includes a range of conduct, including not only physical coercion but also the obligation of law, various sorts of pressures, and sometimes—notably in violations of structural limits—no force or pressure at all. Accordingly, rather than begin by asking about coercion, one must start by inquiring more broadly about a range of federal action.

- *Force or Pressure amid Consent.* Even when, as in most violations of rights, some sort of force or pressure is requisite, consent does not put an end to the inquiry about force or pressure. To be sure, a conditional restriction that violates a right may be without legal obligation. But if consent to the condition is induced with the force of law or constitutionally significant pressure—or if the condition can be enforced with such force or pressure—then the condition is unconstitutional and void.

- *Regulatory Licensing.* Conditions imposed through regulatory licensing—that which offers relief from a background prohibition—are always induced with the force of law.

- *Undue Influence and Public Policy.* Leaving aside whether a condition is void under the Constitution, one must consider whether it is void and unenforceable under traditional doctrines governing consensual transactions—in particular, the doctrines on undue influence and public policy. Thus, even when a lack of force or pressure saves a condition from being held void under the Constitution, the recitation of the condition in any resulting consensual arrangements can be held void and unenforceable under the doctrines on consensual transactions.

Beyond Consent

- *Regulatory Extortion.* Is the condition imposed through threats of regulatory harassment, including threats to delay or adjust government decisions enforcing or adjudicating regulation? When government secures consent to conditions by threatening to adjust its regulatory decisions (notably including regulatory licensing decisions), there is an abuse of office, extortion, and a denial of due process—quite apart from any takings and other constitutional violations that are specified in the conditions.

- *Regulatory Agents.* Does the condition ask states or private institutions to regulate on its behalf, thereby defederalizing or even privatizing federal legislative and judicial power? Does the condition ask states or private institutions to impose unconstitutional restrictions? The federal government cannot avoid its constitutional limits by enlisting states or private institutions to act in its place; nor can those state or private agents thereby avoid their constitutional or other legal limits.

This checklist is no substitute for careful reasoning, but it at least suggests the range of relevant questions.

Relation to Precedent

Although this book goes further than existing doctrine, its analysis is not as much in conflict with existing precedent as may be supposed. In some areas—such as spending, general welfare, and federalism— this book urges judges to reconsider precedent. But that is not its usual approach.

In many regards, the book more or less echoes precedent. The argument, for example, has much in common with *Speiser v. Randall* on the effect of conditions on procedural rights, *National Federation of Independent Business v. Sebelius* regarding conditions commandeering the states, *Trinity Lutheran Church v. Comer* on the limited need for force or coercion, and *Home Insurance Company v. Morse* as to conditions limiting the exercise of rights in the future. Even when the book is not so closely aligned with precedent, it often picks up on existing doctrinal concerns—for example, about germaneness and proportionality—in order to pursue them more systematically.

In fact, far from generally asking judges to reverse or follow precedent, this book typically presses them to attend to questions they have not previously considered. The courts, for example, have not contemplated how regulatory conditions divest and privatize legislative and judicial power. They have not noticed that when direct restrictions abridge the freedom of speech, similar conditions also abridge this freedom. Though they understand that unconstitutional conditions can be void and unenforceable on constitutional grounds, they have not recognized that such conditions can be void and unenforceable for being contrary to public policy. And they have yet to confront the role of conditions as mechanisms for extortion and for creating regulatory agents.

The bulk of this book's analysis is thus, if not quite terra incognita, then at least undeveloped intellectual territory, which is ripe for exploration. The judges should therefore be less concerned about precedent than about recognizing the landscape of power that lies before them.

The People and the Judges

Underlying the threat from conditions are the failures of Americans and their judges. Not merely government, but the people and their judges have failed to understand the seriousness of the problem and the possibility of concrete legal solutions.

Judges should recognize that the purchase of submission threatens to sideline much of the Constitution, including not only rights but also structural freedoms, such as representative government, adjudication in the courts, and federalism. It may be supposed that conditions have introduced only marginal adjustments to the Constitution—peripheral emendations that are justified as necessary for the public good. But whatever the judges' theories of constitutional change at the margins, they cannot pretend that the constitutional stakes are so negligible, for the purchase of submission has become a massive evasion, which brushes aside one constitutional freedom after another. Far from a minor change, this is a massive repudiation of the Constitution's rights and even structural freedoms.

Having understood the danger, judges should realize that they already have a host of practicable solutions. Instead of wringing their hands about the difficulties of fashioning new approaches, they need only pick up the tools lying in front of them. Some such tools are in the Constitution, which vests legislative powers in Congress and judicial power in the courts, and which secures rights in provisions that often indicate when consent matters and when it does not. Other tools can be found in familiar ideas about force in the inducement and in enforcement and about undue influence and public policy. The concrete character of these solutions should give comfort to judges and should encourage those who seek their decisions.

What is needed, in short, is a sober recognition of the problem and the law's responses. Rather than run to extremes—whether an indifference about the danger or an eagerness for newfangled remedies—the judges should simply do their duty. They should candidly recognize the reality of how Americans are governed these days, and should acknowledge how the law itself bars the purchase of submission.

Thus far, however, many Americans, including the judges, seem blind to how this country is ruled. Many still imagine they live in a republic under laws entirely adopted by elected legislators. Others recognize that an administrative state has developed within the Constitution's United States, but only see that agencies rule through administrative edicts and do not adequately appreciate that they also purchase submission. Sadly, when it comes to the purchase of submission, few judges have the stomach to acknowledge the realities.[4]

But the people of this country cannot afford to live in a judicial fantasy in which the Constitution serves as a fig leaf of legality and a host of legal fictions scarcely cover up the obscene reality of agency power. Whether exercised by administrative or pecuniary means, none of this is law, and much of it slices through the Constitution's structures and rights.

The judges in particular need to understand all of this because the judiciary itself is at risk. Their failure to enforce the Constitution against administrative power has been endorsed as a praiseworthy abnegation of law, and perhaps the same will be said of their failure to confront the unconstitutionality of purchasing submission. But these two wayward pathways have by now gone so far in displacing constitutional avenues of power, and in disregarding constitutionally enumerated powers and rights, that Americans have reason to question whether the judges are really doing their job. And if, in the courts, Americans cannot find what John Locke called *indifferent judges*, the judges should not be surprised if many Americans eventually feel tempted to take their appeals elsewhere.

The judges thus have plenty to worry about. Although there is much blame to go around for the purchase of submission, the judges serve as the nation's constitutional shortstop and have dropped the ball. They are therefore especially at fault. And having done so much to let the problem get out of hand, they should consider fixing it—not by taking any extraordinary measures but simply by following the law.

Political Theory

The purchase of submission sheds much light on the way we are governed now. Americans are currently governed not so much along the Constitution's avenues of power—acts of Congress and of the courts— as along the irregular pathways of administrative commands and conditions on privileges. Though Americans can still vote for their congressional legislators and in this sense are still self-governing, Americans are more typically subject to administrative command or are simply bought off—their tax dollars being used to purchase their submission.

Republican self-government evidently has given way to a strange combination of bureaucratic command and inducement. Yet the combination is not really strange when one considers how government agencies are run by, and more generally are aligned with, the knowledge class—the class of Americans who are more attached to the authority of their academic-style knowledge than to their localities and the authority of local representative choices. From the perspective of most members of the knowledge class, the alleged expertise of agencies gives them or people like them sufficient authority to rule—whether through administrative command or through the purchase of submission. Seemingly opposite modes of control thus flourish together, both being expressions of class dominance.

One of the dangers, as Tocqueville observed, is that government command and largess, though designed with benevolence, can lull the people into acquiescence, leaving them enervated and no longer capable of political self-government.[5] Even when some programs are designed to preserve real choices (for example, by offering only small-scale nudges), the overall tendency is to create what Max Weber called *Ordnungsmenschen*—individuals who feel the need for government direction.[6]

The danger is all the greater because the added pathways—administrative and pecuniary—often shade off into even more thuggish versions of themselves. Administrative power frequently becomes government by raised eyebrow and threat of retaliation. And the purchase of submission frequently develops into a mode of extortion and of control through regulatory agents.

Of course, one could imagine the purchase of conditions as it might have been—confined to genuinely voluntary conditions, which did not regulate Americans or deprive them of their freedoms. From this perspective, one might reasonably observe that carrots seem better than sticks, if only because the former are less likely to provoke. But the use of carrots (and sticks masquerading as carrots) to purchase submission to unconstitutional restrictions and modes of governance is unlikely to lead to a peaceable kingdom. Although there is no guarantee of popular satisfaction when the people are governed along the avenues established by the Constitution, the purchase of submission almost inevitably leads to widespread discontent.

In departing from the Constitution's pathway for regulation, this system of control displaces the satisfactions of political participation and self-government. It thereby, moreover, tends to short-circuit the very mechanism that ordinarily gets the government to recognize and avoid popular discontent. And in circumventing the Constitution's route for judicial decisions, this mode of power supplants adjudication by independent judges—leaving Americans with a sense that they cannot get unbiased resolutions of their controversies with the government.

Not only the people but also the government are therefore ill-served by the purchase of submission. And the collision between a people with high constitutional ideals and a government that purchases its way out of representative lawmaking, unbiased judging, and constitutional rights is not apt to end well for anyone.

Conditions are too much with us; late and soon,
Spending and getting, they lay waste our powers;—
Little we see in the Constitution that is ours;
We have given our rights away, a sordid boon!

Notes

Introduction

1. Jenia I. Turner, "Judicial Participation in Plea Negotiations: A Comparative View," *American Journal of Comparative Law* 54 (2006): 199, 205. Throughout this book, I have modernized the spelling and capitalization of quotations (except those from the Constitution) and have often adjusted the capitalization of initial letters in quotations.

2. The Solomon Amendment, adopted in 1995, denied Department of Defense funding to subunits of academic institutions that "in effect, prevent" military recruitment on campus, and when, in 1997, it became clear that this was not enough of a threat, Congress expanded the amendment's reach so that it also cut off federal funds coming through grants and contracts from the Departments of Labor, Health and Human Services, Education, and Transportation. In 2000, the Department of Defense adopted regulations broadening conditions to bar such funding to "all sub-elements of such an institution," thus bringing the economic pressure to bear on entire universities. The department, moreover, interpreted the statutory condition—which merely stated that institutions should not "in effect, prevent" recruitment—to mean that institutions could not deny the Defense Department recruitment access "at least equal in quality and scope" to that enjoyed by other employers.

3. "Economic Report of the President," February 2018, 556, Table B-21. The Budget of the US Government reports somewhat higher numbers for total outlays to state and local governments, but those are the amounts available, not the amounts actually spent.

4. "Office of Management and Budget, Historical Tables, Table 1.1—Summary of Receipts, Outlays, and Surpluses or Deficits, 1789–2025," https:// www.whitehouse.gov/omb/historical-tables/.

5. Terence P. Jeffrey, "1 Federal Department Now Spending $100 Billion per Month," CNSnews, July 10, 2019, https://www.cnsnews.com/commentary /terence-p-jeffrey/1-federal-department-now-spending-100-billion-month.

6. In other words, the doctrines on speech content (such as content and viewpoint discrimination) developed to police the boundaries of the freedom from after-the-fact constraints on speech and should not be considered applicable to the freedom from prior review or licensing, which is a freedom from a particularly dangerous method of control.

7. For Franklin D. Roosevelt, see Betty Houchin Winfield, *FDR and the News Media* (New York: Columbia University Press, 1994), 110. For both FDR and JFK, see Paul Matzko, "The Sordid History of the Fairness Doctrine," Reason (January 30, 2021), at https://reason.com/2021/01/30/the -sordid-history-of-the-fairness-doctrine/. The IRS delayed and denied §501(c)(3) status to groups on the basis of their politics, especially their ties to the Tea Party. See *Linchpins of Liberty et al. v. United States of America*, D.C. Cir. Ct. 2017, https://www.courthousenews.com/wp-content/uploads/2017 /10/LINCHPINS-OF-LIBERTY-CONSENT-ORDER.pdf. A study of IRB licensing reveals political bias in reviewing and censoring conservative research. Stephen J. Ceci, Douglas Peters, and Jonathan Plotkin, "Human Subjects Review, Personal Values, and the Regulation of Social Science Research," *American Psychologist* 40 (1985): 995.

8. Although framed in terms of "contract," Henry Sumner Maine's theory of the shift from status to contract does not rest narrowly on common law notions of contract but encompasses the full range of consensual transactions and is thus applicable to conditions on government privileges, even when they are not contractual.

9. Of course, artificial persons cannot seek habeas corpus, but that is because they naturally cannot be imprisoned, not because the Constitution debars any class of claimants.

10. For further discussion of this equality and its structural significance for the protection of rights, see Philip Hamburger, *Liberal Suppression: Section 501(c)(3) and the Taxation of Speech* (Chicago: University of Chicago Press, 2018), 289.

11. Ruth W. Grant, *Strings Attached: Untangling the Ethics of Incentives* (New York: Russell Sage Foundation, 2012), 6–7, 41. Note also Alanson W. Willcox's comment: "The Federal grant-in-aid is only now beginning to get . . . the attention that is its due as an instrument of government." Alanson W. Willcox, "The Function and Nature of Grants," *Administrative Law Review* 22 (1970): 125. Richard Cappalli observes that the government "converted the federal grant into a powerful instrument of control." Richard B. Cappalli, *Federal Grants and Cooperative Agreements: Law, Policy, and Practice* (Wilmette, IL: Callaghan, 1982), chap. 11, 54, §11:24.

12. Philip Hamburger, *Is Administrative Law Unlawful?* (Chicago: University of Chicago Press, 2014), 1.

13. Grant, *Strings Attached*, 12.

14. Martha Derthick, *The Influence of Federal Grants: Public Assistance in Massachusetts* (Cambridge, MA: Harvard University Press, 1970).

15. James L. Buckley, *Saving Congress from Itself: Emancipating the States and Empowering the People* (New York: Encounter Books, 2014); Thomas R. McCoy and Barry Friedman, "Conditional Spending: Federalism's Trojan Horse," *Supreme Court Review* 85 (1988).

16. Amid the vast literature on conditions unconstitutionally restricting rights is my own flawed effort: "Unconstitutional Conditions: The Irrelevance of Consent," *Virginia Law Review* 98 (2012): 479.

Other contributions include Howard E. Abrams, "Systemic Coercion: Unconstitutional Conditions in the Criminal Law," *Journal of Criminal Law and Criminalization* 72 (1981): 128; Catherine R. Albiston and Laura Beth Nielsen, "Welfare Queens and Other Fairy Tales: Welfare Reform and Unconstitutional Reproductive Controls," *Howard Law Journal* 38 (1995): 473, 489–491; Thomas J. Andrews, "Screening Travelers at the Airport to Prevent Hijacking: A New Challenge for the Unconstitutional Conditions Doctrine," *Arizona Law Review* 16 (1974): 658; Lynn A. Baker, "Conditional Federal Spending after *Lopez*," *Columbia Law Review* 95 (1995): 1911; Lynn A. Baker, "The Prices of Rights: Toward a Positive Theory of Unconstitutional Conditions," *Cornell Law Review* 75 (1990): 1185; Mitchell N.

Berman, "Coercion without Baselines: Unconstitutional Conditions in Three Dimensions," *Georgetown Law Journal* 90 (2001): 1; Mitchell N. Berman, "Commercial Speech and the Unconstitutional Conditions Doctrine: A Second Look at the 'Greater Includes the Lesser,'" *Vanderbilt Law Review* 55 (2002): 693; Mitchell N. Berman, "Coercion, Compulsion, and the Medicaid Expansion: A Study in the Doctrine of Unconstitutional Conditions," *Texas Law Review* 91 (2013): 1283; Peter M. Brody, "Confidentiality Clauses in Research Contracts and Grants: Are They 'Unconstitutional Conditions'?," *Public Contract Law Journal* 22 (1993): 447; Harold H. Bruff, "Unconstitutional Conditions upon Public Employments: New Departures in the Protections of First Amendment Rights," *Hastings Law Journal* 21 (1969): 129; Jesse H. Choper, "The Supreme Court and Unconstitutional Conditions: Federalism and Individual Rights," *Cornell Journal of Law and Public Policy* 4 (1994): 460; David Cole, "Beyond Unconstitutional Conditions: Charting Spheres of Neutrality in Government-Funded Speech," *New York Law Review* 67 (1992): 675; Adam B. Cox and Adam M. Samaha, "Unconstitutional Conditions Questions Everywhere: The Implications of Exit and Sorting for Constitutional Law and Theory," *Journal of Legal Analysis* 5 (2013): 61; Einer Elhauge, "Contrived Threats versus Uncontrived Warnings: A General Solution to the Puzzles of Contractual Duress, Unconstitutional Conditions, and Blackmail," *University of Chicago Law Review* 83 (2016): 503; Richard A. Epstein, "Unconstitutional Conditions, State Power, and the Limits of Consent," *Harvard Law Review* 102 (1988): 4, 197; Daniel A. Farber, "Another View of the Quagmire: Unconstitutional Conditions and Contract Theory," *Florida State Law Review* 33 (2006): 917; Gary Feinerman, "Unconstitutional Conditions: The Crossroads of Substantive Rights and Equal Protection," *Stanford Law Review* 43 (1991): 1369; John D. French, "Unconstitutional Conditions: An Analysis," *Georgetown Law Review* 50 (1961): 234; Laura M. Friedman, "Family Cap and the Unconstitutional Conditions Doctrine: Scrutinizing a Welfare Woman's Right to Bear Children," *Ohio State Law Journal* 56 (1995): 637; Brooks R. Fudenberg, "Unconstitutional Conditions and Greater Powers: A Separability Approach," *UCLA Law Review* 43 (1995): 371; Edward J. Fuhr, "The Doctrine of Unconstitutional Conditions and the First Amendment," *Case Western Reserve Law Review* 39 (1988–1989): 97; Karen Gross, "The Debtor as Modern Day Peon:

A Problem of Unconstitutional Conditions," *Notre Dame Law Review* 65 (1990): 165; Robert L. Hale, "Unconstitutional Conditions and Constitutional Rights," *Columbia Law Review* 35 (1935): 321; Rachel Hannaford, "Trading Due Process Rights for Shelter: Rucker and Unconstitutional Conditions in Public Housing Leases," *University of Pennsylvania Journal of Constitutional Law* 6 (2003): 139; Carole M. Hirsch, "When the War on Poverty Became the War on Poor, Pregnant Women: Political Rhetoric, the Unconstitutional Conditions Doctrine, and the Family Cap Restriction," *William and Mary Journal of Women and Law* 8 (2002): 335; Ginny Kim, "Unconstitutional Conditions: Is the Fourth Amendment for Sale in Public Housing?," *American Criminal Law Review* 33 (1995): 165; Seth F. Kreimer, "Allocational Sanctions: The Problem of Negative Rights in a Positive State," *University of Pennsylvania Law Review* 132 (1984): 1293, 1301; Renée Lettow Lerner, "Unconstitutional Conditions, Germaneness, and Institutional Review Boards," *Northwestern Law Review* 101 (2007): 775; William P. Marshall, "Towards a Nonunifying Theory of Unconstitutional Conditions: The Example of the Religion Clauses," *San Diego Law Review* 26 (1989): 243, 243–244; Michael W. McConnell, "Unconstitutional Conditions: Unrecognized Implications for the Establishment Clause," *San Diego Law Review* 26 (1989): 255; James McGrath, "Abstinence-Only Adolescent Education: Ineffective, Unpopular, and Unconstitutional," *University of San Francisco Law Review* 38 (2004): 665; Maurice H. Merrill, "Unconstitutional Conditions," *University of Pennsylvania Law Review and American Law Register* 77 (1929): 879; Thomas W. Merrill, "*Dolan v. City of Tigard*: Constitutional Rights as Public Goods," *Denver Law Review* 72 (1995): 859; Julie A. Nice, "Making Conditions Constitutional by Attaching Them to Welfare: The Danger of Selective Contextual Ignorance of the Unconstitutional Conditions Doctrine," *Denver University Law Review* 72 (1995): 971; Laurence C. Nolan, "The Unconstitutional Conditions Doctrine and Mandating Norplant for Women on Welfare Discourse," *Journal of Gender and the Law* 3 (1994): 15, 17; Robert M. O'Neil, "Unconstitutional Conditions: Welfare Benefits with Strings Attached," *California Law Review* 54 (1966): 443; Michael Stokes Paulsen, "A Funny Thing Happened on the Way to the Limited Public Forum: Unconstitutional Conditions on 'Equal Access' for Religious Speakers and Groups," *University of California Davis Law Review* 29 (1996):

653; Allen Redlich, "Unconstitutional Conditions on Welfare Eligibility," *Wisconsin Law Review* 450 (1970); Dorothy Roberts, "The Only Good Poor Woman: Unconstitutional Conditions and Welfare," *Denver University Law Review* 72 (1995): 931; Jane Rutherford, "The Meek Shall Inherit the Earth: A Power-Based Theory of Unconstitutional Conditions on Religion," *Denver Law Review* 72 (1995): 909; Samuel C. Salganik, "What the Unconstitutional Conditions Doctrine Can Teach Us about ERISA Preemption: Is It Possible to Consistently Identify 'Coercive' Pay-or-Play Schemes?" *Columbia Law Review* 109 (2009): 1482; Frederick Schauer, "Too Hard: Unconstitutional Conditions and the Chimera of Constitutional Consistency," *Denver University Law Review* 72 (1995): 989; David J. Schwartz, "Campaign Finance Reform: Limits on Out-of-State Contributions and the Question of Unconstitutional Conditions," *University of Dayton Law Review* 23 (1997): 87; Paul M. Secunda, "Lawrence's Quintessential Millian Moment and Its Impact on the Doctrine of Unconstitutional Conditions," *Villanova Law Review* 50 (2005): 117; Kenneth W. Simons, "Offers, Threats, and Unconstitutional Conditions," *San Diego Law Review* 26 (1989): 289; Kathleen Sullivan, "Unconstitutional Conditions," *Harvard Law Review* 102 (1989): 1413, 1490; Cass Sunstein, "Why the Unconstitutional Conditions Doctrine Is an Anachronism (with Particular Reference to Religion, Speech, and Abortion)," *Boston University Law Review* 70 (1990): 593.

17. Charles A. Reich, "The New Property," *Yale Law Journal* 73 (1964): 733.

18. The negligible process gains for benefits also came with overt deprivations of due process in cases involving government constraints. See Philip Hamburger, "The Administrative Evasion of Procedural Rights," *New York University Journal of Law & Liberty* 11 (2018): 915, 954–955.

19. Alexis de Tocqueville, "What Type of Despotism Democratic Nations Have to Fear," part IV, chap. 6, in *Democracy in America*, ed. Eduardo Nolla, trans. James T. Schleifer (Indianapolis, IN: Liberty Fund, 2010), 1251, 1254.

Chapter 1: Poorly Understood

1. Richard H. Thaler and Cass R. Sunstein, *Nudge: Improving Decisions about Health, Wealth, and Happiness* (New Haven, CT: Yale University Press, 2008).

2. Seth F. Kreimer, "Allocational Sanctions: The Problem of Negative Rights in a Positive State," *University of Pennsylvania Law Review* 132 (1984): 1293, 1359–1374.

3. Richard A. Epstein, "Unconstitutional Conditions, State Power, and the Limits of Consent," *Harvard Law Review* 102 (1988): 4, 14–15.

4. Kathleen Sullivan, "Unconstitutional Conditions," *Harvard Law Review* 102 (1989): 1413, 1490; see also Dorothy Roberts, "The Only Good Poor Woman: Unconstitutional Conditions and Welfare," *Denver University Law Review* 72 (1995): 931, 939.

5. Martha Derthick writes, "The intergovernmental sharing of functions in general, and the grant system in particular, grew up bit by bit as political institutions responded to particular circumstances in an *ad hoc* fashion . . . without any systematic doctrinal justification." Martha Derthick, *The Influence of Federal Grants: Public Assistance in Massachusetts* (Cambridge, MA: Harvard University Press, 1970), 219.

6. *Hess v. Pawloski*, 274 U.S. 352 (1927).

7. *McAuliffe v. Mayor & Board of Aldermen*, 155 Mass. 216, 220 (1892).

8. https://www.usgovernmentspending.com/federal_spending_chart; https://www.usgovernmentspending.com/spending_chart_1792_2016USp_XXsllil11mcn_F0f_US_Federal_Spending_since_the_Founding.

9. "Economic Report of the President," February 2018, 556, Table B-21. The Budget of the US Government reports somewhat higher numbers for total outlays to state and local governments, but those are the amounts available, not the amounts actually spent.

10. Center on Budget and Policy Priorities, "Federal Aid to State and Local Governments," April 19, 2018, https://www.cbpp.org/research/state-budget-and-tax/federal-aid-to-state-and-local-governments.

11. Martha Derthick writes about grants to states and localities: "Critical public decisions" are arrived at through a process that is "shielded from the public view and from routine participation by legislatures." Derthick, *The Influence of Federal Grants*, 242. She also notes, "Negotiations are carried on privately." Derthick, *The Influence of Federal Grants*, 209. For the limited ability of nonparties to participate in such negotiations, see *National Welfare Rights Organization et al. v. Finch*, 429 F.2d 725 (D.C. Cir. 1970).

12. *Pennhurst State School and Hospital v. Halderman*, 451 U.S. 1, 17 (1981).

13. Similarly, see Paul G. Dembling and Malcolm S. Mason, *Essentials of Grant Law Practice* (Philadelphia: ALI-ABA, 1991), 1.

14. 26 U.S.C. §170; 26 U.S.C. §501(c)(3). Another example from the same era was the Social Security Act of 1935, which taxed employers but allowed an employer to credit or offset against this tax the amount he had contributed under a state unemployment law—provided that the state law had been certified by the Federal Social Security Board to satisfy various federal conditions. One condition, for example, was that by state law, money paid into the state unemployment fund shall be used solely in the payment of compensation, exclusive of expenses of administration. Although this scheme was upheld in *Steward Machine Company v. Davis* (1937), it probably should have been condemned at least as a mode of regulating and commandeering.

A contemporary example of how conditions can adjust incentives for third parties can be found in the Real ID Act, which sets national standards for drivers' licenses. Although states can choose whether or not to adopt such standards, residents of states that do not comply are unable to travel by air, as Homeland Security requires travelers to have "secure" drivers' licenses as a condition of air travel. See Paul Posner, "The Politics of Coercive Federalism in the Bush Era," *Publius* 37 (2007): 390, 398, 400.

15. *Koontz v. St. Johns River Water Management District*, 570 U.S. 595 (2013).

16. *National Endowment for the Arts v. Finley*, 524 U.S. 569 (1998).

17. *National Endowment for the Arts v. Finley*, 524 U.S. 581 (1998).

18. The Community Reinvestment Act of 1977 offers another example of a condition in the form of a consideration. Under this statute, federal financial supervisory agencies must "take into account" a financial institution's record of "meeting the credit needs of its entire community, including low- and moderate-income neighborhoods" when evaluating the institution's application for a deposit facility. 2 U.S.C. §2903(a).

19. Adam B. Cox and Adam M. Samaha, "Unconstitutional Conditions Questions Everywhere: The Implications of Exit and Sorting for Constitutional Law and Theory," *Journal of Legal Analysis* 5 (2013): 61.

20. Sullivan, "Unconstitutional Conditions," 1413, 1490; see also Roberts, "The Only Good Poor Woman," 931.

21. Daniel A. Farber, "Another View of the Quagmire: Unconstitutional Conditions and Contract Theory," *Florida State Law Review* 33 (2006): 917, 930.

22. Laura M. Friedman, "Family Cap and the Unconstitutional Conditions Doctrine: Scrutinizing a Welfare Woman's Right to Bear Children," *Ohio State Law Journal* 56 (1995): 637; Laurence C. Nolan, "The Unconstitutional Conditions Doctrine and Mandating Norplant for Women on Welfare Discourse," *Journal of Gender and the Law* 3 (1994): 15, 17; Catherine R. Albiston and Laura Beth Nielsen, "Welfare Queens and Other Fairy Tales: Welfare Reform and Unconstitutional Reproductive Controls," *Howard Law Journal* 38 (1995): 473, 489–491; Roberts, "The Only Good Poor Woman," 931.

23. Ginny Kim, "Unconstitutional Conditions: Is the Fourth Amendment for Sale in Public Housing?," *American Criminal Law Review* 33 (1995): 165.

24. Rachel Hannaford, "Trading Due Process Rights for Shelter: *Rucker* and Unconstitutional Conditions in Public Housing Leases," *University of Pennsylvania Journal of Constitutional Law* 6 (2003): 139.

25. Hannaford, "Trading Due Process Rights for Shelter," 143.

Chapter 2: Examples

1. *Wyman v. James*, 400 U.S. 309 (1971). Many searches at an earlier period were brutish—as when homes were searched after midnight to determine if men were present. See Charles A. Reich, "The New Property," *Yale Law Journal* 73 (1964): 733, 761.

2. HHS, ASPE, Indicators of Welfare Dependence: Annual Report to Congress, 2001. Aid to Families with Dependent Children (AFDC) and Temporary Assistance for Needy Families (TANF), at https://aspe.hhs.gov /report/indicators-welfare-dependence-annual-report-congress-2001/aid -families-dependent-children-afdc-and-temporary-assistance-needy -families-tanf; Eleanor Baugher and Leatha Lamison-White, *Poverty in the United States: 1995* (Washington, DC: US Department of Commerce, Economic and Statistics Administration, Bureau of the Census, 1995), v.

The ratio of AFDC families to families in poverty is less clear for New York State. It is known, however, that in 1995, just over 450,000 New York families were on AFDC (including over 1,240,000 individuals). Office of Family Assistance, "Caseload Data 1995 (AFDC Total)," https://www.acf.hhs .gov/ofa/resource/caseload-data-afdc-1995-total.

3. Incidentally, "by 1992, the majority of AFDC recipients were single mothers, rather than widows." Olga Khazan, "How Welfare Reform Left Single Moms Behind," *The Atlantic*, May 12, 2014.

4. 23 U.S.C. §158.

5. 8 U.S.C. §1373.

6. 47 U.S.C. §303; 18 U.S.C. §1464.

7. *Red Lion Broadcasting Co., Inc. v. FCC*, 395 U.S. 367 (1969); *Syracuse Peace Council v. Federal Communications Commission*, 867 F.2d 654 (D.C. Cir. 1989); Brooks Boliek, "FCC Finally Kills Off Fairness Doctrine," *Politico*, August 22, 2011. For the suppression of political opponents, see Paul Matzko, "The Sordid History of the Fairness Doctrine," Reason, January 30, 2021, https://reason.com/2021/01/30/the-sordid-history-of-the-fairness-doctrine / .

8. 47 U.S.C. §315.

9. *United States v. Causby*, 328 U.S. 256, 263 (1946).

10. 26 U.S.C. §§170 and 501(c)(3). Note that the organizations must give up more than just their freedoms of speech and the press; they also must sacrifice their right to petition, their free exercise of religion, and even their freedom from an establishment and their due process and jury rights. See Philip Hamburger, *Liberal Suppression: Section 501(c)(3) and the Taxation of Speech* (Chicago: University of Chicago Press, 2018), 190–223. But there is no need to explore all of the losses here. See also Hamburger, *Liberal Suppression*, 243–244.

11. For the complex question of whether the exemption is really a subsidy or tax expenditure, see Hamburger, *Liberal Suppression*, 173–181.

12. 26 U.S.C. §527.

13. Hamburger, *Liberal Suppression*, 32–33, 245–246.

14. Hamburger, *Liberal Suppression*, 243–244.

15. Hamburger, *Liberal Suppression*, 87–89.

16. For the scholarship underlying this account of IRBs, including accounts of Beecher's scholarship and what it failed to disclose, see Philip

Hamburger, "IRB Licensing," in *Who's Afraid of Academic Freedom?* (New York: Columbia University Press, 2014), 153; Philip Hamburger, "Getting Permission," *Northwestern Law Review* 101 (2007): 405; Philip Hamburger, "The New Censorship: Institutional Review Boards," *2004 Supreme Court Review* 271 (2005).

17. Hamburger, "IRB Licensing," 158–159; Hamburger, "Getting Permission," 405, 441; Hamburger, "The New Censorship," 271, 328–329.

18. Hamburger, "IRB Licensing," 158–159; Hamburger, "Getting Permission," 405, 445–446; Hamburger, "The New Censorship," 271, 331n140.

19. The cross collateralization of conditions is accomplished by running all grants for individual researchers through their institutions, which first must submit an assurance to the government. For the Federalwide Assurance for the Protection of Human Subjects, see https://www.hhs.gov/ohrp/register -irbs-and-obtain-fwas/fwas/fwa-protection-of-human-subjecct/index.html.

20. 46 C.F.R. §46.102(e). Italics have been added for emphasis.

21. 46 C.F.R. §46.102(l). Italics have been added for emphasis.

22. 46 C.F.R. §46.104(d)(2).

23. 46 C.F.R. §46.111(a)(2).

24. Office for Human Research Protections, *Institutional Review Board Guidebook*, chap. 3, part A. Although this publication is no longer current, its assumptions persist among IRBs.

25. Peter Pronovost, Dale Needham, Sean Berenholz, et al., "An Intervention to Decrease Catheter-Related Bloodstream Infections in the ICU," *New England Journal of Medicine* 2725 (2006): 355; Allison Lipitz-Snyderman, Dale M. Needham, Elizabeth Colantuoni, et al., "The Ability of Intensive Care Units to Maintain Zero Central Line–Associated Bloodstream Infections," *Journal of the American Medical Association* 171 (2011). Until then, "catheter-related bloodstream infections kill[ed] at least 17,000 patients every year." Kevin B. O'Reilly, "Effort Cuts Down Catheter-Related Infections," Amednews.com, January 22, 2007.

26. 46 C.F.R. §46.111(a)(3).

27. Philip Hamburger, "HHS's Contribution to Black Death Rates," Liberty Law Blog, January 8, 2015, https://www.lawliberty.org/2015/01/08 /hhss-contribution-to-black-death-rates/. More generally, see Vivian W. Pinn, "From Exclusion to Inclusion: Participation in Biomedical Research and the

Legacy of the Public Health Syphilis Study at Tuskegee," in *The Search for the Legacy of the USPHS Syphilis Study*, ed. Ralph V. Katz and Rueben C. Warren (Lanham, MD: Lexington Books, 2011), 1. IRB consent procedures also harm Black individuals. As noted by Simon Whitney, "African American infant mortality in the United States is double that of white infants," but though "the IRB system's stated goals include the pursuit of justice and the protection of vulnerable groups; yet . . . as a result of IRB action," a major study of premature infants at eighteen medical centers over four years ended up being "more applicable to white infants than to black infants." Simon N. Whitney, "The Python's Embrace: Clinical Research Regulation by Institutional Review Boards," *Pediatrics* 129 (March 2012): 576.

28. The consequences for pregnant women—at least under FDA regulations—were recently acknowledged in relation to COVID-19: "When federal regulators approved the first two COVID-19 vaccines for general use in the United States, they gave pregnant people and those who are breastfeeding the option to decide whether to get the immunization. But they stopped short of recommending it outright. That's because pregnancy is a medical condition that typically excludes people from participating in clinical trials to study the safety and effectiveness of a drug. Excluding this group of people meant there was little data available." At the Forefront, "The mRNA COVID-19 Vaccine and Pregnancy: What You Need to Know if You're Pregnant, Trying to Get Pregnant, or Breastfeeding," UChicago Medicine.org, February 4, 2021, https://www.uchicagomedicine.org/forefront /coronavirus-disease-covid-19/mrna-covid-19-vaccine-pregnancy -breastfeeding.

Chapter 3: Regulatory Conditions

1. Lynn A. Baker, "The Prices of Rights: Toward a Positive Theory of Unconstitutional Conditions," *Cornell Law Review* 75 (1990): 1185, 1217; Lynn A. Baker, "Conditional Federal Spending after *Lopez*," *Columbia Law Review* 95 (1995): 1911, 1916; Thomas R. McCoy and Barry Friedman, "Conditional Spending: Federalism's Trojan Horse," *Supreme Court Review* 85 (1988); Renée Lettow Lerner, "Unconstitutional Conditions, Germaneness, and Institutional Review Boards," *Northwestern Law Review* 101 (2007): 775, 788–789.

2. *South Dakota v. Dole*, 483 U.S. 203, 216 (1987).

3. Department of Health and Human Services, Office for Human Research Protections, https://www.hhs.gov/ohrp/.

4. 23 U.S.C. §158.

5. Congress has used crossover conditions since at least 1965, and it has long been understood that such provisions have "altered drastically the traditional legal concept under which each grant is viewed as a quasi-contractual relationship, freely entered into." Advisory Commission on Intergovernmental Relations, *Twelfth Annual Report: Federalism in 1970* (Washington, DC: Advisory Commission on Intergovernmental Relations, 1971), 57. Examples can be found in the Highway Beautification Act of 1965, 23 U.S.C. §131, the National Health Planning and Resource Development Act of 1974, 42 U.S.C. §300m(d), and the Federal Aid Highway Amendments of 1977, 42 U.S.C. §7506(c), §7616. Many crossover conditions are "federalwide" conditions. The Office of Management and Budget found fifty-nine of them in 1980. Martha Derthick, "Crossing Thresholds: Federalism in the 1960s," in *Keeping the Compound Republic: Essays in American Federalism* (Washington, DC: Brookings Institution Press, 2001), 150.

6. *South Dakota v. Dole*, 483 U.S. 203 (1987). Indeed, the Congressional Budget Office recognizes *Dole* as a paradigmatic example of a condition that does not concern the funded activity: "The federal government attaches conditions to many intergovernmental grants requiring recipient state and local governments to take certain prescribed actions [that] may have little direct bearing on the grant program, such as the requirement that, in order to receive highway funding, a state must set a minimum drinking age of 21." Congressional Budget Office, "Federal Grants to State and Local Governments," March 2013, https://www.cbo.gov/sites/default/files/113th-congress-2013-2014/reports/03-05-13federalgrantsonecol.pdf.

7. *South Dakota v. Dole*, 483 U.S. 215 (1987).

8. Lerner, "Unconstitutional Conditions," 775, 778–785.

9. *United States Agency for International Development v. Alliance for Open Society International, Inc.*, 570 U.S. 205 (2013). Incidentally, the Supreme Court acknowledged that "the definition of a particular program can always be manipulated to subsume the challenged condition" but aptly noted that judges must recognize the realities rather than allow the First Amendment to be "reduced to a simple semantic exercise."

10. There were also other changes in the condition. In 1997, Congress expanded the Solomon Amendment's reach so that it cut off federal funds coming through grants and contracts from not only the Department of Defense but also the Departments of Labor, HHS, Education, and Transportation. And in 2000, the Department of Defense interpreted the statutory condition—which merely stated that institutions should not "in effect, prevent" recruitment—to mean that institutions could not deny the Defense Department recruitment access "at least equal in quality and scope" to that enjoyed by other employers.

11. Paul Posner, "The Politics of Coercive Federalism in the Bush Era," *Publius: The Journal of Federalism* 37 (Summer 2007): 390, 401.

12. *FCC v. League of Women Voters*, 468 U.S. 364 (1984).

13. Along the same lines, the government imposes such conditions on idealistic organizations when it authorizes donors to deduct their charitable donations from their income. Although it has good reason to avoid subsidizing the political speech of the idealistic organizations, it could have achieved this end by narrowly denying deductions for the donations that get used for such speech. But instead of limiting deductibility for misused donations, it uses deductibility for donors to impose the same sweeping speech conditions on almost all idealistic organizations. Nor is this a surprise, for suppression of the political speech of churches and churchy organizations was precisely the regulatory goal of nativists and others who demanded such speech limits, including the imperial wizard of the Ku Klux Klan, who initially proposed the speech restrictions. Philip Hamburger, *Liberal Suppression: Section 501(c)(3) and the Taxation of Speech* (Chicago: University of Chicago Press, 2018), 87–89.

14. *National Federation of Independent Business v. Sebelius*, 567 U.S. 519 (2012).

15. *Home Insurance Company v. Morse*, 87 U.S. 445, 451 (1874).

Chapter 4: Spending

1. The history of the spending power is recounted in Jeffrey T. Renz, "What Spending Clause? (Or the President's Paramour): An Examination of the Views of Hamilton, Madison, and Story on Article I, Section 8, Clause 1

of the United States Constitution," *John Marshall Law Review* 33, no. 81 (1999). Although Renz notes it only in passing, there was a surreptitious attempt to create a separate spending power by adding a semicolon after the word *Excise*. Renz, "What Spending Clause?," 105. On September 4, 1787, the Committee of Eleven reported to the convention a draft of what became Section 8, which read: "The Legislature shall have power to lay and collect taxes, duties, imposts, and excises, to pay the debts and provide for the common defense and general welfare of the United States." Max Farrand, ed., *The Records of the Federal Convention of 1787* (New Haven, CT: Yale University Press, 1911), 2:493. On September 12, the Committee on Style reported a version of this paragraph, and the next day, it distributed a printed version of its report. Farrand, *Records of the Federal Convention*, 3:457, appendix A, document cccxliv (memoirs of John Quincy Adams). In this printed report, however, there was not a comma, but a semicolon after the word *Excises*—so that "to pay the Debts and provide for the common Defence and general Welfare of the United States" became an additional power, conjoined to the power to tax, rather than merely a limitation on it. Farrand, *Records of the Federal Convention*, 2:594. The convention, however, recognized this alteration and rejected it. At stake was simply the addition and removal of a single dot above a comma.

Its importance was recognized in early debates about the Constitution. For example, on June 19, 1798, Albert Gallitin told the House of Representatives:

> He was well informed that those words had originally been inserted in the Constitution as a limitation to the power of laying taxes. After the limitation had been agreed to, and the Constitution was completed, a member of the Convention, (he was one of the members who represented the State of Pennsylvania [i.e., Gouverneur Morris]) being one of a committee of revisal and arrangement, attempted to throw these words into a distinct paragraph, so as to create not a limitation, but a distinct power. The trick, however, was discovered by a member from Connecticut, now deceased, and the words restored as they now stand.

Farrand, *Records of the Federal Convention*, 3:379, appendix A, document cclxxxi.

2. Alexander Hamilton, "Opinion on the Constitutionality of an Act to Establish a Bank" (February 23, 1791), *The Papers of George Washington*, Presidential Series (Charlottesville: University Press of Virginia, 1998), 7:425.

3. James Madison, Speech on the Bank Bill, HR (February 2, 1791).

4. Revealingly, the strongest alternative view to that presented in the text is not that the general welfare clause was a stand-alone power but rather that it was designed to be ambiguous. David S. Schwartz, "The Strategic Ambiguity of the General Welfare Clause," SSRN, at https://ssrn.com /abstract=3671883. But this is improbable for several reasons.

First, strategic ambiguity in drafting was not generally endorsed by the framers or ratifiers. On the contrary, almost all of them who discussed drafting indicated their desire for the Constitution to be as clear as possible. Indeed, the only formal principles of drafting to come out of the framing convention included an injunction to use "precise language." Philip Hamburger, "The Constitution's Accommodation of Social Change," *Michigan Law Review* 88 (1989): 239, 323.

Second, the strategic ambiguity article dismisses the story about Gouverneur Morris without contrary evidence.

Third, even if the Morris story could be brushed aside, it is difficult to discount the undisputed drafting history—that the word *Excise* was initially followed by a comma, that the Committee of Style changed it to a semicolon, and that the convention then restored the comma. The article questions the relevance of this history by observing that the initial comma appeared in manuscript and claiming that the manuscript would not have been seen by most framers. But even if, improbably, the framers did not read their manuscripts, they obviously saw the semicolon in print and rejected it.

Fourth, the article attempts very nearly to rewrite the Constitution's text by noting that some eighteenth-century writings used commas and semicolons interchangeably. The suggestion is that the comma after "Excises" should be read akin to a semicolon. But the convention rejected a semicolon there, and the Constitution's enumeration of powers is very deliberate in its use of commas and semicolons. The article's attempt to discount the difference between the comma and a semicolon is thus almost a rewriting of the text and practically an admission that the Constitution as written does not support a general spending power, let alone a general welfare power.

Fifth, the argument on behalf of strategic ambiguity and a possible general welfare power would have one believe that the relevant paragraph zigzagged—that it began with a taxing power, switched to a power to pay debts and provide for the general welfare, and then doubled back to qualify the taxing power with a uniformity requirement. It is as if the Constitution were written by a drunk driver.

5. *South Dakota v. Dole*, 483 U.S. 203, 210 (1987).

6. *National Federation of Independent Business v. Sebelius*, 567 U.S. 519 (2012). Note also the Supreme Court's opinion in *Butler:* "If the taxing power may not be used as the instrument to enforce a regulation of matters of state concern with respect to which the Congress has no authority to interfere, may it, as in the present case, be employed to raise the money necessary to purchase a compliance which the Congress is powerless to command?" *United States v. Butler*, 297 U.S. 1, 70 (1936).

7. *Massachusetts v. United States*, 435 U.S. 444 (1978).

8. *Ivanhoe Irrigation District v. McCracken*, 357 U.S. 275, 295 (1958).

9. *South Dakota v. Dole*, 483 U.S. 203, 208 (1987).

10. *National Federation of Independent Business v. Sebelius*, 567 U.S. 519 (2012).

11. *South Dakota v. Dole*, 483 U.S. 203, 207 and n2 (1987).

12. *South Dakota v. Dole*, 483 U.S. 203, 17 (1987).

13. James L. Buckley, *Saving Congress from Itself: Emancipating the States and Empowering Their People* (New York: Encounter Books, 2014), 19–56.

Chapter 5: Divesting and Privatizing Government Powers

1. Gillian E. Metzger, "Privatization as Delegation," *Columbia Law Review* 103 (2003): 1367; Jon Michaels, *Constitutional Coup: Privatization's Threat to the American Republic* (Cambridge, MA: Harvard University Press, 2017).

2. For these jurisdictional qualifications, see Philip Hamburger, *The Administrative Threat* (New York: Encounter Books, 2017), 47–50.

3. See *United States v. Am. Library Association*, 539 U.S. 194, 203 (2003) (plurality opinion), remarking that "Congress has wide latitude to at-

tach conditions to the receipt of federal assistance in order to further its
policy objectives."

4. *Chevron U.S.A., Inc. v. Natural Resources Defense Council, Inc.*, 467
U.S. 837, 844 (1984).

5. Philip Hamburger, "Delegating or Divesting," *Northwestern University Law Review Online* 115 (2020): 88.

6. For withholding or suspending payments, see Richard B. Cappalli, *Federal Grants and Cooperative Agreements: Law, Policy, and Practice* (Wilmette, IL: Callaghan, 1982), chap. 8, 49, §8:09.

For partial or complete suspension or termination of an award, see 2 C.F.R. §200.338–39.

For the return of prior payments, see Cappalli, *Federal Grants and Cooperative Agreements*, chap. 8, 67–82, §8:13–14, and for an example, see 20 U.S. Code §1234a.

For penalties, see Cappalli, *Federal Grants and Cooperative Agreements*, chap. 8, 85–89, §8:17.

For cease-and-desist orders, see Eloise Pasachoff, "Agency Enforcement of Spending Cause Statutes: A Defense of the Funding Cut-Off," *Yale Law Journal* 124 (2014): 248, 282, citing 20 U.S.C. §1234c and §1234e.

In contrast to these relatively serious responses, an agency can more modestly, through its auditing proceedings, disallow payments for particular deviations from the conditions of a grant. Cappalli, *Federal Grants and Cooperative Agreements*, chap. 8, 31–48, §8:07.

7. Cappalli, *Federal Grants and Cooperative Agreements*, chap. 8, 22, §8:05. Speaking merely of internal administrative appeals, not even appeals to the courts, "NSF [National Science Foundation] officials state that the few number of disputes raised before their agency evidence the fact that formal appeal procedures are not necessary. On the other hand, however, these same officials express concern that, if more elaborate procedures existed, more appeals would be brought." Ann Steinberg, "Federal Grant Dispute Resolution," in *Administrative Conference of the United States, Drafting Federal Grant Statutes* (Washington, DC: Administrative Conference of the United States, 1990), 189n89, citing interviews with William Cole, Director of the Division of Grants and Contracts, NSF (Washington, DC, June 1980 and March 5, 1982).

8. A report prepared for the Administrative Conference of the United States notes, "Many disputes are resolved informally without any paper trail or recordation." Steinberg, "Federal Grant Dispute Resolution," 189. For certifications, representations, and additional conditions, see 2 C.F.R. §200.207–08; 2 C.F.R. §200.338.

9. Some state courts have recognized the danger of displacing judicial power—at least in extreme cases. See Richard Briffault, "The Challenge of the New Preemption," *Stanford Law Review* 70 (2018): 1995, 2006, 2017, discussing *State ex rel. Bronovich v. City of Tucson*, 339 P.3rd 663, 672 (Ariz. 2017) (regarding a condition that might "displace this Court from its constitutionally assigned role . . . effectively preventing final judicial resolution of the issue"), and *City of Toledo v. State*, 72 N.E.3rd 692, 699 (Ohio Ct. App.) appeal allowed, 83 N.E.3d 938 (Ohio 2017) (rejecting the "end-run around the trial court's injunction").

10. Charles A. Reich, "The New Property," *Yale Law Journal* 73 (1964): 733, 770.

11. Philip Hamburger, *Is Administrative Law Unlawful?* (Chicago: University of Chicago Press, 2014), 397.

12. Rachel E. Barkow, "The Prosecutor as Regulatory Agency," in *Prosecutors in the Boardroom: Using Criminal Law to Regulate Corporate Conduct*, ed. Anthony Barkow and Rachel Barkow (New York: New York University Press, 2009), 177.

13. Philip Hamburger, *Law and Judicial Duty* (Cambridge, MA: Harvard University Press, 2008), 319, 464.

14. Hamburger, *Law and Judicial Duty*, 106n11.

Chapter 6: Short-Circuiting Politics

1. Martha Derthick writes, "Because federal requirements are typically stated in general terms, administrators have a high degree of flexibility in negotiating terms of conformance. Within the broad guidelines they have laid down, they have been able to adapt to the political administrative circumstances of each state." Martha Derthick, *The Influence of Federal Grants: Public Assistance in Massachusetts* (Cambridge, MA: Harvard University Press, 1970), 210. Some federal statutes candidly acknowledge the variation

from state to state. Under the Highway Beautification Act of 1965, for example, a state loses 10 percent of its federal highways funds if it fails to maintain "effective control" of outdoor advertising (notably, billboards) in accord with its "customary use" as stipulated in an agreement with the secretary of the Department of Transportation. Indeed, the outdoor speech standards set in the resulting fifty-two agreements are not entirely uniform.

2. Martha Derthick writes, "Grant statutes and their expansion are an inviting vehicle for members of Congress who want to achieve grand policy objectives incrementally, with little scrutiny or debate." Martha Derthick, "On the Mutability of American Laws," in *What Would Madison Do? The Father of the Constitution Meets Modern American Politics*, ed. Benjamin Wittes and Pietro Nivola (Washington, DC: Brookings Institution Press, 2015), 132.

3. Robert Cover, "Federalism and Administrative Structure," *Yale Law Journal* 92 (1983): 1342. See also Richard A. Epstein, "Unconstitutional Conditions, State Power, and the Limits of Consent," *Harvard Law Review* 102, no. 4 (1988): 197.

4. For more on the structural role of equality, especially the danger of allocating different speech rights to individuals and institutions, see Philip Hamburger, *Liberal Suppression: Section 501(c)(3) and the Taxation of Speech* (Chicago: University of Chicago Press, 2018), 287–290.

5. Carrots can also be better than sticks when government does not want all individuals to carry out a task and does not know which individuals are apt to do it. Gerrit De Geest and Giuseppe Dari-Mattiacci, "The Rise of Carrots and the Decline of Sticks," *University of Chicago Law Review* 80 (2013): 341, 345. But this use of rewards instead of punishments describes only a small corner of the universe of conditions, and it does not explain, let alone justify, the vast bulk of regulatory conditions, the conditions imposing unconstitutional restrictions, the regulatory extortion through conditions, and so forth.

Chapter 7: Denying Procedural Rights

1. For a relatively early, though incomplete, observation about the systematic danger to procedural rights, see Robert M. O'Neil, "Unconstitutional

Conditions: Welfare Benefits with Strings Attached," *California Law Review* 54 (1966): 443, 474–475.

2. Philip Hamburger, *Is Administrative Law Unlawful?* (Chicago: University of Chicago Press, 2014), 170.

3. St. George Tucker, Law Lectures, p. 4 of four loose pages inserted in notebook 2, Tucker-Coleman Papers, Mss. 39.1 T79, Box 62, Special Collections Research Center, Earl Gregg Swem Library, College of William and Mary, https://digitalarchive.wm.edu/handle/10288/13361. When, in the main body of his lecture notes, he discussed the courts, he commented, "No person shall be deprived of life, liberty, or property, (and these we shall remember are the objects of all rights) without due process of law; which it is the province of the judiciary to grant." St. George Tucker, Law Lectures, 5:203–204.

4. James Kent, *Commentaries on American Law* (New York: 1826), 2:13.

5. Joseph Story, *Commentaries on the Constitution* (Boston: 1833), 3, §1783. These conclusions about due process should not be surprising, as legal process—whether the original process commencing an action, mesne process during the proceedings, or final process enforcing judgment—could be obtained only from a court. Of course, the due process of law came to be understood more broadly, but its development from ideas of legal process explain why the due process of law so clearly required government to work through the courts when bringing proceedings against persons, even if only to have them answer questions.

6. For the *Ten Pound Cases* and the limited room left for small claims proceedings, see Philip Hamburger, *Law and Judicial Duty* (Cambridge, MA: Harvard University Press, 2008), 428–429.

7. For the loss of due process for researchers subjected to IRBs, see Carl E. Schneider, *The Censor's Hand: The Misregulation of Human-Subject Research* (Cambridge, MA: MIT Press, 2015), 141.

8. Judicial review of agencies is limited in many ways. For example, a court will typically defer to an agency's interpretation of its authorizing statutes and its rules and even to its administrative record. With this deference to agencies on both the law and the facts, the opportunities for real review are rather confined.

9. As loosely anticipated already in *Lemon v. Kurtzman*, "The history of government grants of a continuing cash subsidy indicates that such pro-

grams have almost always been accompanied by varying measures of control and surveillance." *Lemon v. Kurtzman,* 403 U.S. 602, 621 (1971).

10. Office for Human Research Protections, "Institutional Review Board Written Procedures: Guidance for Institutions and IRBs (2018), IV. Reporting of Unanticipated Problems, Serious or Continuing Noncompliance, and Any Suspension or Termination of IRB Approval," https://www .hhs.gov/ohrp/regulations-and-policy/guidance/institutional-issues /institutional-review-board-written-procedures/index.html. In *Grove City College v. Bell,* 465 U.S. 555 (1984), the Supreme Court upheld an assurance of compliance without recognizing the depth of what was at stake.

11. In *Speiser v. Randall,* the Supreme Court observed that "while the fairness of placing the burden of proof on the taxpayer in most circumstances is recognized, this Court has not hesitated to declare a summary tax collection procedure a violation of due process when the purported tax was shown to be in reality a penalty for a crime." *Speiser v. Randall,* 357 U.S. 513, 524–525 (1958).

12. *Speiser v. Randall,* 357 U.S. 513 (1958).

13. In speaking of "licensing conditions," the text here refers to the conditions attached to regulatory licensing, not conditions on mere licenses of proprietary rights.

14. Brook Chambery, *A Court without Justice: Administrative Law, the Constitution, and Me* (2020), 335–367.

15. 5 U.S.C. §§554, 556, 557, and 558(c). On revocations of licenses, see Geraldine F. Baldwin, "Section 558(c) of the Administrative Procedure Act: Is a Formal Hearing to Demonstrate Compliance Required before License Revocation or Suspension?" *Fordham Law Review* 51 (1983): 1436, 1438, arguing that "informal compliance proceedings can satisfy" §588(c).

16. Note that the federal government sometimes uses not conditions but direct requirements to shift licensing and other adjudicatory decisions to private bodies—as when the Health Insurance Portability and Accountability Act privacy rule requires IRB or privacy board approval for sharing or otherwise publishing specified health or scientific information. See 45 C.F.R. pts. 160 and 164, promulgated under the Health Insurance Portability and Accountability Act of 1996, Pub. L. No. 104–191, 110 Stat. 2021–2031 (1996).

More typically, however, the shift of adjudicatory decisions is accomplished by means of conditions.

17. Charles Reich talks about procedures that "in varying degrees, represent short-cuts that tend to augment the power of the grantor at the expense of the recipient." Charles A. Reich, "The New Property," *Yale Law Journal* 73 (1964): 733, 751.

18. For the administrative side of this problem, see Philip Hamburger, "The Administrative Evasion of Procedural Rights," *New York University Journal of Law & Liberty* 11 (2018): 915, 960.

19. Hamburger, "The Administrative Evasion of Procedural Rights," 915, 960.

20. U.S. Department of Education, Dear Colleague Letter (April 4, 2011), https://www2.ed.gov/print/about/offices/list/ocr/letters/colleague-201104.html.

21. Robert L. Shibley, *Twisting Title IX* (New York: Encounter Books, 2016), 35.

22. For details of the bias among administrative law judges at the Securities and Exchange Commission, see Brief of the New Civil Liberties Alliance as Amicus Curiae in Support of Petitioners, *Lucia v. Securities and Exchange Commission*, on Writ of Certiorari to the U.S. Court of Appeals for the District of Columbia Circuit, No. 17–130.

23. Recall Martha Derthick's comments about the administrative "flexibility" arising from the fact that "federal requirements are typically stated in general terms." Martha Derthick, *The Influence of Federal Grants: Public Assistance in Massachusetts* (Cambridge, MA: Harvard University Press, 1970), 210.

Chapter 8: Federalism

1. Jessica Bulman-Pozen, "From Sovereignty and Process to Administration and Politics: The Afterlife of American Federalism," *Yale Law Journal* 123 (2014): 1920.

2. Martha Derthick, *The Influence of Federal Grants: Public Assistance in Massachusetts* (Cambridge, MA: Harvard University Press, 1970), 210.

3. For the euphemism "cooperative federalism" and the possibility that it was coined by Edwin Corwin in 1937, see Richard B. Cappalli, *Federal*

Grants and Cooperative Agreements: Law, Policy, and Practice (Wilmette, IL: Callaghan, 1982), chap. 1, 13, §1:06. Jonathan Adler writes, "Though generally described as 'cooperative federalism,' the relationship between the states and federal government in environmental policy is typically anything but 'cooperative.' To the contrary, many state officials 'resent what they believe to be an overly prescriptive federal orientation toward state programs, especially in light of stable or decreasing grant awards.'" Jonathan H. Adler, "Letting Fifty Flowers Bloom: Using Federalism to Spur Environmental Innovation," in *The Jurisdynamics of Environmental Protection: Change and the Pragmatic Voice in Environmental Law,* ed. Jim Chen (Washington, DC: Environmental Law Institute, 2003), 265.

4. Derthick, *The Influence of Federal Grants,* 220 (Cambridge, MA: Harvard University Press, 1970).

5. *New York v. United States,* 505 U.S. 144, 181 (1992).

6. Robert Cover, "Federalism and Administrative Structure," *Yale Law Journal* 92 (1983): 1342, 1342–1343.

7. Cover was worried about the full range of federal spending in aid to the states, not merely that which regulates or asks states to regulate. But the costs for Americans are all the greater when the federal government uses its spending to secure regulation.

8. See, for example, *Carleson v. Remillard,* 406 U.S. 598 (1972); *Townsend v. Swank,* 404 U.S. 282 (1971). See also Cappalli, *Federal Grants and Cooperative Agreements,* chap. 1, 16–17, §1:09; Paul G. Dembling and Malcolm S. Mason, *Essentials of Grant Law Practice* (Philadelphia: ALI-ABA, 1991), 23.

9. [Alexander Hamilton], "Federalist No. 33," in *The Federalist,* ed. Jacob E. Cooke (Middletown, CT: Wesleyan University Press, 1961), 207.

10. Bradford R. Clark, "The Procedural Safeguards of Federalism," *Notre Dame Law Review* 83 (2008): 1681, 1711–1712.

11. Jessica Bulman-Pozen argues that executive preemption threatens "values of diversity, contestation, and political community." Jessica Bulman-Pozen, "Preemption and Commandeering without Congress," *Stanford Law Review* 70 (2018): 2029, 2051. Although she largely confines her argument to rules issued without notice and comment, her concerns are more broadly relevant. Bulman-Pozen, "Preemption and Commandeering without Congress," 2042. Note also Thomas W. Merrill, "Preemption and Institu-

tional Choice," *Northwestern University Law Review* 102 (2008): 727; Ernest A. Young, "Executive Preemption," *Northwestern University Law Review* 102 (2008): 869.

12. James M. Landis, *The Administrative Process* (New Haven, CT: Yale University Press, 1938), 15.

13. *New York v. United States*, 505 U.S. 144, 168–169 (1992).

14. *New York v. United States*, 505 U.S. 144, 162, 178 (1992).

15. *Steward Machine Co. v. Davis*, 301 U.S. 548, 595 (1937).

16. *National Federation of Independent Business v. Sebelius*, 567 U.S. 519 (2012).

17. *National Federation of Independent Business v. Sebelius*, 567 U.S. 519 (2012).

18. *National Federation of Independent Business v. Sebelius*, 567 U.S. 519 (2012).

19. *National Federation of Independent Business v. Sebelius*, 567 U.S. 519 (2012).

20. *National Federation of Independent Business v. Sebelius*, 567 U.S. 519 (2012).

21. *National Federation of Independent Business v. Sebelius*, 567 U.S. 519 (2012). The phrase echoed in *Sebelius* about "the simple expedient of not yielding" developed as mere dictum in *Massachusetts v. Mellon*, 262 U.S. 447, 482 (1923) and became a holding in *Oklahoma v. United States Civil Service Commission*, 330 U.S. 127, 143 (1947). See Cappalli, *Federal Grants and Cooperative Agreements*, chap. 1, 12, §1:06.

22. *New York v. United States*, 505 U.S. 144, 182 (1992). Similarly, the court said, "State officials . . . cannot consent to the enlargement of the powers of Congress beyond those enumerated in the Constitution." *New York v. United States*, 505 U.S. 144, 182 (1992).

23. 42 U.S.C. §7509(a)–(b). See Jonathan H. Adler, "Judicial Federalism and the Future of Federal Environmental Regulation," *Iowa Law Review* 90 (2005): 377, 449–450; Samuel R. Bagenstos, "The Anti-Leveraging Principle and the Spending Clause after NFIB," *Georgetown Law Review* 101 (2013): 861, 916–917.

24. Martha Derthick, "Crossing Thresholds: Federalism in the 1960s," in *Keeping the Compound Republic: Essays in American Federalism* (Washington, DC: Brookings Institution Press, 2001), 149. Derthick writes that in

the 1960s, "one after another, constitutional thresholds were crossed. By the mid-1970s, American federalism had become something very different from what it had been fifteen years before. Place had lost much of its importance in the American polity." Derthick, "Crossing Thresholds," 138. She adds, "The change in American federalism . . . in the 1960s was more profound than any that occurred in the New Deal." Derthick, "Crossing Thresholds," 151. "It was one thing for the national government to make radically broadened claims for authority to regulate commerce, and another to make rules applying to the states governments' own conduct." Derthick, "Crossing Thresholds," 151. Anita Harbert writes:

> Before the 1960s, the typical grant-in-aid programs were not used to resolve problems of national concern but were established to help state or local governments accomplish their respective objectives—"to help them get farmers out of the mud." . . . In general, federal agencies saw their role as one of technical assistance rather than of control: they offered advice and worked with the states to improve programs initiated by the states, and they did not substitute their policy judgment for those of state and local agencies. . . . Federal review and control of grant distribution in earlier decades was designed to accomplish the objectives of efficiency and economy in order to safeguard the federal treasury, and was not generally intended to affect the substance of grant programs.

Anita S. Harbert, *Federal Grants-in-Aid: Maximizing Benefits to the States* (New York: Praeger, 1976), 4. That changed in the 1960s.

25. Bulman-Pozen, "From Sovereignty and Process to Administration and Politics," 1920, 1932, 1957.

26. Congressional Budget Office, *Federal Grants to State and Local Governments* (Washington, DC: CBO, 2013), 10, https://www.cbo.gov/sites/default/files/113th-congress-2013-2014/reports/03-05-13federalgrantsonecol.pdf.

27. Derthick, *The Influence of Federal Grants*, 7.

28. Congressional Budget Office, *Federal Grants to State and Local Governments*, 23.

29. Congressional Budget Office, *Federal Grants to State and Local Governments*, 23.

30. Richard Cappalli writes that "the lever of federal funds had pried open state and local agencies to federal policies which they would have rejected or would have accepted only grudgingly and slowly." Cappalli, *Federal Grants and Cooperative Agreements*, chap. 1, 12, §1:06.

31. Congressional Budget Office, *Federal Grants to State and Local Governments*, 3.

32. Congressional Budget Office, *Federal Grants to State and Local Governments*, 20.

33. Heather K. Gerken and Jessica Bulman-Pozen, "Uncooperative Federalism," *Yale Law Journal* 118 (2009): 1256, 1259, 1265.

34. Bill W. Thurman, Paul L. Posner, and Stephen M. Sorett, "Federal Grants and Intergovernmental Relations," in *Federal Grant Law*, ed. Malcom S. Mason (Chicago: American Bar Association, 1982), 213 ("the priorities and programs of state and local governments have increasingly come to reflect federal decisions" and that federal grants "alter state and local government policies toward federally favored ends"). State policies thereby end up "different, probably very different, from what they would be in the absence of federal action." Derthick, *The Influence of Federal Grants*, 214.

35. Derthick, *The Influence of Federal Grants*, 235, quoting Walter W. Heller.

36. Bulman-Pozen, "From Sovereignty and Process to Administration and Politics," 1920, 1932, 1957.

37. Derthick, *The Influence of Federal Grants*, 193.

38. Derthick, *The Influence of Federal Grants*, 237.

39. Derthick, *The Influence of Federal Grants*, 223, quoting Richard N. Goodwin, a speech writer for President Johnson. Derthick notes that "if the influence on structures and processes is extensive and enduring enough, the result must be to influence policy outcomes as well—*all* policy outcomes, not just those in which the federal government is actively interested." Derthick, *The Influence of Federal Grants*, 207. Richard Cappalli writes that "the federal grant has been used to structure state and local governments along the lines of federal policy and practice." Cappalli, *Federal Grants and Cooperative Agreements*, chap. 11, 54, §11:24.

40. Cappalli, *Federal Grants and Cooperative Agreements*, chap. 11, 11, §11:24.

41. Advisory Commission on Intergovernmental Relations, *Contracting with America: ACIR Recommendations 1961–1995* (Washington, DC: ACIR, c. 1996), 52.

42. Advisory Commission on Intergovernmental Relations, *Twelfth Annual Report: Federalism in 1970* (Washington, DC: ACIR, January 31, 1971), 17.

43. Advisory Commission on Intergovernmental Relations, *Contracting with America*, 52.

44. Emmett McGroarty, Jane Robbins, and Erin Tuttle, *Deconstructing the Administrative State: The Fight for Liberty* (Washington, DC: American Principles Project, 2017), 235–243. Similarly, "direct federal-city relations . . . bypassed the states." Harbert, *Federal Grants-in-Aid*, 7.

45. Cappalli, *Federal Grants and Cooperative Agreements*, chap. 11, 55, §11:24.

46. Derthick, *The Influence of Federal Grants*, 203, 205, 241. Such conditions typically require "a single state or local government department, agency, board or commission, as the single administrative focal point of an aided program" and even sometimes "dictate a specific headquarters-field administrative relationship within a state or substate governmental department or agency." Advisory Commission on Intergovernmental Relations, *Twelfth Annual Report*, 56. For examples, see Dembling and Mason, *Essentials of Grant Law Practice*, 53.

47. Derthick, *The Influence of Federal Grants*, 205, 241. At the same time, some block grants have required state legislative action, thus preventing states from leaving such matters to their executives. Cappalli, *Federal Grants and Cooperative Agreements*, chap. 1, 96, §1:42.

Incidentally, Derthick observes that when federal administrators are pursuing their administrative ends, they are most likely to go beyond their congressional authorization:

> Administrators, whose proposals to Congress and whose day-to-day conduct are dominant in determining the content of such conditions, attach high priority to attainment of administrative ends. Although they concentrate on such ends partly because Congress has given them the authority to do so, it is in pursuit of administrative ends that they are most likely to test the bounds of congressional tolerance. When public

assistance administrators stretch statutory provisions it is generally for the sake of reforming state administrative structure procedure. One such case was their attempt, between 1935 and 1939, to require the states to set up merit systems even though Congress in 1935 had declined to enact such a requirement. In general the pursuit of professionalization, including imposition of the educational requirement, was carried on without explicit sanction from Congress. Another example was the decision to interpret the requirement of statewide operation as if it were a requirement of statewide uniformity.

Derthick, *The Influence of Federal Grants*, 198.

48. Derthick, *The Influence of Federal Grants*, 241.

49. 5 U.S.C. §1501-08, upheld in *Oklahoma v. United States Civil Service Commission*, 330 U.S. 127 (1947). See also Derthick, *The Influence of Federal Grants*, 206, 216, 222; Cappalli, *Federal Grants and Cooperative Agreements*, chap. 1, 11, §1:06; chap. 1, 102, §1:43; chap. 18, 15–23, §18.06-09.

50. Derthick, *The Influence of Federal Grants*, 158–189, 194, 216. Derthick notes, "An alliance between federal and state administrative agencies, formed and perfected through the working of the grant system, can become a powerful force in state politics, perhaps the dominant force in the making of policy for the program in question." Derthick, *The Influence of Federal Grants*, 206.

Derthick is careful to note that it "cannot be shown that federal action caused these changes," in the sense of being the sole cause. She adds:

It is perfectly clear, however, that the changes were accelerated and in important ways shaped by federal action. Change took place faster than it would have in the absence of federal participation, and took specific forms and directions that it might not otherwise have taken. Had federal influence not been felt, the Massachusetts public assistance program in 1965 would have been far different: less legal, less uniform, less centralized, less bureaucratized, and less professionalized. Although the state role in policymaking and the supervision of administration would surely have grown, it would not have grown so much. It is most unlikely that state administration would have been adopted by 1967. In the absence of federal insistence to the contrary, selectmen in the smallest Massachusetts towns to this day might be administering the towns' few public assistance cases themselves.

Derthick, *The Influence of Federal Grants*, 194.

51. Advisory Commission on Intergovernmental Relations, *Twelfth Annual Report*, 2. Note also President Johnson's distaste for the "irrationalities of present state and local jurisdictional boundaries." Jill M. Fraley, "Stealth Constitutional Change in the Geography of Law," *Drexel Law Review* 4 (2012): 467, 469; quoted by Jessica Bulman-Pozen, "Our Regionalism," *University of Pennsylvania Law Review* 166 (2018): 377, 408.

52. Daniel P. Moynihan, "The Future of Federalism," in *American Federalism: Toward a More Effective Partnership* (Washington, DC: Advisory Commission on Intergovernmental Relations, 1975), 94.

53. See note 51.

54. Commenting on the deliberate character of the change, Derthick writes, "What was distinctive about the 1960s was that, for the first time in a century, changing federalism became an end in itself, consciously pursued by numerous holders of national power who were trying to reconstruct American society and politics. It was not just an incidental by-product of war or modernization." Derthick, "Crossing Thresholds," 152. Even decentralization in the grant system was a mode of control: "Decentralization was conceived . . . as a way of making state governments and their subdivisions better administrators of federal programs." Derthick, *The Influence of Federal Grants*, 234.

55. Advisory Commission on Intergovernmental Relations, *Twelfth Annual Report*, 56.

56. *New York v. United States*, 505 U.S. 144, 185 (1992).

57. For example, the Supreme Court has held that the president may not violate his duty to take care that the laws are faithfully enforced. See U.S. Constitution, Article II, §3; *Youngstown Sheet & Tube Co. v. Sawyer*, 343 U.S. 579 (1952); *Kendall v. United States ex rel. Stokes*, 37 U.S. 524 (1838); Jack Goldsmith and John F. Manning, "The Protean Take Care Clause," *University of Pennsylvania Law Review* 164 (2016): 1849–1851.

58. *South Dakota v. Dole*, 483 U.S. 203, 210 (1987).

59. *United States v. Butler*, 297 U.S. 1, 75 (1936). Justice Anthony Kennedy has written that "the Spending Clause power, if wielded without con-

cern for the federal balance, has the potential to obliterate distinctions between national and local spheres of interest and power by permitting the
federal government to set policy in the most sensitive areas of traditional state
concern, areas which otherwise would lie outside its reach." *Davis v. Monroe
County Board of Education*, 526 U.S. 629, 654–655 (1999) (Kennedy
dissenting).

Part III

1. *Doyle v. Continental Insurance Company*, 94 U.S. 535, 543 (1876). The
court has also said that "the right to continue the exercise of a privilege
granted by the state cannot be made to depend upon the grantee's submission to a condition prescribed by the state which is hostile to the provisions
of the federal constitution." *Frost & Frost Co. v. Railroad Commissioner*, 271
U.S. 583, 594 (1926).

Chapter 9: Consent No Relief from Constitutional Limits

1. *Gonzales v. Raich*, 545 U.S. 1 (2005). More completely, Stevens
wrote: "Just as state acquiescence to federal regulation cannot expand the
bounds of the Commerce Clause, . . . so too state action cannot circum-
scribe Congress' plenary commerce power." *Gonzales v. Raich*, 545 U.S. 1
(2005). And earlier, the Supreme Court observed about Congress's power
over interstate commerce: "That power can neither be enlarged nor diminished by the exercise or non-exercise of state power." *United States v. Darby*,
312 U.S. 100 (1941).
2. Frank Easterbrook, "Insider Trading, Secret Agents, Evidentiary
Privileges, and the Production of Information," *Supreme Court Review*
(1981): 309, 347.
3. Like Anti-Federalists, Federalists understood constitutional rights to
be exceptions to powers. Alexander Hamilton, in defense of the US Constitution, explained that "by a limited constitution, I understand one which
contains certain specified exceptions to the legislative authority; such, for
instance, as that it shall pass no bills of attainder, no ex-post-facto laws, and
the like." Alexander Hamilton, "Federalist Number 78," in *The Federalist*,

ed. Jacob E. Cooke (Middletown, CT: Wesleyan University Press, 1961), 524. Similarly, when James Madison overcame his objections to a bill of rights, he introduced the initial draft of the Bill of Rights on the floor of the House of Representatives with the observation that "a bill of rights" would "enumerat[e] particular exceptions to the grant of power." Speech of James Madison (June 8, 1789), in *Creating the Bill of Rights: The Documentary Record from the First Federal Congress*, ed. Helen E. Veit, Kenneth R. Bowling, and Charlene Bangs Bickford (Baltimore: Johns Hopkins University Press, 1991), 83.

Chapter 10: Consent within and beyond the Constitution

1. William P. Marshall, "Towards a Nonunifying Theory of Unconstitutional Conditions: The Example of the Religion Clauses," *San Diego Law Review* 26 (1989): 243, 243–244; Cass Sunstein, "Why the Unconstitutional Conditions Doctrine Is an Anachronism (with Particular Reference to Religion, Speech, and Abortion)," *Boston University Law Review* 70 (1990): 593.

2. Mitchell N. Berman, "Coercion without Baselines: Unconstitutional Conditions in Three Dimensions," *Georgetown Law Journal* 90 (2001): 1, 6.

3. The Fifth Amendment's compulsion has been held to include the threat of being fired. In *Gardner v. Broderick* (1968), a police officer was subpoenaed to appear before a grand jury that was investigating alleged corruption among police officers. He was told that the grand jury proposed to examine him concerning the performance of his official duties and that he would be fired if he refused to waive his right against self-incrimination. He refused and was discharged. The Supreme Court held that because the questioning was in the course of a criminal inquiry, his right against self-incrimination had been violated.

4. For details, see Philip Hamburger, *Is Administrative Law Unlawful?* (Chicago: University of Chicago Press, 2014), 149–150, 169–172.

5. Thomas W. Merrill, "*Dolan v. City of Tigard*: Constitutional Rights as Public Goods," *Denver Law Review* 72 (1995): 859.

6. Philip Hamburger, "Equality and Diversity: The Eighteenth-Century Debate about Equal Protection and Equal Civil Rights," *Supreme Court Review* (1992): 295, 370–371, 374.

7. See, for example, Tsilly Dagan and Talia Fisher, "Rights for Sale," *Minnesota Law Review* 96 (2011): 90, 92.

8. *Planned Parenthood v. Casey*, 505 U.S. 833 (1992).

9. Allen Redlich, "Unconstitutional Conditions on Welfare Eligibility," *Wisconsin Law Review* (1970): 450, 452.

10. Carole M. Hirsch, "When the War on Poverty Became the War on Poor, Pregnant Women: Political Rhetoric, the Unconstitutional Conditions Doctrine, and the Family Cap Restriction," *William and Mary Journal of Women and Law* 8 (2002): 335, 338–339.

11. *United States v. Scott*, 450 F.3d 863, 866–867 (9th Cir. 2006). Considering another version of this sort of inquiry, Melanie Wilson notes that the Supreme Court "has never resolved whether someone *convicted* of a crime validly waives his Fourth Amendment rights by 'agreeing' to a blanket-search provision as part of his post-conviction release on probation or his post-incarceration supervised release." Melanie D. Wilson, "The Price of Pretrial Release: Can We Afford to Keep Our Fourth Amendment Rights?" *Iowa Law Review* 92 (2006): 159, 162.

12. Another example of a condition on juries running into the future is familiar from *Fox River Paper Co. v. Railroad Commission*, 274 U.S. 651 (1927). A 1925 Wisconsin statute had provided that a riparian owner could operate and maintain a dam only with a permit from the state's Railroad Commission, and further that such a permit was to be granted subject to the express condition that, after thirty years, the state could acquire the dam for the cost of reproducing it in its then-existing condition plus the value of the underlying land prior to the grant of the permit—all as determined by the commission. A dam owner applied for a permit but refused to include consent to these conditions. The state's constitution guaranteed that property "shall not be taken for public use, without just compensation," and the owner's consent would have waived his future right to get just compensation and his future right to have this decided by a court rather than the Railroad Commission. Although this was upheld by an equally divided court in *Fox River*, it is difficult to justify the restrictions on the future exercise of the rights.

Similarly, one must wonder about state workers' compensation statutes. Such statutes permit the resolution of disputes about injuries in administrative hearings—so as to avoid the cost and delay of lawsuits. Mandatory versions of these statutes were widely considered unconstitutional (until the Supreme Court upheld them in 1917) as they deprived employers of their due process of law and their right to a jury. Other statutes therefore offered voluntary workers' compensation. Under the voluntary statutes, employers could annually choose to participate—on the condition that they gave up their jury rights. Such statutes were upheld in *Oceanic Steam Navigation Co. v. Stranahan*, 214 U.S. 320 (1909) and *Booth Fisheries Co. v. Industrial Commission*, 271 U.S. 208 (1926). Notwithstanding the decisions upholding the mandatory and voluntary sacrifice of jury rights, it is difficult to be sanguine about these cases. The mandatory deprivation looks unconstitutional, and so too does the consensual sacrifice of jury rights in future cases.

13. For the relinquishment of a future claim for just compensation, see *Fox River Paper Co. v. Railroad Commission*, 274 U.S. 651 (1927), discussed in the prior endnote.

14. *Home Insurance Company v. Morse*, 87 U.S. 445, 451 (1874).

15. Incidentally, it may be suggested that the germaneness or relevance of a condition to the underlying spending is crucial for understanding whether a condition violates the freedom of speech. For example, it may be said that a condition against hiring Republicans for government jobs violates the freedom of speech of applicants for teaching positions at state universities, but does not violate the freedom of speech of persons considered for cabinet positions—on the theory that political affiliation is relevant or germane for the latter.

But there ordinarily is no need to consider germaneness in evaluating a condition restricting speech—the reason being that if germaneness would matter in evaluating a direct version of the restriction, it will have already been taken into account. Imagine a direct version of the condition mentioned above—that is, a direct prohibition on hiring Republicans. One might well distinguish between such a rule for teachers and such a rule for cabinet officers—partly on germaneness grounds, and partly for other reasons, such as the president's appointment power. And once it is evident that such a rule for teachers abridges the freedom of speech, it is clear that a similar condition abridges this freedom. So there is no need to reintroduce the question of whether the restriction is germane, as this has already been taken into account.

16. *Speiser v. Randall*, 357 U.S. 513, 518 (1958).

17. *National Endowment for the Arts v. Finley*, 524 U.S. 569, 581 (1998).

18. *Rust v. Sullivan*, 500 U.S. 173 (1991).

19. In addition, if the funding and thus the condition in *Rust* reached most family planning doctors, the condition would have been regulatory and should have been held void for divesting Congress and the courts of their powers.

20. Although the relevant statutes are not ordinarily understood in terms of fiduciary duties, they are most easily understood in such terms. Indeed, such statutes impose their duties on a person who has been "entrusted with" documents and so forth or who has "lawful possession" of them, 18 U.S.C. §793(f), or who is an "officer or employee of the United States." 18 U.S.C. §1905.

21. Secrecy Agreement (May 28, 1951), https://www.cia.gov/library /readingroom/docs/CIA-RDP80B01676R004000050031-1.pdf.

22. See *Connick v. Myers*, 461 U.S. 138 (1983); *Garcetti v. Ceballos*, 547 U.S. 410 (2006).

23. *Pickering v. Board of Education*, 391 U.S. 563 (1968).

24. 5 U.S.C. §7323.

25. *Board of Trustees of Leland Stanford Jr. University v. Sullivan*, 773 F. Supp. 472 (D.D.C. 1991).

Chapter 11: Varieties of Federal Action

1. *Sherbert v. Verner*, 374 U.S. 398, 404 (1963).

2. *Goldberg v. Kelly*, 397 U.S. 254, 264 (1970); *Board of Regents of State Colleges v. Roth*, 408 U.S. 564, 571 (1972). For a prominent application of such views to conditions, see Seth F. Kreimer, "Allocational Sanctions: The Problem of Negative Rights in a Positive State," *University of Pennsylvania Law Review* 132 (1984): 1293, 1359–1374.

3. *Goldberg v. Kelly*, 397 U.S. 254, 264 (1970); *Mathews v. Eldridge*, 424 U.S. 319 (1976).

4. *Hamdi v. Rumsfeld*, 542 U.S. 507 (2004).

5. Philip Hamburger, "The Administrative Evasion of Procedural Rights," *New York University Journal of Law and Liberty* 11 (2018): 915, 954–955.

6. Put another way, this book does not embrace the generalized blurring of property rights and government benefits that was popularized by Charles A. Reich, "The New Property," *Yale Law Journal* 73 (1964): 733.

7. H. L. A. Hart, *The Concept of Law* (Oxford: Clarendon, 1990), 19–24, 30–31, 77–79.

8. For the most famous modern account of legal obligation, see Hart, *The Concept of Law*, 79–88.

9. *Frost & Frost Trucking Co. v. Railroad Commission*, 271 U.S. 583, 593 (1926).

10. *South Dakota v. Dole*, 483 U.S. 203, 204, 211 (1987), quotation marks omitted.

11. *United States v. Butler*, 297 U.S. 1, 70–71 (1936).

12. See, for example, *Atlantic Packers' Association v. Domenico*, 117 F. 99 (9th Cir. 1902); *Lefkowitz v. Turley*, 414 U.S. 70 (1973).

13. *Trinity Lutheran Church of Columbia, Inc. v. Comer*, 582 U.S. (2017).

Chapter 12: Force and Other Pressure amid Consent

1. *National Federation of Independent Business v. Sebelius*, 567 U.S. 519 (2012).

2. Although the pressure on states is not quite *comply or die*, states cannot afford to allow their inhabitants to be taxed to support subsidies for other states.

3. *South Dakota v. Dole*, 483 U.S. 203, 211 (1987), omitting interior quotation marks.

4. For the return of prior payments, see Richard B. Cappalli, *Federal Grants and Cooperative Agreements: Law, Policy, and Practice* (Wilmette, IL: Callaghan, 1982), chap. 8, 67–82, §8:13–14, and for example, 20 U.S. Code § 1234a; 42 U.S.C. §609(a)(1)(B).

5. Richard B. Cappalli, *Federal Grants and Cooperative Agreements: Law, Policy, and Practice*, chap. 8, 85–89, §8:17.

6. 20 U.S.C. §1234c and §1234e; Eloise Pasachoff, "Agency Enforcement of Spending Cause Statutes: A Defense of the Funding Cut-Off," *Yale Law Journal* 124 (2014): 248, 281–282.

7. For injunctions sought by government, see Cappalli, *Federal Grants and Cooperative Agreements*, chap. 8, 103–106, §8:24; Paul G. Dembling and Malcolm S. Mason, *Essentials of Grant Law Practice* (Philadelphia: ALI-ABA, 1991), 175 (under the heading of "Specific Performance"). For private claims, see Leonard Weiser-Varon, "Injunctive Relief from State Violations of Federal Funding Conditions," *Columbia Law Review* 82 (1982): 1236; Caroline Bermeo Newcombe, "Implied Private Rights of Action: Definition, and Factors to Determine Whether a Private Action Will Be Implied from a Federal Statute," *Loyola University Chicago Law Journal* 49 (2017): 117, 126–127.

8. 31 U.S.C. §3729.

9. 18 U.S.C. §1001.

10. Martha Derthick describes defunding as a "weapon in reserve." Martha Derthick, *The Influence of Federal Grants: Public Assistance in Massachusetts* (Cambridge, MA: Harvard University Press, 1970), 209. She adds, "In cases of federal-state conflict, federal negotiators keep open the possibility of withholding during the process of negotiation, referring to it in oblique and subtle terms. They seek to obscure the low probability that they will actually use it. By not making overt threats to withhold, federal administrators protect their credibility; the state is kept guessing." Derthick, *The Influence of Federal Grants*, 210–211. In fact, although some federal agencies are open to negotiation, others demand unqualified submission. And as Derthick recognizes, the shift from formula grants to project grants increases the pressure for compliance. Derthick, *The Influence of Federal Grants*, 224. For the rareness of formal defunding proceedings, see Pasachoff, "Agency Enforcement of Spending Cause Statutes," 248, 284.

A 1979 RAND study for the Department of Health, Education, and Welfare concluded that "the federal management of Title I lies far more on techniques of informal political pressure, less on formal methods of centralized enforcement, than is generally recognized." For example, the department uses "the oversight process itself as a sanction, instead of as groundwork for fiscal sanctions." Overall, "most of the effects of federal management are achieved through the informal management system." Paul T. Hill, *Enforcement and Informal Pressure in the Management of Federal Categorical Programs in Education* (Santa Monica, CA: RAND, 1979), viii, 1.

Although Pasachoff argues that agencies should more commonly pursue funding cutoffs and other formal remedies, it is unsurprising that agencies prefer their informal remedies. One reason is legal, for according to 2 C.F.R. §200.338, an agency cannot resort to its formal remedies until it has determined that "noncompliance cannot be remedied by imposing additional conditions." And even when the law does not impede resort to formal remedies, agencies know that such remedies are final agency actions, which come with the risk of judicial review.

11. In this sense—that the government both sets the terms of the agreements and backs them up with force—the federal action here is much clearer than in *Shelley v. Kraemer*, 334 U.S. 1, 20 (1948).

12. *United States v. Butler*, 297 U.S. 1, 73 (1936).

13. *Steward Machine Co. v. Collector*, 301 U.S. 548, 575 (1937).

14. Oliver Wendell Holmes Jr., "The Path of the Law," *Harvard Law Review* 10 (1897): 457, 462.

Chapter 13: Irrelevance of Force and Other Pressure

1. On undue influence, see Richard A. Epstein, "Unconstitutional Conditions, State Power, and the Limits of Consent," *Harvard Law Review* 102, no. 4 (1988): 8.

2. E. Allan Farnsworth, *Contracts* (New York: Aspen Publishers, 2004), 318.

3. Elisha Greenwood, *The Doctrine of Public Policy in the Law of Contracts Reduced to Rules* (Chicago: Callaghan, 1886), 2.

4. Greenwood, *The Doctrine of Public Policy*, 2.

5. Restatement of Contracts, 2nd, §178.

6. Greenwood, *The Doctrine of Public Policy in the Law of Contracts Reduced to Rules*, 3.

7. Joseph Story, *Commentaries on Equity Jurisprudence*, 4th ed. (Boston: Little & Brown, 1846), 1:744.

8. Story, *Commentaries on Equity Jurisprudence*, 6.

9. *Frost & Frost Trucking Co. v. Railroad Commission*, 271 U.S. 583, 600–01 (1926).

10. John D. French, "Unconstitutional Conditions: An Analysis," *Georgetown Law Review* 50 (1961): 234, 239. On the applicability of general

contract principles in federal courts, see Richard L. Revesz, "Restatements and the Federal Common Law," American Law Institute *Quarterly Newsletter* (September 27, 2016), https://www.ali.org/news/articles/restatements -and-federal-common-law/.

11. The Restatement assumes legislative or judicial foundations for public policies, explaining that "in weighing a public policy against enforcement of a term, account is taken of . . . the strength of that policy as manifested by legislative or judicial decisions." Restatement of Contracts, 2nd, §178(3).

12. In *Hurd v. Hodge* (1948), the Supreme Court wrote, "The power of the federal courts to enforce the terms of private agreements is at all times exercised subject to the restrictions and limitations of the public policy of the United States as manifested in the Constitution, treaties, federal statutes, and applicable legal precedents. Where the enforcement of private agreements would be violative of that policy, it is the obligation of courts to refrain from such exertions of judicial power." *Hurd v. Hodge*, 334 U.S. 24, 35 (1948).

Chapter 14: Regulatory Extortion

1. Charles Reich hints at the danger of extortion (for example, by the FCC). Charles A. Reich, "The New Property," *Yale Law Journal* 73 (1964): 733, 750.

2. For a somewhat similar distinction between bribery and this sort of extortion, see *Roma Construction Company v. aRusso*, 96 F.3d 566 (1st Cir. 1996); James Lindgren, "The Theory, History, and Practice of the Bribery-Extortion Distinction," *University of Pennsylvania Law Review* 141 (1993): 1695, 1698–1704.

3. J. Thomas Rosch, "Consent Decrees: Is the Public Getting Its Money's Worth?" April 7, 2011, 11, https://www.ftc.gov/sites/default/files /documents/public_statements/consent-decrees-public-getting-its-moneys -worth/110407roschconsentdecrees.pdf.

4. 16 C.F.R. §2.32 (2010) ("Every agreement also shall waive further procedural steps and all rights to seek judicial review or otherwise to challenge or contest the validity of the order").

5. Rosch, "Consent Decrees," 32.

6. *Doyle v. Continental Insurance Company*, 94 U.S. 535, 543 (1876).

7. Legislatures traditionally also enjoyed the power to compel appearance and testimony, but otherwise, subpoenas and other such demands were judicial powers.

8. Notwithstanding the overall benefits, it is evident that some of the employers who cooperated with OSHA took advantage of the reduced inspections to avoid meeting safety standards. There consequently was union opposition to OSHA's program. See, for example, "Maine 200, Workers 0," *UE News*, November 1996, http://www.ranknfile-ue.org/h&s1196.html.

9. For such delays, see Reich, "The New Property," 733, 750.

10. The Supreme Court in *Nollan* casually discussed extortion but apparently as a way of addressing the takings problem, saying that "unless the permit condition serves the same governmental purpose as the development ban, the building restriction is not a valid regulation of land use, but an out-and-out plan of extortion." *Nollan v. California Coastal Commission*, 483 U.S. 825, 837 (1987), internal quotation marks omitted. And the opinion in *Dolan* merely referred back to *Nollan*. *Dolan v. City of Tigard*, 512 U.S. 374, 386, 391 (1994).

11. *Nollan v. California Coastal Commission*, 483 U.S. 825, 837 (1987); *Dolan v. City of Tigard*, 512 U.S. 374, 386, 391 (1994).

12. *Koontz v. St. Johns River Water Management District*, 570 U.S. 595 (2013).

13. *Koontz v. St. Johns River Water Management District*, 570 U.S. 595 (2013).

14. St. George Tucker, Law Lectures, p. 4 of four loose pages inserted in notebook 2, Tucker-Coleman Papers, Mss. 39.1 T79, Box 62, Special Collections Research Center, Earl Gregg Swem Library, College of William and Mary, https://digitalarchive.wm.edu/handle/10288/13361; James Kent, Commentaries on American Law, 2: 13 (New York: 1826). See also Joseph Story, Commentaries on the Constitution, 3: §1783 (Boston: 1833).

15. These extorted conditions requiring state regulation apparently were initiated in the 1965 Water Quality Act. Martha Derthick, "Crossing Thresholds: Federalism in the 1960s," in *Keeping the Compound Republic: Essays in American Federalism* (Washington, DC: Brookings Institution Press, 2001), 150. This extorted mode of commandeering was upheld by the Supreme Court in *Hodel v. Virginia Surface Mining and Reclamation*

Association, 452 U.S. 264 (1981). Some such federal extortion, such as the Clean Air Act, combines regulatory threats with more mundane financial pressure—that is, "the imposition of more stringent regulatory requirements and the revocation of federal highway funds." Jonathan H. Adler and Nathaniel Stewart, "Is the Clean Air Act Unconstitutional? Coercion, Cooperative Federalism and Conditional Spending after *NFIB v. Sebelius*," *Ecology Law Quarterly* 43 (2017): 671, 673.

Chapter 15: Regulatory Agents

1. See, for example, Evangelical Council for Financial Accountability, Integrity Standards for Nonprofits, Standard 4, http://www.ecfa.org/Content /Comment4; United States Conference of Catholic Bishops, Office of General Counsel, Political Activity and Lobbying Guidelines for Catholic Organizations (March 1, 2015), http://www.usccb.org/about/general -counsel/upload/USCCB-PACI-Guide-2015.pdf; Church of Jesus Christ of Latter-day Saints, Handbook 2, Administering the Church, §21.1.29 regarding Political and Civic Activity (March 2019), https://www.lds.org/study /manual/handbook-2-administering-the-church/selected-church-policies -and-guidelines/selected-church-policies?lang=eng#title_number46.

2. Richard A. Epstein, "Unconstitutional Conditions, State Power, and the Limits of Consent," *Harvard Law Review* 102, no. 4 (1988): 14.

3. HHS is rumored to have at least briefly shut down research at over 15 institutions, and elsewhere, it has threatened to shut down research. At one university, HHS threatened a shutdown merely because a single researcher filed an out-of-date form. And as put with satisfaction by a former head of the Office for Human Research Protections, "the suspensions created a crisis of confidence and a climate of fear." Greg Koski, "Beyond Compliance . . . Is It Too Much to Ask?," *Ethics and Human Research* 25, no. 5 (2003).

4. Charles Reich explains that "recipients are likely to be overzealous in their acceptance of government authority so that a government contractor may be so anxious to root out 'disloyal' employees that he dismisses men who could probably be retained consistently with government policy. . . . This penumbral government power is, indeed, likely to be greater than the

sum of the granted powers. Seeking to stay on the safe side of an uncertain, often unknowable line, people dependent on largess are likely to eschew any activities that might incur official displeasure. Beneficiaries of government bounty fear to offend, lest ways and means be found, in the obscure corners of discretion, to deny these favors in the future." Charles A. Reich, "The New Property," *Yale Law Journal* 73 (1964): 733, 751.

5. HHS, for example, long set only minimum standards for the censorship conducted by IRBs, leaving IRBs to go further by taking into account their institution's "prevailing community standards." Office for Protection from Research Risks, *Protecting Human Research Subjects: The Institutional Review Board Guidebook* (Washington, DC: Department of Health and Human Services, 1993), chap. III, part A.

6. In a late-nineteenth-century case, the Supreme Court said, "Congress cannot, by authorization or ratification, give the slightest effect to a State law or constitution in conflict with the Constitution of the United States." *Gunn v. Barry*, 82 U.S. 610, 623 (1872).

7. See, for example, Evangelical Council for Financial Accountability, Integrity Standards for Nonprofits, Standard 4, http://www.ecfa.org/Content /Comment4; the United States Conference of Catholic Bishops, Office of General Counsel, Political Activity and Lobbying Guidelines for Catholic Organizations (March 1, 2015), http://www.usccb.org/about/general-counsel /upload/USCCB-PACI-Guide-2015.pdf; the Church of Jesus Christ of Latter-day Saints, Handbook 2, Administering the Church, §21.1.29 regarding Political and Civic Activity (March 2019), https://www.lds.org/study/manual /handbook-2-administering-the-church/selected-church-policies-and -guidelines/selected-church-policies?lang=eng#title_number46.

8. An interesting example can be found in the conditions requiring federal contractors not to discriminate against any employee or job applicant on account of race, color, religion, sex, sexual orientation, gender identity, national origin, or disability. To this, the conditions add "affirmative action" requirements and "goals" measured by percentages of employees. The initial anti-discriminatory purpose of the conditions was not unappealing. But the conditions clearly are regulatory. And because the conditions require contractors to impose similar conditions on their subcontractors, they reveal how federal conditions turn vast numbers of businesses into regulatory agents, with controlling effects that reach far into American society.

Conclusion

1. Philip Hamburger, *Is Administrative Law Unlawful?* (Chicago: University of Chicago Press, 2014), 441–478.

2. *Frost & Frost Trucking Co. v. Railroad Commission,* 271 U.S. 583, 594 (1926).

3. *Perry v. Sindermann,* 408 U.S. 593, 597 (1972).

4. Attempts to get the judges to recognize the realities of commandeering have thus far fallen on deaf ears. In 1971, the Advisory Commission on Intergovernmental Relations vainly expressed its "hope that the federal judiciary, when judging grantor-grantee disputes, will recognize that compulsion rather than voluntariness and coercion rather than inducement now characterize many federal grants-in-aid and their requirements." Advisory Commission on Intergovernmental Relations, *Twelfth Annual Report: Federalism in 1970* (Washington, DC: Advisory Commission on Intergovernmental Relations, 1971), 58.

5. Alexis de Tocqueville, "What Sort of Despotism Democratic Nations Have to Fear," in *Democracy in America,* ed. Eduardo Nolla, trans. James T. Schleifer (Indianapolis, IN: Liberty Fund, 2010), 4:1245–1261.

6. Hamburger, *Is Administrative Law Unlawful?,* 508nb.

Acknowledgments

Fellow scholars contributed much to this book. I am deeply grateful to Nicholas Campbell, Mark Chenoweth, Aaron Gordon, John Harrison, Bert Huang, Jeremy Kessler, Josh Kleinfeld, Ethan Leib, Renée Lerner, James Lindgren, Julia Mahoney, Thomas Merrill, Henry Monaghan, Caleb Nelson, Michael Rappaport, and Peter Strauss—all of whom read and commented on the entire manuscript. I also was fortunate in being able to draw upon the knowledge of Richard Briffault, Jessica Bulman-Pozen, Joseph Landau, Daniel Richman, Kristen Underhill, and Dean Zerbe. Columbia Law School enabled me to present some chapters at the Faculty Workshop, and Dean Gillian Lester generously funded a conference on the manuscript. Not least, I am much indebted to my friend and agent, Lynn Chu, for her remarkable editing.

Index